CULTURES OF THE HINDUKUSH
AFTER JETTMAR

CULTURES
OF THE
HINDUKUSH
AFTER JETTMAR

✳

A BIBLIOGRAPHY

ALBERTO M. CACOPARDO

With a contribution by
IMTRAUD STELLRECHT

Orchid Press

CULTURES OF THE HINDUKUSH AFTER JETTMAR
A Bibliography

Alberto M. Cacopardo

ORCHID PRESS
P.O. Box 70,
Trinity TB, NL A0C 2S0
Canada
www.orchidbooks.com

Cover illustrations: Front: Wooden carving in the form of a ram's head at the entrance to a Kalasha *Jeshtak han* temple. Rear: The village of Grom in Rumbur Valley, Chitral District, Khyber Pakhtunkhwa, Pakistan. Images by K. Novakovic, July 2017.

ISBN: 978-1-7782522-0-4

CONTENTS

PUBLISHER'S NOTE

Orchid Press first considered publishing a full English translation of Karl Jettmar's German publication on his work in Peristan, *Die Religionen des Hindukusch* (Kolhammer 1975) early in the present century. Various obstacles, many relating to the complexities of translating such a work following the author's death in 2002, delayed the completion of this task until four years ago, when *The Religions of the Hindukush* (Orchid Press, Bangkok 2018) was finally released. We believe that, as his work was so fundamental to all that has occurred in the field since, anyone today wishing to fully understand the development of modern Peristan studies from its foundations must first start with Jettmar's monumental work.

Despite the long years of preparation, our 2018 edition still suffered from two major deficiencies. The bibliography did not reflect the huge volume of scholarship that has been published since 1975. And the index of the 2018 edition was deficient, a flaw for which Orchid Press must take responsibility, and offer its sincere regrets.

The current volume admirably corrects the first of these deficiencies. Dr. Cacopardo's documentation of some 1200 additional bibliographical references, both earlier works omitted in Jettmar's original bibliography and subsequent publications right up to 2022, provides the scholar with an indispensable resource to follow on from Jettmar, and to bring him/her to the present state of research in the field. Further, the bibliography expands on Jettmar to provide guidance in a broad spectrum of aspects of Peristan studies, including archaeology, ethnology, geography, genetics and physical anthropology, history, linguistics and bibliography.

As for the other deficiency, Orchid Press is pleased to announce that a second edition of *The Religions of the Hindukush* (ISBN 978-1-7782522-1-1), with revised index, will be released in conjunction with the present, companion volume.

ACKNOWLEDGEMENTS

The compilation of this bibliography has been largely discussed with Augusto Cacopardo, who has also contributed a useful part of the material tasks. Without his help, this work would not be quite the same.

We are grateful to Elena Bashir, Almuth Degener, Jürgen Wasim Frembgren, Birgitte Glavind Sperber, Jan Heegard Petersen, Wolfgang Holzwarth, Henrik Liljegren, Hermann Kreutzmann, Luca Maria Olivieri, Ruth Laila Schmidt, Wlodek Witek, who have all been helpful in various ways with this bibliography. Special thanks are due to Irén Hegedűs, who has generously contributed many valuable indications and to Max Klimburg, who gave the original impulse and has followed the enterprise with friendly attention. We further owe very special thanks to Sviatoslav Kaverin of Moscow, who, with his great enthusiasm for Peristan studies, has provided invaluable assistance about Russian and Eastern European research and many other precious indications. Needless to say, none of them is in any way responsible for any aspect of the selection or compilation.

FOREWORD

AFTER JETTMAR:
NEW PERSPECTIVES IN PERISTAN STUDIES

The pre-Islamic cultures of the Hindukush, largely known as "Kafir" in the literature, have been the subject of intense attention in the West at various times during the last couple of centuries. These fair-skinned, polytheistic, wine-drinking, Indo-European-speaking peoples, who believed to be "cousins of the Franks", were bound to be construed as the only living testimony to the remote pre-Christian heritage of the Europeans and to be candidates for a very special place in the ethnographic record.

After the intriguing (and most valuable) second-hand report about them published by Lord Montstuart Elphinstone in 1815, attempts to reach their remote homeland multiplied during the 19th century, but it was only at its close that George S. Robertson succeeded in spending a whole year among them. His famous book *The Kafirs of the Hindu Kush* was published in 1896, just after what is now Nuristan was conquered by the Afghan monarchy, which officially declared the Kafirs converted to Islam.

For a long time that milestone work, which was actually quite faulty in many respects, was considered the definitive and exhaustive work about the "Kafirs". It was mainly for this reason, as well as for the political conditions obstructing field work, that for the next half century research came to a virtual halt. While the results of the 1935 German Hindukush Expedition were largely disappointing and published only in German, the only real progress in this first half of the 1900's was the vast work of the Norwegian linguist Georg Morgenstierne. This was the second milestone in the field.

Curiously, Robertson had totally ignored the Kalasha of Chitral, who, having chanced to fall on the British side of the imperial border drawn in 1893-95, had remained unconverted, as they mostly are to this day. The Kalasha were later to become a most important source of knowledge and focus of research, but throughout the colonial period the whole of Northern Pakistan remained closed to civilian traffic for military reasons, and the only notice about them was the travelogue of an eccentric British officer published in 1938, Schomberg's *Kafirs and Glaciers*. This was the starting point of Kalasha studies. Then, the second half of the 1900's became the golden age of field work on the pre-Islamic cultures of the Hindukush.

On the one hand, a number of scholars managed to negotiate the Afghan government's restrictions on access to Nuristan, to find that memories about the Kafir past that had escaped the Germans in 1935 were still vivid enough to allow great improvement in our knowledge. On the other hand, on the Pakistan side of the border, research made huge progress with field work and participant observation among the Kalasha, and could even record sparse but important traces of pre-Islamic cultures in the rest of the country's north, from Chitral to Gilgit and Astor.

Perhaps the most seminal event in this period was the German Hindu Kush Expedition of 1955-56, led by Adolf Friedrich, with the participation of Karl Jettmar, Peter Snoy and Georg Buddruss. Stellrecht's essay in this volume is a unique investigation into the context, scientific premises, vicissitudes (and methodological limitations) of that memorable endeavour. The expedition was not particularly fortunate, and was devastated by the tragic death of Friedrich before he could return.

Yet it was the starting point of a life-long commitment of the other three scholars to research on the cultures and languages of the Hindukush/Karakorum, which was to stimulate and inspire the involvement of a whole generation of new researchers in the following decades. Karl Jettmar became a pivotal driving force in this wave of scientific enthusiasm: even for scholars who were not directly associated with him, a visit to him and his Südasien Institut in Heidelberg became an indispensible step in their research activity.

The publication of his weighty volume *Die Religionen des Hindukusch* in 1975 thus became the new milestone in the study of "Kafir" cultures. Building on Jettmar's own field work as well as on the 900-page manuscript of Friedrich's field notes, it made a vast reconnaissance of all the data so far available not only on Nuristan and the Kalasha, but also on the pre-Islamic traces in the rest of northern Pakistan, providing a comprehensive investigation of these cultures that no one had attempted before. Its vast bibliography of over six-hundred titles became a pathfinder for any newcomer to the field.

Nevertheless, the work was not exempt from shortcomings, especially in the depiction of the obscure history of the Hindukush/Karakorum in the last millennium and of the processes of Islamization and state creation in that period. The image of Nuristan as a long-standing cultural isolate within an Islamized world, as well as Jettmar's bold and mostly sourceless historical narratives, owed much to an old tradition of fictional historiography produced by both Western and local writers over the span of a century, since the days of Biddulph and Aziz ud-Din (see *e.g.* Holzwarth 1996; Cacopardo & Cacopardo 2001: 25ff). "Hypothetical constructions" prevailed, as the author himself later recognized (Jettmar 2018: xxvi).

Furthermore, and more visibly at the time, Jettmar's theoretical background rooted in Father Schmidt's old Vienna school of anthropology, was blatantly out of fashion on the international scenery in the Seventies. It was probably also for this reason that the book was not readily translated into English. While a deeply revised Russian translation was published with wide circulation in 1986, only the Nuristan section became available in English the same year.

Thus anglophone readers were left without access to the only existing comprehensive treatment of "Kafir" cultures—until Orchid Press' courageous decision to publish the full English version of its original form in 2018. At that point a true revision and updating of the volume would have been absolutely impossible: it would have meant rewriting the whole text from top to bottom. It will take time before anybody can undertake such an attempt to emulate and improve Jettmar's enterprise on the basis of the new findings that are still in progress today.

It was not impossible, however, to update his 1975 bibliography, providing an indispensible basis not only for such an ambitious future endeavour, but for any kind of future research in the field. This is the task we have undertaken with the present publication. Readers must therefore be aware that, since we could not include here the titles present in Jettmar's original listing, this work is not complete without reference to its antecedent. The two listings are strictly complementary. Wherever we have referred to titles from the original listing, we have simply added a "J" to the date of the publication: thus, for example, Snoy (1962J) means that the entry must be sought in the bibliography to Jettmar (2018).

The new historiographic studies triggered by Wolfgang Holzwarth's pioneering research in the Nineties have by now transformed the very concept of "Kafiristan", which can no longer be simply identified with present-day Nuristan: it is now established that "Kafir" cultures still formed in the 17th century a vast continuous region that covered the whole of Northern Pakistan up to the borders of Kashmir, extending from Nuristan and the Pashai areas in Afghanistan all the way to the borders of Kashmir, where Gilgit and Astor remained largely unconverted till the close of the 1700's (see Maps in Figs. 1 to 4, from Cacopardo 2016). Though this chronological framework was never grasped by Jettmar, this is the region that captured his attention in his *magnum opus* and throughout his life, and it is therefore the region covered in this work. Because of the derogatory connotations of the term "Kafir" to the ear of the present Muslim inhabitants of the area, "Peristan" is the name that is now gaining foot in the literature to refer to its pre-Islamic past.

We have based our selection on the concept that all aspects of the Peristani cultures, technology, economy, language, art, social and political institutions, are inextricably connected to "religion", which is really an exogenous category to these cultures. We have therefore included all research and documents that are directly or indirectly relevant to an understanding of "Kafir" cultures in this holistic sense.

The bibliography includes in the first place post-Jettmar research that has to do with such matters. This recent research comprises at least five distinct lines of inquiry.

Ethnographic work *stricto sensu* is the first. In Afghanistan, however, field work was severely hindered by political conditions since the outbreak of the long wars in the late Seventies, when it was already rapidly exhausting its resources in collective memory: what was once a matter of ethnography has by now turned into a matter of history, as new insights are coming mainly from the disclosure of new written sources. Results of field work in Nuristan, however, are still being published, the most prominent example being the publications of Max Klimburg, who is still working at his important volume on the intriguing culture of the Parun valley. In Pakistan, field work has continued to increase our knowledge about the Kalasha, in recent times with contributions from several Pakistani anthropologists. In the rest of Eastern Peristan, field work has mostly concentrated on issues of development and contemporary Muslim society that are not relevant to Jettmar's subject. The vast body of studies produced in the Nineties by the Pak-German "Culture Area Karakorum Project" (CAK) is an example. Many of these works, however, can shed light on aspects of the pre-Islamic past and the processes of Islamization, through inquiries into oral traditions, research on written documents and investigation of traditional practices and institutions. For just one example, it is in a study of Gilgit's contemporary bazaars (Dittman 1997: 123) that we incidentally find the proof that there were no bazaars at all in Gilgit in 1886: a not-marginal insight about the pre-colonial economy of Peristan. We have therefore included some of these studies in our list.

Historiographic research on written documents from the surrounding regions, in Persian and other languages, is a second field that has already produced important results included in this list, and is open to further, highly promising inquiries. The pathbreaking role of Holzwarth in this sphere has already been highlighted. New evidence is also emerging from colonial time sources in the English language. Historiography is bound to remain in the future one of the most important paths of investigation on Peristani cultures.

The numerous languages of pre-Islamic Peristan, which are of extraordinary interest for Indo-European linguistics, are fortunately still alive, with very few exceptions. Linguistic studies, which Jettmar had always followed, have therefore continued without hindrance in recent years, and this is perhaps the field that has witnessed the most intense production. We have included the most important works, but we have had to leave out some of the many writings on detailed points, while privileging the ones that include transcriptions of oral texts, which can often shed some light on Jettmar's concerns. Encounters with various forms of spirits, for example, are one of the favourite subjects of these texts.

Archaeology is a fourth area. After his discovery of the Karakorum highway petroglyphs in the early 1980's, the study of these most important findings of the Buddhist period became a central concern in the latter part of Jettmar's life, as testified in the Epilogue to his volume. We have therefore included subsequent studies on this subject and on the regional archaeological issues that are directly connected with it. Recent archaeological research in Swat, Ladakh, Wakhan and Chitral has added to our knowledge of the Buddhist period in Peristan and is here included. Apart from Swat, excavations in Northern Pakistan are still at a pioneer stage and there is enormous scope for future investigation, while the archaeology of "Kafir" sites, augured by Jettmar in his 2001 Preface (Jettmar 2018: xxviii), still belongs entirely to the future, both in Afghanistan and in Pakistan.

We have included a fifth field of research that did not exist at all in Jettmar's times: genetic studies on the peoples of Peristan are now in a pioneer phase, but, especially if coordinated with linguistic, ethnographic, archaeological and historical evidence, they are likely to shed in the future much light on the remote, and less remote, past of the region.

But the bibliography is not limited to recent post-Jettmar research. In order to provide the reader with an as-far-as-possible complete documentation, we have also included previous publications that are directly relevant to Jettmar's treatment, but, for various reasons, were not listed in his extensive bibliography.

This component includes: 20th century studies published after the original 1975 edition, or, for Nuristan, after the 1986 English version, including Jettmar's own publications; other 20th century studies that had somehow escaped Jettmar's attention; and a number of relevant works from colonial and pre-colonial times that were not perused by him. As a rule, we have not listed unpublished archive materials, but we have made some exceptions, particularly for a few important confidential reports of the British intelligence, some of which are now freely available online.

The reader should note that we have refrained from listing works already included in Schuyler Jone's 1966 annotated bibliography of Nuristan and the Kalasha, which has had a wide circulation and is now fully available online. Researchers are strongly advised to consult this highly useful work in order to obtain a complete picture.

We must also refer the student to a number of other bibliographies that can be useful for particular aspects; in Snoy (1983J) there is a complete list of Jettmar's publications until that date; the same for Morgenstierne, in Morgenstierne (1973bJ); for Buddruss in Söhnen-Thieme & Hinüber (1994a); and for Edelberg in Børdahl (2021b). Ovesen (1979) is an annotated bibliography for the Pashai; Olivieri (2015a) provides an extensive coverage of the publications of the Italian Archaeological Mission in Swat, which Jettmar followed particularly through Giorgio Stacul; and Jettmar, König & Thewalt (1989) list all the works of the Pak-German team for the Karakorum Highway petroglyphs till that date. For linguists, there is a diligent bibliography of Dardic languages in Schmidt, Koul & Kaul (1984), and one for the languages of Northern Pakistan in Baart & Baart (2001), available online, which is not particularly exhaustive, but does list several works not included here, such as Bailey's papers from the 1920's on Shina. Allan (1998) covers Karakorum/Himalaya, thus including part of our area; while Stellrecht (1998a) is a monumental bibliography of Northern Pakistan compiled for the CAK project, which lists some 4000 titles from a wide range of subjects, including ethnography and linguistics, as well as natural sciences, development, agriculture and forest management, exploration, contemporary issues, mountaineering, and history. It is worth noting that it includes a list of as many as 28 titles by Gottlieb W. Leitner, to which we refer readers interested in this memorable and peculiar author. Lorimer is also well represented. Finally, we must also point out that readers can now find online the monumental, unpublished work by McCoy Owens, Riccardi & Lewis (n.d. [1987]), which lists over 7000 titles on the whole Himalayan area, including sections on the "Pakistan Himalayan Region", with many little-known items, also on Nuristan.

It is a great shame for Peristan studies that most Western scholars do not read Russian. In fact, in recent times attention towards the pre-Islamic cultures of our region has been perhaps more vivid in Russia than anywhere else, following a long-standing tradition dating back to the days of the Great Game. It is surprising to find that even Jettmar and Snoy, who mastered the language, apparently ignored much of the Russian works listed here. We have provided an English translation of the titles, in the hope of encouraging Western scholars to overcome the language barrier, and perhaps also Russian scholars to write in English a bit more often. Russophone readers are begged to excuse some minor inconsistencies in the transcription systems. On the other hand, we must regret not being able to break with Western academic tradition by listing works in Eastern languages, such as Persian, Urdu, Chinese or Japanese. There can be a lot to learn from such works, but the task was just beyond our reach.

Future research on the cultural history of Peristan will have to be concerned with the often little-known history of the immediately adjoining areas, which were mostly the extreme peripheries of the great civilizations of the plains. Baltistan, the Yarkand region, Wakhan, Shughnan, Badakhshan, Panjshir, the Kabul Kohistan, Laghman and Ningrahar, Bajaur, Swat, Buner, the Hazara and Kishanganga valleys, and Kashmir itself, are all places that have hardly been investigated in the perspective of Peristan studies. We have included in our selection only a few works on some of these areas, particularly if carried out by scholars competent on Peristan, but our selection in this direction is probably rather arbitrary and certainly incomplete. This is another promising field for future research that will deserve attention.

On the other hand, the reader must note that we have left out of our selection most of the vast literature on the military and political events of the Great Game and the colonial struggle in the late 19th century. Matters like the siege of Chitral or the politics of Kashmir in Gilgit, were not things that Jettmar was interested in and are carefully avoided in his *opus magnum*. Therefore we have only included works about them when they happened to have some incidental relevance for the knowledge of pre-Islamic cultures. It must be kept in mind, however, that this literature does have relevance to Peristani studies in the sense that it is useful to a critical understanding of early colonial sources on the "Kafirs", since most of their authors were officers directly involved in that military and political struggle.

At any rate, the resulting collection of over a thousand titles would have been hard to use efficiently without some kind of index. To avoid overlappings and ambiguities, we have chosen to classify the entries by only two categories: "Ethno-Geographical Area" and "Topic". The 15 local areas are easily recognizable by anyone acquainted with the region. The seven topics are each vast enough to avoid uncertainties, but we must specify that: Ethnography is a sweeping label for all aspects of a culture, including religion, economy, politics, kinship, art, music, architecture, material culture, oral literature; Linguistics includes sociolinguistics; History includes ethnohistory; Archaeology includes anything concerning antiquity; Genetics includes physical anthropology and phenetics; Geography is used in a narrow, not an extensive sense; while Bibliography, for one, needs no qualification.

A few last practical and technical notes. As a rule, we have chosen to exclude, not without regret, unpublished dissertations and papers, or, in general, hard-to-find unpublished materials, though we have had to make several exceptions for works that are particularly important or relevant to Jettmar's subject. Researchers should keep in mind, however, that there is a vast corpus of unpublished materials that often deserve scrutiny. There are many dissertations by important scholars, such as Parkes, Strand, Stellrecht, Holzwarth and Jettmar himself that have never been published and are not online. More recent works of this kind, on the contrary, are usually available on the Internet, such as the several valuable dissertations by Henrik Liljegren's students at Stockholm University.

As a rule, we have also excluded entries to encyclopaedias and other repertoires, as well as recent non-academic literature. Here again, however, with some exceptions, each with its own good reasons. We have included a number of reviews and review articles, because these can often be very informative: but our choice in this field is practically fortuitous.

We must further warn the reader that there are a number of volumes of collective essays that are entirely, or almost entirely, dedicated to our area: since we could not list separately all of the items therein, we have selected only the ones that are more important or directly relevant. Researchers should be aware that they might find, in each of such volumes, further materials of their interest. These include especially: the Proceedings of the 2nd (Chitral, 1990) and 3rd (Chitral, 1995) Hindukush Cultural Conferences, i.e. Bashir & Israr-ud-Din (1996) and Israr-ud-Din (2008); the first three volumes of the ANP series, namely Jettmar, König & Thewalt (1989), Jettmar, König & Bemmann (1993) and Fussman, Jettmar & König (1994); volumes 2 to 5 of the CAK series, edited or co-edited by Stellrecht; as well as Kreutzmann (2006), Bianca (2007), Skyhawk (2008), Baart, Liljegren & Payne (2022); the two recent collections of essays with Kalasha focus by Chelazzi *et al.* (2016) and Pir *et al.* (2019); and the one on Hunza edited by Holden (2018). Let us also add that a most important collection of essays focussed on the pre-Islamic cultures of Peristan in all their aspects, is due to appear in 2023. The Proceedings of the "Roots of Peristan" conference, held in Rome in October 2022 under the auspices of ISMEO, will include dozens of papers by the most important scholars of the field, investing all the research areas mentioned here. It is hoped that this will help to inspire a new leap forward in Peristan studies.

Note that all Muslim and Eastern names are listed hereunder the last term appearing in print, whether it be a title, or whatever else: with the exception of Munphool Mir, who published under three different "last names" and is listed under "Munphool", and Izzet Ullah, listed under "I" being better known as Izzatullah.

Finally, as a rule, we have not carried the Internet URLs at which listed works can be found, even for online journals, with the exception of a few cases of important publications that one might not expect to find so easily accessible (such as the ANP and MANP series), or of links that are not so easy to discover. Readers should be aware that a very large portion of the listed items, whether recent or ancient, is nowadays immediately available on the web, and can be easily found by digiting its title in inverted commas after the author's name.

The fabulous age when "all the books of the world will be online", prophesied by one US president over twenty years ago, seems to be coming up fast: and this is making life a lot easier for researchers—and for bibliographers as well. Nevertheless, we know of no bibliography where something isn't missing: readers and authors are begged to excuse us if we failed to make the exception.

SELECTED BIBLIOGRAPHY OF WORKS RELATED TO THE PRE-ISLAMIC CULTURES OF PERISTAN

ABBREVIATIONS:

AAE	Archivio per l'Antropologia e la Etnologia
AJHG	The American Journal of Human Genetics
ANP	Antiquities of Northern Pakistan. Reports and Studies
CAJ	Central Asiatic Journal
CAK	Culture Area Karakorum Scientific Studies
E&W	East and West
JCA	Journal of Central Asia (now Journal of Asian Civilizations)
JAC	Journal of Asian Civilizations
JASB	Journal of the Asiatic Society of Bengal
JIES	Journal of Indo-European Studies
JRAS	The Journal of the Royal Asiatic Society of Great Britain and Ireland (after 1991: Journal of the Royal Asiatic Society)
IsMEO	Istituto Italiano per il Medio ed Estremo Oriente
IsIAO	Istituto Italiano per l'Africa e l'Oriente (Heir of IsMEO)
J	When an item is referred to within an entry, a "J" after its date indicates that it is listed in Jettmar's bibliography, in Jettmar 2022: 524ff.
MANP	Materialien zur Archäologie der Nordgebiete Pakistans
MSS	Münchener Studien zur Sprachwissenschaft
NIFTH	National Institute for Folk and Traditional Heritage of Pakistan (Lok Virsa)
NTS	Norsk Tidsskrift for Sprogvidenskap
NIPS	National Institute of Pakistan Studies, Quaid-i-Azam University
RGGU	Rossijskij Gosudarstvennyj Gumanitarnyj Universitet (= RSUH, Russian State University for the Humanities)
SII	Studien zur Indologie und Iranistik
SIL	Summer Institute of Linguistics
SOAS	School of Oriental and African Studies of the University of London

SPbGU   Sankt-Peterburgskij gosudarstvennyj universitet (= SPbSU,
           Saint Petersburg State University)
SSNP   Sociolinguistic Survey of Northern Pakistan
TAASA
Review   Journal of The Asian Arts Society of Australia
ZAS   Zentralasiatische Studien des Seminars für Sprach und
           Kulturwissenschaft Zentralasiens der Universität Bonn
ZDMG   Zeitschrift der Deutschen Morgenländischen Gesellschaft.

Abaeva, Tamara G. (1971) Neizvestnye materialy po narodnym verovanijam Prigindukuš'ja [Unknown materials on the popular beliefs of the Hindukush area]. In: Taškentskij gosudarstvennyj universitet im. V. I. Lenina. Naučnye trudy. ["V.I. Lenin" State University of Tashkent, Scientific Transactions], Vol. 404. Tashkent, pp. 129-33.

———. (1973) "Indija" Beruni kak istočnik po istoričeskoj geografii Prigindukuš'ja. [Beruni's "India" as a source on the historical geography of the Hindukush area] Obŝestvennye nauki v Uzbekistane, 7-8: 102–104.

———. (1975) Issledovanija A.V. Staniševskogo (Aziza Niallo) o Pamire [Research of A.V. Stanishevsky (Aziz Niallo) on the Pamirs] In: Zelinskij, A. N., ed., Strany i narody Vostoka [Countries and Peoples of the East], Vol. 16, Pamir. Nauka, Moscow, pp. 262-91.

———. (1978) K voprosu ob arhaičnyh slojah kafirskoj mifologii [On the question of the archaic layers of Kafir mythology.]. In: Babahodžaev, M. A., ed., Afganistan: (Voprosy istorii, èkonomiki i filologii) [Afghanistan: Questions of History, Economics and Philology]. Fan, Tashkent, pp. 104-21.

———. (1980) A. E. Snesarev i izučenie Južnogo Prigindukuš'ja [A.E. Snesarev and the study of the Southern Hindukush]. In: Gankovskij J. V., ed., Strany Srednego Vostoka (istorija, èkonomika, kul'tura) [Countries of the Middle East (history, economy, culture)]. Nauka, Moscow, pp. 253-63.

———. (1984) Kafiristan v agressivnyh planah Anglii v Afganistane v konce XIX veka [Kafiristan in the aggressive plans of England in Afghanistan at the end of the XIX century]. In: Babakhodzhaev, M.A., ed., Strany Bližnego i Srednego Vostoka v meždunarodnyh otnošenijah (XIX-XX vv.) [Countries of the Middle East in International Relations (XIX-XX centuries)]. Fan, Tashkent, pp. 6-19.

———. (1987) Pamiro-Gindukušskij region Afganistana v konce XIX - načale XX v. (Očerk istorii) [The Pamir-Hindukush Region of Afghanistan in the Late 19th - early 20th Century. An essay in history]. Gosizdat SSSR, Tashkent.

Aerde, Marike van (2019) Routes beyond Gandhara: Buddhist Rock Carvings in the Context of Early Silk Roads. In: Yang, L.E., H.-R. Bork, X. Fang & S. Mischke, eds., Socio-Environmental Dynamics along the Historical Silk Road. Springer Open – Springer Nature Switzerland, Cham (Switzerland), pp. 455-80.

Ahmed, Ajaz (2007) Non-Timber Forest Products: A Substitute for Livelihood of the Marginal Community in Kalash Valley, Northern Pakistan. Ethnobotanical Leaflets UAS, 11: 97–105.

Ahmed, Akbar S. (1986) Pakistan Society: Islam, Ethnicity and Leadership in South Asia. Oxford U.P., Karachi. [With a chapter "The Islamization of the Kalash Kafirs"].

Ahmed, Musavir (2016) A Descriptive Study of the Phonology of Gurezi Shina. Acta Orientalia Academiae Scientiarum Hungaricae, 69,1: 87-106.

———. (2019) A Descriptive Grammar of Gurezi Shina. SIL Digital Resources. [Online publication].

Ahmad, Zahir, J.C. Postigo, F. Rahman & A. Dittman (2021) Mountain Pastoralism in the Eastern Hindu Kush: The Case of Lotkuh Valley, Pakistan. Mountain Research and Development, 41, 4: R16-R28. [Online open access].

Akhtar, Aasim (1997) Indus Kohistan. The Distant Steppe. Alliance Française, Islamabad.

Akhunzada, Fakhruddin (2018) Madaklashti: A Persian Speaking Community of Northern Pakistan. AAE, 148: 35-48.

Akhunzada, F. & M. Liljegren (2009) Kalkatak, a Crossroads of Cultures in Chitral. Forum for Language Initiatives, Islamabad.

Alauddin, Mohammad (2006) Kalash, The Paradise Lost. Ushba Publishing International, Karachi.

Alekseev, Sergej V. (2012) Mehanizmy skladyvanija èlit: arhaičeskoe i tradicionnoe obŝestvo [Mechanisms of élite formation: the archaic and traditional society]. In: Alekseev S.V., ed., Èlita Rossii v prošlom i nastojaŝem: social'no-psihologičeskie i istoričeskie aspekty. Sbornik naučnyh statej [Russia's Élite in the Past and Present: socio-psychological and historical aspects]. Vol. 2. Izd. Nacional'nogo instituta biznesa, Moscow, pp. 73-80.

Ali, Abida (2018) Governance and Customary Laws of Hunza in Burushaski Folktales: An Emic Approach. In: Holden (2018): 51-82.

Ali, Ihsan, C.M. Batt, R.A.E. Coningham & R.L. Young (2002) New Exploration in the Chitral Valley, Pakistan: An Extension of the Gandharan Grave Culture. Antiquity, 76 (293): 647-53.

Ali, I., D. Hamilton, P. Newson, M. Qasim, R. Young & M. Zahir (2008) New Radiocarbon Dates from Chitral, NWFP,

Pakistan, and their Implications for the Gandharan Grave Culture of Northern Pakistan. Antiquity, 82 (318). Online "Project Gallery" (acc. Feb. 5, 2019): http://www.antiquity. ac.uk/projgall/youngr318/

Ali, I., I. Shah, A. Hameed & A. Ahmad (2010) Gankorineotek (Chitral) Excavations, Second Field Season (2008), Pakistan Heritage, 2,1: 209-237.

Ali, I., I. Shah, A. Samad, M. Zahir & R. Young (2013) Heritage and Archaeology in Chitral, Pakistan: exploring some local views and issues. International Journal of Heritage Studies, 19,1: 78-97.

————. (2016) Preliminary Results of Archaeological Survey in Chitral, Khyber Pakhtunkhwa, Pakistan. In: Widorn, V., U. Franke & P. Latschenberger, eds., Contextualizing Material Culture in South and Central Asia in Pre-Modern Times. Papers from the 20th Conference of the European Association for South Asian Archaeology and Art [Vienna, 2010]. Brepols Publishers, Turnhout (Belgium), pp. 177-86.

Ali, I., I. Shah, R. Young & A. Samad (2010) Latest Archaeological Explorations in the Chitral Valley (2009). Pakistan Heritage, 2,1: 125-35.

Ali, I. & M. Zahir (2005a) Excavation of Gandharan Graves at Parwak, Chitral, 2003-4. Frontier Archaeology, 3: 135-82.

Ali, I., M. Zahir & M. Qasim (2005b) Archaeological Survey of District Chitral, 2004. Frontier Archaeology, 3: 91-106.

Ali, M. Kashif (2020) A Historical Narrative of the Bashali: The Menstrual House as Cultural Identity of the Kalasha Women of the Hindu Kush (Chitral-Pakistan). Journal of the Research Society of Pakistan, 57,3: 204-18.

Ali, M. Kashif & M. I. Chawla (2019) Socio-Cultural Life of the Kalasha People of Chitral: A Study of their Festivals. Pakistan Vision, 20,2: 42-57. [A synthetic description based on literature, with some field data].

Ali, M. Kashif, G. Shabbir & M.I. Chawla (2021) Library Sources Available on Pre-Islamic Religious Traditions of the Eastern Hindu Kush and on Shamanism among the Kalasha People. Library Philosophy and Practice (e-journal). 5286. [Though based on literature, this paper also includes some field data].

Ali, Tahir (1981) Ceremonial and Social Structure among the Burusho of Hunza. In: Fürer-Haimendorf, C. von, ed., Asian Highland

Societies in Anthropological Perspective. Sterling Publishers, New Delhi, pp. 231-49.

———. (1983) The Burusho of Hunza: Social Structure and Household Viability in a Mountain Desert Kingdom. PhD Dissertation. University of Rochester, Rochester, NY.

Allan, Nigel (1986) Communal and Independent Mountain Irrigation Systems in North Pakistan. In: Rahman, M., ed., Proceedings of the International Geographical Union Irrigation Conference. IGU & WAPDA, Lahore, pp. 82-102.

———. (1998) Karakorum Himalaya: A Bibliography. Orchid Press, Bangkok.

Allchin, F. Raymond (1970) A Pottery Group from Ayun, Chitral. Bulletin of the SOAS, 33, 1-4.

———. (1981) Archeological and Language-Historical Evidence for the Movement of Indo-Aryan Speaking Peoples into South Asia. In: Asimov, M.S. *et al.*, eds., Ethnic Problems in the History of Central Asia in the Early Period (2nd millennium B.C.). Nauka, Moscow, pp. 336-48.

Allen, Nick (1991) Some Gods of Pre-Islamic Nuristan. Revue de l'Histoire des Religions. 208, 2: 141-68.

———. (1999) Review of Pstrusińska (1999). Journal of the Anthropological Society of Oxford, 30, 2: 200-201.

———. (2000) Imra, Pentads and Catastrophes. Ollodagos: actes de la Société Belge d'Études Celtiques, 14: 278-308.

Allison, John (1976) The Ashkun: Foundation for an Ethnography. PhD Dissertation. Indiana University, Bloomington.

Amella, Marie-Véronique (2020) Viviane Lièvre & Jean-Yves Loude, avec la collab. d'Hervé Nègre, *Le Chamanisme des Kalash du Pakistan. Des montagnards polythéistes face à l'islam.* L'Homme, 233,1: 173-77. [A review of the 2018 re-edition of Lièvre & Loude (1990), published on the occasion of the exhibition «Fêtes himalayennes, les derniers Kalash», held at Musée des Confluences, Lyon, 23 Oct., 2018 – 1 Dec., 2019].

Andersen, Peter, S. Castenfeldt & S. Soren (2010/11): Den tredje danske centralasiatiske ekspedition – Halfdan Siigers indsamlinger og feltstudier. Tværkultur: Årbog for ToRS, 2: 69-74.

Anderson, Dorothy (2003) The last visitor to Kafiristan: George Scott Robertson, 1890-91. Soldiers of the Queen, 113: 11-16.

————. (2008) The Unlikely Hero. The History Press, Stroud (UK). [A biography of George S. Robertson, with a distinct colonial military flavour, and astonishingly scarce attention to the formidable Kafiristan feat for which he is down in history].

Anderson, Gregory D.S. (2022) Burushaski: Some Areal-typological Comments on the Phonemics, Case Marking, and Complex Predicate Structure. In: Baart, Liljegren & Payne (2022): 1-38.

Andreev, Mihail S. & A.A. Polovtsov (1911) Materialy po ètnografii iranskih plemen Srednej Azii: Iškašim i Vahan [Materials on the ethnography of Iranian tribes of Central Asia: Ishkashim and Wakhan] (= Sbornik Muzeja antropologii i ètnografii, 1,9). Tipografija Imperatorskoj Akademii Nauk, St. Petersburg.

Andrews, Peter A. & K. Jettmar, eds. (2000) Sazin. A Fortified Village in Indus-Kohistan. With a contribution by G. Buddruss. ANP, Vol. 4. Philipp von Zabern, Mainz. Permalink: https://digi. hadw-bw.de/view/anp4

Anonym [Davies, Robert H.] (1862) Report on the Trade and Resources of the Countries on the North-Western Boundary of British India. Printed at the Governmnt Press, Lahore. [This source informs us, *inter alia*, that the "Dangiri" of Chitral, i.e. the Palula, were still considered "idolaters" at the time, see p. ccclxii].

Anonym (1879) Major Biddulph's Tour in Chitral and Yassin. Proceedings of the Royal Geographical Society, N.S., 1: 794-96.

Anonym (1882) Biddulph's Routes near Gilgit. Proceedings of the Royal Geographical Society, N.S., 4: 548-49.

Anonym (1934) The Non-Pathan Tribes of the Valley of the Hindu-Kush. Journal of the Royal Central Asian Society, 21,2: 305-308.

Anonym (1965) Ancient Routes through the Pamirs. Central Asian Review, 13, 1: 44-54.

Anonymous Missionary (1896) The Amir's Paean, the Mitai Valley, and the Kafirs. The Imperial and Asiatic Quarterly Review and Oriental and Colonial Record, 2 (3rd s.): 278-90.

Arbabzada, Nushin & N. Green (2022) Between Afghan "Idolography" and Kafir "Autoethnography": A Muslim Convert Describes His Former Religion. Journal of the American Oriental Society, 142, 3: 643-70.

Arsenault, Paul & A. Kochetov (2011) Retroflex harmony in Kalasha: Agreement or spreading? In: Lima, S., K. Mullin & B. Smith, eds., NELS 39: Proceedings of the thirty-ninth annual meeting of the North East Linguistic Society, vol. 1. GLSA [Graduate Linguistics Students Association] Publications, Amherst, Mass., pp. 55–66.

————. (2022) Two Types of Retroflex Harmony in Kalasha: Implications for Phonological Typology. In: Baart, Liljegren & Payne (2022): 39-75.

Ay, Zahide (2019) The Wakhis of Gojal (Upper Hunza): An Historical Analysis within the Context of Ismailism in Badakhshan. Alevilik-Bektaşilik Araştırmaları Dergisi/Journal of Alevism-Bektashism Studies, 19: 81-111. [Though showing a surprising distraction about the Peristani-Kafir background of the region and only partial knowledge of the relevant literature, this study has a valuable original inquiry into little-known ancient sources and present oral traditions that can help to shed light on the Islamization of Peristan].

Aziz, M. Abdul, A.M. Abbasi, Z. Ullah & A. Pieroni (2020) Shared but Threatened: The Heritage of Wild Food Plant Gathering among Different Linguistic and Religious Groups in the Ishkoman and Yasin Valleys, North Pakistan. Foods, 9, 601: 1-22. [An MDPI online journal]

Aziz, Shahid, M. Nawaz, S.G. Afridi & A. Khan (2019) Genetic Structure of Kho Population from North-Western Pakistan Based on mtDNA Control Region Sequences. Genetica. An International Journal of Genetics and Evolution, 147,2: 177-83. [Online publication].

Baart, Joan L.G. (1997) The sounds and tones of Kalam Kohistani, with wordlist and texts. NIPS & SIL, Islamabad.

————. (1999) A sketch of Kalam Kohistani grammar. NIPS & SIL, Islamabad.

Baart, J. & E.L. Baart-Bremer (2001) Bibliography of Languages of Northern Pakistan. NIPS & SIL, Islamabad

Baart, J.L.G., H. Liljegren & T. E. Payne, eds. (2022) Languages of Northern Pakistan and Surrounding regions: Linguistic studies dedicated to the memory of Carla Radloff. Oxford U.P., Karachi. [With contributions by Bashir, Mock, Strand, Tikkanen and others].

Baart, J.L.G. & M. Zaman Sagar (2004) Kalam Kohistani Texts. NIPS & SIL. Islamabad.

Backstrom, Peter C. & Carla F. Radloff (1992) Languages of Northern Areas. SSNP, Vol. 2. NIPS & SIL, Islamabad.

Baig, R. Karim (1994) Hindu Kush Study Series: Volume One. Rehmat Printing Press, Peshawar.

———. (1997) Hindu Kush Study Series: Volume Two. Rehmat Printing Press, Peshawar. [Both volumes with data on Chitral mehtarship and Kho traditions].

Bailey, T. Grahame (1927) R sounds in Kafir Languages. JRAS, 558-59.

Bakker, Peter & A. Daval-Markussen (2016) Linguistic and Genetic Roots of the Kalasha. In: Johnsen *et. al.* (2016): 93-114.

Bakker, Peter, K.F. Bøeg & Y.U. Goldshtein (2021) The languages of Edelberg's Nuristan and environs. In: Johnsen *et al.* (2021): 69-87.

Balneaves, Elizabeth (1952) The Happy Valley of Swat. Pakistan Quarterly, 2, 4: 1-19.

———. (1964) Kalash Kafirs of the Hindukush. Canadian Geographical Journal, 68: 98-107.

Balslev Jørgensen, Jørgen, L. Edelberg, C. Krebs & H. Siiger (1964) Anthropological Studies in the Hindukush and the Punjab. Folk, 6, 2: 37-51.

Bandini-König, Ditte = König, Ditte, see also.

Bandini-König, Ditte, ed. (1999) Die Felsbildstation Hodar. MANP, Vol. 3. Philipp von Zabern, Mainz. Permalink: https://digi. hadw-bw.de/view/manp3

———. ed. (2003) Die Felsbildstation Thalpan: 1. Kataloge Chilas-Brücke und Thalpan (Steine 1 – 30). MANP, Vol. 6. Philipp von Zabern, Mainz. Permalink: https://digi.hadw-bw.de/ view/manp6

———. ed. (2005) Die Felsbildstation Thalpan: 2. Katalog Thalpan (Steine 31 – 195). MANP, Vol. 7. Philipp von Zabern, Mainz. Permalink: https://digi.hadw-bw.de/view/manp7

———. ed. (2007) Die Felsbildstation Thalpan: 3. Katalog Thalpan (Steine 196 – 450). MANP, Vol. 8. Philipp von Zabern, Mainz. Permalink: https://digi.hadw-bw.de/view/manp8

———. ed. (2009) Die Felsbildstation Thalpan: 4. Katalog Thalpan (Steine 451 – 811). MANP, Vol. 9. Philipp von Zabern, Mainz. Permalink: https://digi.hadw-bw.de/view/manp9

———. (2011) Die Felsbildstation Thalpan. MANP, Vol. 10. Philipp von Zabern, Mainz. Permalink: https://digi.hadw-bw.de/view/manp10

Bandini-König, D., M. Bemmann & H. Hauptmann (1997) Rock Art in the Upper Indus Valley. In: Hauptmann, H., ed., The Indus.

Cradle and Crossroads of Civilizations. Embassy of the Federal Republic of Germany, Islamabad, pp. 29-70.

Bandini-König, D. & O. von Hinüber, eds. (2001) Die Felsbildstationen Shing Nala und Gichi Nala. MANP, Vol. 4. Philipp von Zabern, Mainz. Permalink: https://digi.hadw-bw.de/view/manp4

Barbour, Philip L. (1921) Buruçaski, a Language of Northern Kashmir. Journal of the American Oriental Society, 41: 60-72.

Barrington, Nicholas, J.T. Kendrick & R. Schlagintweit (2005) A Passage to Nuristan: Exploring the Mysterious Afghan Hinterland. I.B. Tauris, London. [Three young diplomats on a tour in Nuristan in July 1960, with many BW photos].

Barrow, Edmund G. (1888) Gazetteer of the Eastern Hindú Kush, in four Parts: Part I. Wakhán, Ish-Kásham, and Zébak. Part II. Dárdistán. Part III. Káfiristán. Part IV. Routes in the Hindú Kush. Government Central Press. Simla. Permalink: http://pahar.in/wpfb-file/1888-gazetteer-of-the-eastern-hindu-kush-by-barrow-s-pdf/ [An important confidential report by a member of the 1885-86 Lockhart expedition, first confirmed European visitors to Nuristan, with a valuable list of British confidential reports on Peristan].

Bartasheva, Nina L. = Lužeckaja, Nina L, see also.

Bartasheva, Nina L. (1975) Toponimika Kafiristana v «Siradž at-tavarih» [Toponymy of Kafiristan in "Siraj at-tavarikh"]. In: Pis'mennye pamjatniki i problemy istorii kul'tury narodov Vostoka [Written Documents and Problems in the Cultural History of the Peoples of the East]. XI godičnaja naučnaja sessija LO IV AN SSSR (kratkie soobŝenija i avtoannotacii). Čast' 1. GRVL, Moscow, pp. 88-91. [With an account of a 10-day visit to Nuristan in July 1960].

Barth, Fredrick (1956) Ecologic Relations of Ethnic Groups in Swat, North Pakistan. American Anthropologist, 58: 1079-1089.

Barth, F. & Morgenstierne, G. (1958) Vocabularies and Specimens of Some S.E. Dardic Dialects. NTS, 18: 118-36.

Bartol'd, Vasily V. (1896) Kafiristan v XVI v. [Kafiristan in the 16th century]. Sredne-Aziatskij vestnik, 7: 54-56 [= Sočinenija, VIII (1973). Raboty po istočnikovedeniju, pp. 21-22].

Bashir, Elena (1988) Topics in Kalasha Syntax: An Areal and Typological Perspective. Ph.D. Dissertation. University of Michigan, Ann Arbor.

———. (1990) Involuntative Experience in Kalasha. In: Verma, M.K. & K.P. Mohanan, eds., Experiencer Subjects in South Asian Languages. Center for the Study of Language and Information. Stanford University, Stanford, pp. 297-318.

———. (1995) Some Place Names in Chitral and their Possible Historical Significance. Paper presented at the Third International Hindukush Cultural Conference, Chitral 26-30 August 1995. Unpublished. [For unknown reasons, this valuable paper was not included in the Proceedings in Israr ud-Din (2008)].

———. (1996a) Mosaic of tongues: Quotatives and complementizers in Northwest Indo-Aryan, Burushaski, and Balti. In: W.L. Hanaway & W. Heston, eds., Studies in Pakistani Popular Culture. Lok Virsa Publishing House and Sang-e-Meel Publications, Lahore, pp. 187–286.

———. (1996b) The areal position of Khowar: South Asian and other affinities. In: Bashir & Israr-ud-Din (1996), pp. 167-79.

———. (2000) A Thematic Survey of Burushaski Research. History of Language, 6,1: 1-14.

———. (2001a) Spatial Representation in Khowar. In: Proceedings of the 36th Annual Meeting of CLS. Chicago Linguistic Society, Chicago, pp. 15-29.

———. (2001b) Khowar-Wakhi Contact Relationships. In: Lönne, D.W., ed., Tohfa-e-Dil. Festschrift Helmut Nespital. Dr. Inge Wezler Verlag, Reinbek bei Hamburg, pp. 3-17.

———. (2003) Dardic. In: Cardona G. & Dhanesh Jain, eds., The Indo-Aryan Languages. Routledge, London, pp. 818-94.

———. (2007a) Contact-induced change in Khowar. In: Shafqat, S., ed., New Perspectives on Pakistan: Contexts, Realities and Visions of the Future. Oxford U.P., Karachi, pp. 205-38.

———. (2007b) Review article of Zoller (2005). Himalayan Linguistics Review. 2: 1-6.

———. (2008) Artificial glaciers: Trajectories of a practice and an idea. In: Skyhawk (2008a): 210-40.

———. (2009) Review article of Schmidt & Kohistani (2008). Studia Orientalia, 70: 235-42.

———. (2010a) Introduction to: Inam Ullah, Torwali-Urdu Dictionary. Center for Research in Urdu Language Processing, University for Computer and Emerging Sciences, Lahore.

———. (2011) Kalasha: Past, present, and possible futures. In: Everhard & Mela-Athanasopoulou (2011): 13-36.

————. (forthcoming in 2022) Khowar and Kalasha: Similarities and differences in their micro-areal contexts. In: Degener & Hill (2022)

Bashir, E. & Israr-ud-Din, eds. (1996) Proceedings of the Second International Hindukush Cultural Conference. Oxford U.P., Karachi.

Baskhanov, Mihail K., A.A. Kolesnikov & M.F. Matveeva, eds. (2015) Derviš Gindukuša. Putevye dnevniki generala B.L. Grombčevskogo [Dervish of the Hindukush. Travel diaries of General B.L. Grombchevsky]. Nestor-Istorija, St. Petersburg.

Baskhanov, M.K., A.A. Kolesnikov, M.F. Matveeva & A.I. Gluhov, eds., (2017) Pamir, Hunza i Kašgarija v èkspedicionnyh fotografijah generala B.L. Grombčevskogo [Pamir, Hunza and Kashgaria in the Expedition Photographs of General Grombchevsky]. Pelikan, Moscow.

Beben, Daniel (2021) The Ismailis of Badakhshan. Conversion and narrative in highland Asia. In: Formichi, C., ed., Routledge Handbook on Islam in Asia. Routledge, Taylor & Francis, London, pp. 109-24.

Becka, Jiři (1981a) Review of Edelberg & Jones (1979J). Archiv orientální. 49: 286-87.

————. (1981b) Review of Lenz (1939J). Archiv orientální. 49: 203-204.

Bemmann, Martin, ed. (2005) Die Felsbildstation Dadam Das. MANP, Vol. 5. Philipp von Zabern, Mainz. Permalink: https://digi. hadw-bw.de/view/manp5

Bemmann, M. & D. Bandini-König, eds. (1994) Die Felsbildstation Oshibat. MANP, Vol. 1. Philipp von Zabern, Mainz. Permalink: https://digi.hadw-bw.de/view/manp1

Benassi, Andrea & I. Scerrato (2008) Brevi appunti su una ricognizione nella media Valle dell'Indo: rapporto tra petroglifi, miti di fondazione e pratiche rituali dei Brok-pa. Paper presented at the 3rd Italian Congress of Ethnoarchaeology, Mondaino (Italy), 17-19 March, 2004. http://files.landscape2.webnode. it/200006158-7529e7620b/Brok-pa%20della%20valle%20 dell%20Indo.pdf (acc. June 5, 2019) [With data on the Dards of Da-Hanu].

Bengtson, John D. (2014) Burushaski and the Western Dene-Caucasian Language Family: Genetic and Cultural Linguistic Links. Mother Tongue, 19: 181-222.

Benveniste, Émile (1952) Le Nouristan. In: Massé, H. & R. Grousset, eds., La Civilisation Iranienne. Perse, Afghanistan, Iran extérieur. Payot, Paris, pp. 240-43.

Berger, Hermann (1983) Etymologische Bemerkungen zu einigen auf Geister und Geisterglaube bezügliche Wörter im Burushaski. In: Snoy (1983J): 29-33.

————. (1985) A Survey of Burushaski Studies. JCA, 8,1: 33-37.

————. (1998) Die Burushaski-Sprache von Hunza und Nager. Teil 1: Grammatik; Teil II: Texte mit Übersetzungen; Teil III: Wörterbuch Burushaski-Deutsch, Deutsch-Burushaski. Harrassowitz Verlag, Wiesbaden.

————. (2008a) Burushaski – Destinies of a Central Asian Language Remnant. In: Skyhawk (2008a): 147-67.

————. (2008b) Beiträge zur historischen Laut- und Formenlehre des Burushaski. Harrassowitz Verlag, Wiesbaden.

Bhatt, Ram P., H.W. Wessler & C.P. Zoller (2014) Fairy lore in the high mountains of South Asia and the hymn of the Garhwali fairy 'Daughter of the Hills'. Acta Orientalia, 75: 79-166.

Bhasin, Veena (1992) Brok-pa of Ladakh: A Case of Adaptation to Habitat. Journal of Human Ecology, 3,2: 81-113.

————. (2008) Social Change, Religion and Medicine among Brokpas of Ladakh. Studies on Ethno-Medicine, 2,2: 77-102.

Bianca, Stefano, ed. (2007) Karakoram. Hidden Treasures in the Northern Areas of Pakistan. Second edition revised. Umberto Allemandi & C. for The Agha Khan Trust for Culture, Turin.

Bianchi, Nicola (2011) Review of Cacopardo, A.S. (2010a). Quaderni di storia, 74: 275-81.

Bibi, Lakshan (2019) Kalasha. What I Know. My Perspectives of Kalasha's Mystery, History and Faith. [This book by a famous Kalasha lady was apparently printed in the US, but has no indication of publisher or place, and seems not available in any library. One copy has been on sale on the web from Spain].

Bielmeier, Roland (1994) Zu den Bono-Na Liedern der Darden von Da-Hanu. In: Söhnen-Thieme & von Hinüber (1994): 11-32.

Bigoni, Francesca (2016) I Kalasha dell'Hindu Kush: origini tra mito, immaginario e scienza. In: Chelazzi et al. (2016): 7-20. [An overview of genetics research on the Kalasha].

Blaylock, Sarah R. & B. Hemphill (2007) Are the Koh an Indigenous population of the Hindu Kush? II: A Dental Morphology

Investigation. American Journal of Physical Anthropology, 132: 76.

Blažek, Václav & I. Hegedűs (2012) On the position of Nuristani within Indo-European. In: Sukač, R. & O. Šefčík, eds., The Sound of Indo-European 2: Papers on Indo-European Phonetics, Phonemics and Morphophonemics. Lincom, München, pp. 40-66.

Bonvalot, Gabriel (1889) Du Caucase aux Indes. Plon, Nourrit & Cie, Paris. [English transl.: Through the Heart of Asia. Over the Pamir to India. 2 Vls. Chapman & Hall, London, 1899]. [With Capus in Chitral in 1888].

Børdahl, Per E. (2021a) Lennart Edelberg. A bibliography I. In: Johnsen *et al.* (2021): 262-72.

———. (2021b) Lennart Edelberg. A bibliography II. In: Johnsen *et al.* (2021): 273-78.

Borriello, Manuela (1974) I Kalash dell'Hindu Kush: vita e costume. Tesi di laurea. University of Florence. [Based on fieldwork with A. & A. Cacopardo in 1973].

Bozorova, Muslima (2014) Some Hypotheses about the Origin of Infidel (Kafir) Tribes of the Eastern Hindu Kush. Inostrannye jazyki v Uzbekistane, 4,4: 145-49.

Bräker, Annette & H.H. Geerken (2017) The Karakoram Highway and the Hunza Valley, 1998: History, Culture, Experiences. BoD – Books on Demand, Norderstedt (Germany). [Orig. German edition: Der Karakorum Highway und das Hunzatal. BoD, 2016 – This work has valuable original archaeological data from Gilgit/Hunza].

Brandl, Rudolf M. (1997) Zum Gesang der Kafiren. In: Baumann, M.P., R.M. Brandl & K. Reinhard, eds., Neue ethnomusikologische Forschungen. Festschrift Felix Hoerburger. Laaber Verlag, Laaber, pp. 191–207.

Bredi, Daniela (1994) L'uso delle fonti nella storiografia indo-musulmana nella prima metà del XX sec.: Hashmatullah Khan e lo Shighar-namah. Rivista degli Studi Orientali, 68, 3-4: 267-289.

———. (1996) A proposito dell'islamizzazione delle Northern Areas del Pakistan. In: Bredi, D. & G. Scarcia, eds., Ex libris Franco Coslovi. Poligrafo, Venezia, pp. 147-61.

Bruneau, Laurianne (2007) L'architecture bouddhique dans la vallée du Haut Indus: un essai de typologie des représentations rupestres de stūpa. Arts asiatiques, 62: 63-75.

————. (2010) Animal style of the steppes in Ladakh: a presentation of newly discovered petroglyphs (in collaboration with M. Vernier). In: Olivieri, L.M., L. Bruneau & M. Ferrandi, eds., Pictures in Transformation: Rock Art Researches between Central Asia and the Subcontinent. Archaeopress, Oxford, pp. 27-36

————. (2013) L'art rupestre du Ladakh (Jammu et Cachemire, Inde): ses liens avec l'Asie centrale protohistorique. Cahiers d'Asie centrale, 21-22: 487-98.

————. (2015) The Rock Art of Ladakh: A Historiographic and Thematic Study. In: Kumar, A., ed., Rock Art: Recent Researches and New Perspectives (Festschrift to Padma Shri Dr. Prof. Yashodhar Mathpal). New Bharatiya Book Corporation, Delhi, pp. 79-99.

Bucherer-Dietschi, Paul, ed. (1988) Bauen und Wohnen am Hindukush. Aufsätze über Aspekte und Probleme traditioneller Bau- und Wohnformen im Gebiet des afghanischen Hindukush. Stiftung Bibliotheca Afghanica, Liestal.

Buddruss, Georg (1975) Zur Benennung der Schlange in einigen nordwestindischen Sprachen. MSS, 33: 7-14.

————. (1976) Review of Morgenstierne (1973aJ). ZDMG, 126, 2: 401-402.

————. (1977) Nochmals zur Stellung der Nûristân Sprachen des Afghanischen Hindukusch. MSS, 36: 19-38.

————. (1979a) Review of Lentz (1939J). Der Islam, 56: 350-52.

————. (1979b) Review of Robertson (1896J). Orientalistisches Literaturzeitung, 74: 278-79. N - E

————. (1985) Linguistic Research in Gilgit and Hunza: some results and perspectives. JCA, 8,1: 27-32.

————. (1986) Wakhi-Sprichwörter aus Hunza. In: Schmitt, R. & P.O. Skjærvø, eds., Studia Grammatica Iranica, Festschrift für Helmut Humbach. R. Kitzinger, München, pp. 27-44.

————. (1987) Ein Ordal der Waigal-Kafiren des Hindukusch. Cahiers Ferdinand de Saussure, 41: 31-43.

————. (1992) Waigali Sprichwörter. SII, 16-17: 65-80.

————. (1993) German linguistic research in the northern areas of Pakistan. In: Zingel-Avé Lallemant, S. & W.-P. Zingel, eds., Neuere deutsche Beiträge zu Geschichte und Kultur Pakistans. Deutsch-Pakistanisches Forum e.V., Bonn, pp. 38-49.

————. (1998) Eine Einheimische Sammlung von Wakhi-Sprichwörter aus Hunza: Text, Übersetzung, Glossar. In: Kushev *et al.* (1998): 30-45.

————. (2002) Vom mythischen Weltbild eines Hochgebirgsvolkes im Hindukusch. In: Zeller, D., ed., Religion und Weltbild. LIT Verlag, Münster, pp. 117-34.

————. (2005) Māra's Mühlenbau. Analyse eines Prasun-Textes aus dem afghanischen Hindukush. In: Kazanski, N.N., ed., *Hṛdā Mánasā*. Studies presented to Professor Leonard G. Herzenberg on the occasion of his 70. Birthday. Nauka, St. Petersburg, pp. 446-69.

————. (2006a) Drei Texte in der Wama-Sprache des afghanischen Hindukush. In: Bogoljubov, M.N. ed., Indo-Iranian Linguistics and the Typology of Linguistic Situations. Prof. A.L. Grjunberg (1930-1995) Memorial Volume. Nauka, St. Petersburg, pp. 177-200.

————. (2006b) Linguistic Diversity in the Hunza Valley. In: Kreutzmann (2006a): 236-45.

————. (2008) Reflections of the Islamization of Kafiristan in Oral Tradition. In: Skyhawk (2008a): 16-35. [Translation of Buddruss (1983J)]

Buddruss, G. & A. Degener (2015) Materialien zur Prasun-Sprache des Afghanischen Hindukusch. Teil 1: Texte und Glossar. Harvard U.P., Cambridge, Mass. & London. [With very important texts on pre-Islamic mythology].

————. (2017) Materialien zur Prasun-Sprache des Afghanischen Hindukusch. Teil 2: Grammatik. Harvard U.P., Cambridge, Mass. & London.

Buddruss, G. & P. Snoy (2006) Die Deutsche in Hindukusch-Expedition (DHE) 1955-56. In: Brandstetter, A.-M. & C. Lentz, eds., 60 Jahre Institut für Ethnologie und Afrikastudien. Ein Geburtstag. Rüdiger Köppe Verlag, Köln, pp. 49-60.

————. (2008) The German Hindu Kush Expedition (DHE) 1955-56. In: Skyhawk (2008a): 1-15. [Translation of Buddruss & Snoy (2006)]

Buksh, Munshi Faiz (1872) Journey from Peshawar to Kashgar and Yarkand in Eastern Turkestan. JRAS, 42: 448-73. [Report of an early "pundit" crossing Peristan].

[Buksh, M. Faiz =] F.B. (1883) Report on Chitral. Selections from the records of the Government of Punjab and its dependencies.

Confidential Series, no. A XI. Punjab Government Secretariat Press, Lahore. [An important early report on Chitral and its history, not always reliable. Online at: http://www.mahraka.com/fb.html]

Burton-Page, John (1986) Muslim Graves of the "Lesser Tradition". Gilgit, Punial, Swat, Yusufzai. JRAS, N.S., 2: 248-54.

Butz, David & N. Cook (2018) Autoethnography, Knowledge Governance and the PANOS Oral Testimony Program in Shimshal, Pakistan. In: Holden (2018): 33-50.

Cacopardo, Alberto M. (1974) I Kalash dell'Hindu Kush: Economia e Società. Tesi di laurea. University of Florence.

——. (1977) Circuiti di scambio economico e cerimoniale presso i Kalash (Pakistan). Uomo & Cultura, 19-22: 106-19. [This work was mistakenly printed as co-authored by Augusto S. Cacopardo].

——. (1985) Kalash, gli infedeli dell'Hindu Kush. L'Universo, 65, 6: 700-23.

——. (1991) The Other Kalasha. A Survey of Kalashamun-Speaking People in Southern Chitral. Part I: The Eastern Area. E&W, 41, 1-4: 273-310.

——. (1996) The Kalasha in Southern Chitral. Part I: The Eastern Area. In: Bashir & Israr-ud-Din (1996): 247-70.

——. (1999) Review article of Klimburg (1999). E&W, 49, 1-4: 320-22.

——. (2005) Intorno al Peristan, ai Kafiri, ai valichi. In: La Cecla, F. & M. Tosi, eds., Le frontiere dell'Afghanistan. Bononia U.P., Bologna, pp. 97-106.

——. (2007) Some Findings of Archaeological, Historical and Ethnographic Interest in Chitral. E&W, 57, 1-4: 377-89.

——. (2008) Review of Hinüber (2004). E&W, 58, 1/4: 475-77.

——. (2009) Chi ha inventato la democrazia? PhD dissertation. University of Sassari, Sassari. [Political and economic anthropology of Kho, Kalasha, Kati, Kom and Gilgit-Chilas].

——. (2013) La democrazia degli altri. Antiche gentes e democrazia. Nuvole. (Online journal).

——. (2016) Fence of Peristan. The Islamization of the "Kafirs" and Their Domestication. In: Chelazzi et al. (2016): 69-101.

——. (2019) Chi ha inventato la democrazia? Modello paterno e modello fraterno del potere. Meltemi, Milan.

————. (forthcoming in 2022) The counter-civilization of the Hindukush/Karakorum: The state of ethnohistorical research. In: Degener & Hill (2022)

Cacopardo, A.M. & A.S. Cacopardo (1989) The Kalasha (Pakistan) Winter Solstice Festival. Ethnology, 28, 4: 317-29.

————. (1992) The Other Kalasha. A Survey of Kalashamun-Speaking People in Southern Chitral. Part III: Jinjeret Kuh and the Problem of Kalasha Origins. E&W. 42, 2-4: 333-75.

————. (1995) Unknown Peoples of Southern Chitral. Part I: The Dameli. E&W, 45, 1/4: 233-82.

————. (1996) The Kalasha in Southern Chitral. Part III: Jinjiret Kuh and the Problem of Kalasha Origins. In: Bashir & Israr-ud-Din (1996): 299-313.

————. (2001) Gates of Peristan. History, Religion and Society in the Hindu Kush. IsIAO, Rome.

————. (2011) Anthropology and Ethnographic Research in Peristan. In: Olivieri & Rahman (2011): 285-93.

Cacopardo, A.M. & R. L. Schmidt, eds. (2006) My Heartrendingly Tragic Story: Shaikh Muhammad Abdullah Khan 'Azar'. Instituttet for sammenlignende kulturforskning. Novus forlag, Oslo.

Cacopardo, A.M. & S. Pellò (2021) Whose Past and Whose Future: Free Love and Love Marriage among "Kafirs" of the Hindukush in an Early Nineteenth-Century Persian Ethnography. Iran and the Caucasus, 25, 2: 366-78.

————. eds. (forthcoming) The "A'in-i Kafiran" by Haji Allahdad: A Persian Ethnography on the "Kafirs" of the Hindukush (ca. 1837). ISMEO, Rome.

Cacopardo, Augusto S. (1974) I Kalash dell'Hindu Kush: Tradizioni Religiose. Tesi di laurea. University of Florence.

————. (1985) Chaumos: la festa del solstizio d'inverno. L'Universo, 65, 6: 724-53.

————. (1991) The Other Kalasha. A Survey of Kalashamun-Speaking People in Southern Chitral. Part II: The Kalasha of Urtsun. E&W, 41, 1/4: 311-50.

————. (1996) The Kalasha in Southern Chitral. Part II. The Pre-Islamic Culture of the Urtsun Valley. In: Bashir & Israr-ud-Din (1996): 271-98.

————. (1999) Shamans and the Space of the Pure Among the Kalasha of the Hindu Kush (Pakistan). In: Mastromattei, R & A.

Rigopoulos, eds., Shamanic Cosmos, from India to the Polar Star. Venetian Academy of Indian Studies & D.K. Printworld, New Delhi, pp. 57-71.

———. (2006) Anthropomorphic Representations of Divinities among the Kalasha of Chitral (Pakistan). Acta Orientalia, 67: 127-58.

———. (2008) The Winter Solstice Festival of the Kalasha of Birir: Some Comparative Suggestions. Acta Orientalia, 69: 77-120.

———. (2010a) Natale pagano. Feste d'inverno nello Hindu Kush. Sellerio Editore, Palermo.

———. (2010b) Texts from the Winter Feasts of the Kalasha of Birir. Acta Orientalia, 71: 187-242.

———. (2011) Are the Kalasha Really of Greek Origin? The Legend of Alexander the Great and the Pre-Islamic World of the Hindu Kush. Acta Orientalia, 72: 47-92.

———. (2012) La ricerca sui Kafiri prima e dopo Graziosi. Lo "stato dell'arte". AAE, 142: 87-106.

———. (2013) La lingua Kalasha e il suo contesto. AAE, 143: 87-106.

———. (2016a) A World In-between. The Pre-Islamic Cultures of the Hindu Kush. In: Pellò S., ed., Borders. Itineraries on the Edges of Iran. Edizioni Ca' Foscari, Venice, pp. 243-70.

———. (2016b) Pagan Christmas. Winter Feasts of the Kalasha of the Hindu Kush. Gingko Library, London.

Canonne, Marie & J. Herment (2020) Fonds Loude-Lièvre-Nègre (dit fonds Kalash). Répertoire numérique détaillé. musée des Confluences, Lyon. [This is the 77-pages catalogue, available in print and online, of the archives and collection donated to the Museum in 2016 and 2018] https://www. museedesconfluences.fr/sites/default/files/3j_vf_web.pdf (acc. July, 29, 2021)

Capus, Guillaume (1889a) Le Kafiristan et les Kafirs Siah-Pouches. In: Quatrième Congrès International des Sciences Géographiques, Le Mans, pp. 5-47. [= Capus (1890)]

———. (1889b) "Vocabulaire de langues pré-pamiriennes". Bulletins de la Société d'Anthropologie de Paris, 12: 203–216.

———. (1890) Le Kafiristan et les Kafirs Siah-Pouches. Societé d'éditions scientifiques, Paris. [A re-edition in booklet form of Capus (1889a), with new pagination].

Carbajo Usano, Matilde (2020) La casa menstrual como espacio liminal: una lectura de la sociedad Kalasha (Pakistán) a través de su materialidad. Universidad Complutense de Madrid, Facultad de Geografía e Historia. Máster en Arqueología Prehistórica. Trabajo Fin de Máster. [Unpublished Master's thesis available online].

Cardini, Anna Maria (2016) Riordino del corredo fotografico di Paolo Graziosi dei viaggi del 1955 e del 1960 nelle tre valli Kalasha. In: Chelazzi *et al.* (2016): 173-95.

Carther, Martha, L. (1993) Petroglyphs at Chilas II: Evidence for a Pre-Iconic Phase of Buddhist Art in Gandhara. In: Gail, A.J. & G. Merissen, eds., South Asian Archaeology 1991. Franz Steiner Verlag, Stuttgart, pp. 349-66.

Castenfeldt, Svend (1996) A Pre-Muslim Temple in 'Kafiristan'. In: Bashir & Israr-ud-Din (1996): 109-16.

———. (1999) Bjergfolk I Hindu Kush og på Moesgård. In: Høiris, I.O. *et al.*, eds., Menneskelivets mangfoldighed. Arkæologisk og antropologisk forskning på Moesgård. Moesgård, Højbjerg, pp. 47-54.

———. (2016) Halfdan Siiger's Religio-Ethnographic Fieldwork in Central and South Asia, 1948. In: Johnsen *et al.* (2016): 71-92.

———. (2021) The Kafir Temple in the Parun Valley. In: Johnsen *et al.* (2021): 89-98.

Castenfeldt, S. & H. Siiger (2003) Historical Kalasha picture book: photos from the Kalasha people of Chitral, Pakistan, 1948. Moesgaard Museum, Århus.

Castenfeldt, S. & H. Søholt (1985) Nuristan, Beklædning, band og bælter. Aarhus Amtscentral for undervisningsmidler, Højbjerg.

Čašule, Iliya (2014) Evidence for a Burushaski-Phrygian connection. Acta Orientalia, 75: 3-30.

———. (2017) Burushaski Etymological Dictionary of the Inherited Indo-European Lexicon. Lincom Europa, Munich.

———. (2020) The Indo-European Origin of the Burushaski Verbal Prefixation and its Verbal Morphology. Journal of Indo-European Studies, 48, 3-4: 353-87. [Readers will find in this recent article, available on the Internet, full reference to the author's numerous publications on his Burushaski/Indo-European hypothesis, including four monographs and many articles, which cannot be listed in detail here, as well as to the discussion of the hypothesis by many scholars, including

Bashir, Bengtson & Blažek, Edel'man, Hamp, Vrabie and others].

Cathcart, Chundra (2011) *RUKI* in the Nuristani languages: An assessment. In: Jamison, S.W., H. Craig Melchert & B. Vine, eds., Proceedings of the 22nd Annual UCLA Indo-European Conference. Hempen, Bremen, pp. 1-11.

Catu, Robert (1995) Le peuple Pashai. Central Asian Survey, 14, 3: 449-61.

Charles, Christian (1981) Hommes et Glaciers de la Vallée de la Hunza (Karakorum-Pakistan). Revue de Géographie Alpine. 69,4: 607-15.

Chaudhary, M. Azam (1997) Maruts – Gold-Washers of the Indus. In: Stellrecht & Winiger (1997): 431-62.

————. (1998) Blood Feuds in Chilas, Past and Present. In: Stellrecht (1998cII): 443-62.

Chelazzi, Guido, *et al.* (2016) Alti sentieri d'Asia: vita, cultura e miti dei popoli dell'Hindu Kush. AAE, 146.

Chiellini, Maddalena (2013) The Measure of a Man: Science and Orientalism in the Works of Paolo Graziosi on the Kafirs of Chitral, Pakistan. In: Proglio, G., ed., Orientalismi italiani 3. Antares Edizioni, Alba (CN), pp. 76-93.

Chohan, Amar Singh (1989) A History of Kafferistan (Socio-Economic and Political Conditions of the Kaffers). Atlantic Publishers, New Delhi.

————. (1997) Historical Study of Society and Culture in Dardistan and Ladakh (2nd ed.). Atlantic Publishers, New Delhi.

————. (1998) The Gilgit Agency 1877-1935 [rev. 2nd ed.]. Atlantic Publishers, New Delhi.

Choudhry, Fahad R., M.S. Park, K. Golden & I.Z. Bokharei (2017) "We are the soul, pearl and beauty of Hindu Kush Mountains": exploring resilience and psychological wellbeing of Kalasha, an ethnic and religious minority group in Pakistan. International Journal of Qualitative Studies on Health and Well-Being, 12:1. (Online Journal).

Choudhry F.R., T.M. Khan, M.S. Park & K.J. Golden (2018) Mental Health Conceptualization and Resilience Factors in the Kalasha Youth: An Indigenous Ethnic and Religious Minority Community in Pakistan. Frontiers in Public Health, 6:187. (Online journal).

Ciruzzi, Sara (1981) Donazione della raccolta "P. Graziosi" al Museo di Antropologia di Firenze. AAE, 111: 285-88.

Ciruzzi, Sara, S. Mainardi & M.G. Roselli, eds. (2004) "Pakistan 1955" – Appunti di viaggio di Paolo Graziosi. AAE, 134: 3-100. [This is the full text of Graziosi's field notes from 1955, with many previously unpublished photos by him, reproductions of the notebooks' pages with drawings, photos of his collection of artifacts, and a brief presentation by Ciruzzi, but no footnotes or further comments].

―――. eds. (2007) "Pakistan 1960" – Appunti di viaggio di Paolo Graziosi. AAE, 137: 3-133. [This is the full text of Graziosi's field notes from 1960, with many previously unpublished photos by him, reproductions of the notebooks' pages with drawings, and a brief presentation by Ciruzzi, but no footnotes or further comments].

Clemens, Jürgen & M. Nüsser (2008) Animal Husbandry and Utilization of Alpine Pastures in the Nanga Parbat Region of Northern Pakistan: Comparison of Raikot and Rupal Valleys. In: Israr-ud-Din (2008): 71-81.

Cobb, Evelyn H. (1951) The Frontier States of Dir, Swat and Chitral. Journal of the Royal Central Asian Society, 38: 170-76.

Cockerill, George K. (1895) Appendix to Barrow's Gazetteer of Eastern Hindu Kush. Government Central Printing Office, Simla.

Court, C. Auguste (1836) Conjectures on the march of Alexander (communicated by Captain C.M. Wade). JASB, 5: 387-95. [Amidst its hazy and puzzling geographical information, this paper has, esp. at pp. 391-93, some interesting notices on the Kafirs' country, including one about the river "*Khonár*, which flows through *Kaféristán*"]

―――. (n.d., ca. 1837) Notice sur le Kafféristan dressée sur la demande qui m'en fut faite par la Societé asiatique de Paris. In: Mémoires, Vol. 4, pp. 81-104. Archives of Musée Guimet, Paris. [Unpublished manuscript].

―――. (1839) Collection of Facts which may be useful for the comprehension of Alexander the Great's exploits on the Western banks of the Indus (with map). JASB, 8: 304-13.

Cristoforetti, Simone (2014) Review of Cacopardo A.S. (2010). Acta Orientalia, 75: 59-62.

Csáji, László K. (2011) Flying with the vanishing fairies: Typology of the shamanistic traditions of the Hunza. Anthropology of Consciousness, 22,2: 159–87.

―――. (2018) Ethnic Levels and Ethnonyms in Shifting Context:

Ethnic Terminology in Hunza (Pakistan). Hungarian Historical Review, 7,1: 111-35.

Curzon, George N. (1898) The Pamir and the Source of the Oxus. The Royal Geographical Society, London. [Revised and reprinted from The Geographical Journal, 8, 1896, pp. 15-59, 97-120, 239-64. With exhaustive discussion of ancient and modern notices and explorations of Peristan and the Pamirs].

Dainelli, Giotto (1924) Paesi e genti del Karakorum. Pampaloni, Florence.

Dambricourt Malassé, Anne & C. Gaillard (2011) Relations between the Climatic Changes and Prehistorical Human Migrations during Holocene between Gissar Ranges, Pamir, Hindu-Kush and Kashmir, the Archaeological and Ecological Data. Quaternary International, 22: 123-31.

Dani, Ahmad H. (1983a) Chilas. The city of Nanga Parvat (Dyamar). A.H. Dani, Islamabad

————. (1983b) Carvings on a Thalpan Rock. In: Snoy (1983J): 89-95.

————. (1985) The Sacred Rock of Hunza. JCA, 8, 2: 5-124.

————. (1987a) Medieval Kingship in Gilgit. Journal of the Asiatic Society of Bangladesh (Hum.), 32, 2. [Note that the chronological framework of this paper is unlikely to be sound].

————. ed. (1987b) Shah Rais Khan's History of Gilgit. Director, Centre for the Study of the Civilizations of Central Asia, Quaid-i-Azam University, Gilgit/Islamabad.

————. (1989a) History of Northern Areas of Pakistan. National Institute of Historical and Cultural Research, Islamabad. [This work had an updated 2nd edition in 2001. Note that the chronology of both is strongly questioned by subsequent research]

————. (1989b) Islamic Architecture. The Wooden Style of Northern Pakistan. National Hijra Council, Islamabad.

————. (1995) Human Records on Karakorum Highway. Sang-e-Meel Publications, Lahore.

————. (1998) Origin of the Dardic Culture: A New Discovery in the Northern Areas of Pakistan. JCA, 21, 1: 153-85.

————. (2001) History of Northern Areas of Pakistan: up to 2000 A.D. Sang-e-Meel Publications, Lahore. [Updated 2nd edition, after the first of 1989. Note that the chronology of this work is strongly questioned by subsequent research]

Darling, E. Gillian (1979) Merit Feasting among the Kalash Kafirs of North Western Pakistan. M.A. Dissertation. The University of British Columbia, Vancouver.

Daushvili, Georgij Dž. (2002) K voprosu o genezise doislamskoj kultury zapadnyh dardov (pašai) [On the genesis of the pre-Islamic culture of the Western Dards (Pashai)]. Vestnik Vostočnogo instituta (Acta Institutionis Orientalis), 2(12), vol. 6 [2000]: 112-62.

———. (2003) K voprosu o pervom tjurksko-dardskom kontakte v Kabulistane. [On the first Turkic-Dardic contact in Kabulistan]. Vestnik Vostočnogo instituta (Acta Institutionis Orientalis), 1(15), vol. 8 [2002]: 56-66.

———. (2008) K rekonstrukcii doislamskoj kultury zapadnyh dardov pašai – Vostočnyj Gindukuš (vključaja novyje svedenija o srednevekovom kafirskom vooruženii). [Reconstruction of the pre-Islamic culture of the Pashai Western Dards, Eastern Hindukush (including new evidence on medieval Kafir weapons)]. Vestnik SPbGU: Jazyk i literatura, 4, 2: 262-74.

———. (2009a) O dvuh «kafirskih» tehničeskih terminah iz darijazyčnogo teksta vtoroj poloviny XVI v. (Vostočnyj Afganistan). [Two «Kafir» technical terms from a Dari text of the second half of XVI century]. In: D′jakov, N.N., ed., Tezisy dokladov XXV meždunarodnoj konferencii po istočnikovedeniju i istoriografii stran Azii i Afriki [Proceedings of the 25th International Conference on Oriental and African Studies]. Vostočnyj fakul′tet SPbGU, St. Petersburg, pp. 85-87.

———. (2009b) O neizvestnom torgovom puti iz Badahšana v Vostočnyj Afganistan. [An unknown trade route from Badakhshan to Eastern Afghanistan]. In: D′jakov, N.N., ed., Tezisy dokladov XXV meždunarodnoj konferencii po istočnikovedeniju i istoriografii stran Azii i Afriki [Proceedings of the 25th International Conference on Oriental and African Studies]. Vostočnyj fakul′tet SPbGU, St. Petersburg, pp. 84-85.

———. (2014) K proishoždeniju nazvanij Kabul i Gindukuš. [The origin of the names "Kabul" and "Hindukush"]. In: D′jakov, N.N. & A.S. Matveev, eds., Tezisy dokladov XXVII meždunarodnoj konferencii po istočnikovedeniju i istoriografii stran Azii i Afriki [Proceedings of the 27th International Conference on Oriental and African Studies]. Vostočnyj fakul′tet SPbGU, St. Petersburg, pp. 48-49.

————. (2015) "K etimologii gidronima Kunar (Vostočnyj Gindukuš). [Etymology of the hydronym "Kunar" (Eastern Hindukush)]" In: D'jakov, N.N. & A.S. Matveev, eds., Tezisy dokladov XXVIII meždunarodnoj konferencii po istočnikovedeniju i istoriografii stran Azii i Afriki [Proceedings of the 28th International Conference on Oriental and African Studies]. Vostočnyj fakul'tet SPbGU, St. Petersburg, p. 87.

Davidson, John (1900) Some Notes on the Language of Chitral, and Idiomatic Sentences and Translations of Ten Popular Stories. Indian Antiquary, 29: 214-20 & 246-50.

Davies, Robert H. (1862) Report... ... - see Anonym (1862)

Davies, Wendy, ed. (2004) Voices from the Mountain. Oral Testimonies from Shimshal, the Karakoram, Pakistan. The Panos Institute, London. (acc. Aug. 1, 2021) https://b-ok.global/book/887388/dfb24b?id=887388&secret=dfb24b

De Filippi, Filippo (1924) Storia della spedizione scientifica italiana nel Himàlaia, Caracorùm e Turchestàn Cinese (1913-1914). Nicola Zanichelli Editore, Bologna.

————. (1932) The Italian Expedition to the Himalaya, Karakoram and Eastern Turkestan (1913-14). Edward Arnold & C., London. [Translation of De Filippi (1924)]

Decker, Kendall (1992) Languages of Chitral. SSNP, Vol. 5. NIPS & SIL, Islamabad.

Degener, Almuth (1994) Unauffälliges aus Nisheygram. SII, 19: 61-69.

————. (1995) Jägerglaube in Nuristan. Spektrum Iran, 8, 4: 28-35.

————. (1998a) Waigali Lieder zur Islamisierung Kafiristans. In: Kushev et al. (1998): 51-61.

————. (1998b) Die Sprache von Nisheygram im afghanischen Hindukush. Harrassowitz Verlag, Wiesbaden.

————. (2001) Hunter's Lore in Nuristan. Asian Folklore Studies, 60, 2: 329-44.

————. (2002) The Nuristani languages. In: Sims-Williams, N., ed., Indo-Iranian Languages and People. Oxford U.P., London, pp. 103–17.

————. (2008a) Golden Gilgit. A poem in the Shina of Gilgit. In: Skyhawk (2008a): 241-52.

————. (2008b) Shina Texte aus Gilgit (Nord-Pakistan). Sprichwörter und Materialien zum Volksglauben gesammelt von Mohammad Amin Zia. Harrassowitz Verlag, Wiesbaden.

————. (2016) The Prasun Verbal System and Its Terminology. Historische Sprachforschung / Historical Linguistics, 129: 184–95.

————. (forthcoming in 2022) The Wolf and the Kids in the Devozi dialect of Tregami. In: Degener & Hill (2022).

Degener, A. & E. Hill, eds. (2022) Proceedings of the International Workshop "The Nuristani Languages in Synchrony and Diachrony", 1–2 November 2019, University of Cologne. International Journal of Diachronic Linguistics and Linguistic Reconstruction, 19.

Denwood, Philip (2007) The Tibetans in the Western Himalayas and Karakoram. Seventh-Eleventh Centuries: Rock Art and Inscriptions. Journal of Inner Asian Art & Archaeology, 2: 49-58.

Di Carlo, Pierpaolo (2007) The Prun Festival of the Birir Valley, Northern Pakistan, in 2006. E&W, 57, 1-4: 45-100.

————. (2009) Costruzione del sé e dono simbolico: due aspetti della poesia kalasha, Pakistan settentrionale. Systema Naturae, 8: 117-25.

————. (2010a) Take Care of the Poets! Verbal Art Performances as Key Factors in the Preservation of Language and Culture. Anthropological Linguistics, 52, 2: 141-59.

————. (2010b) I Kalasha del Hindu Kush. Ricerche linguistiche e antropologiche. Firenze University Press, Florence.

————. (2010c) I Kalasha del Hindu Kush: ricerche linguistiche e antropologiche. In: Maraschio, N. & D. De Martino, eds., Se telefonando... ti scrivo: l'italiano dal parlato al digitato. Accademia della Crusca, Florence, pp. 163-74.

————. (2011a) Two Clues of a Former Hindu Kush Linguistic Area? In: Everhard & Mela-Athanasopoulou (2011): 101-14.

————. (2011b) Kalasha Language Maintenance through Tradition Vitality. In: Everhard & Mela-Athanasopoulou (2011): 235-46.

————. (2016) Retroflex vowels? Phonetics, phonology, and history of unusual sounds in Kalasha and other languages of the Hindu Kush region. In: Chelazzi et al. (2016): 103-21.

Di Castro, Angelo A. (2015) Goat Heads and Goddesses in Swāt, Gandhāra and Kashmir and Connected Problems. In: Di Castro, A.A. and D. Templeman, eds., Asian Horizons. Giuseppe Tucci's Buddhist, Indian, Himalayan and Central Asian Studies. Monash University Publishing, Melbourne, pp. 263-95.

Di Cristofaro, Julie, *et al.* (2013) Afghan Hindu Kush: Where Eurasian Sub-Continent Gene Flows Converge. PLoS ONE 8(10). (Online Journal).

Dittmann, Andreas (1997) Central Goods and Ethno-Linguistic Groups in the Bazaars of Northern Pakistan: an Example of Central Place Theory Modifications in Mountainous Environments. In: Stellrecht & Winiger (1997): 119-33.

————. ed. (2001) Mountain Societies in Transition. Contributions to the Cultural Geography of the Karakorum. CAK, Vol. 6. Rüdiger Köppe Verlag. Cologne.

Dittmann, A. & M. Nüsser (2002) Siedlungsentwicklung im östlichen Hindukusch: Das Beispiel Chitral Town (North-West Frontier Province, Pakistan). Erdkunde, 56, 1: 60-72.

D'jačok, Mihail T. (2004) Kurut (ob odnoj altajsko-arijskoj izoglosse) [Kurut (about one Altai-Aryan isogloss)]. In: Techné grammatiké (Iskusstvo grammatiki), Vol. 1. Izdatel'stvo Novosibirskogo gosudarstvennogo universiteta, Novosibirsk, pp. 132-38.

Douglas, J.A. (1895) Notes on Chilàs Tradition. Proceedings of the Asiatic Society of Bengal 1894: 67-69.

Douglas, J.A. & C.H. Powell (1894) Report on Gor. Printed at the Government Central Printing Office, Simla. [Confidential].

Downes, Edmund (1873) Kafiristan: an account of the country, language, religion and customs of the Siah Posh Kafirs: considering especially Kafiristan as a suitable field for missionary labour. Printed by W.E. Ball. Lahore.

Drew, Frederick (1876) Notes on the Castes and on Certain Customs of the Dards. In: Douglas, R.K., ed., Transactions of the Second Session of the International Congress of Orientalists Held in London in September 1874. Trübner & Co., London, pp. 400-404.

————. (1879) Dârd Clans. Indian Antiquary, 8: 256.

Driem, George van (2001) Languages of the Himalayas: An Ethnolinguistic Handbook of the Greater Himalayan Region, containing an Introduction to the Symbiotic Theory of Language, 2 vols. Brill, Leiden. [With paragraphs on "Nuristani", pp. 1078-86; "Aryan society and languages", with notes on Indo-Aryan languages of Peristan, pp.1086-1103; "Burushaski and Beyond", pp. 1177-1221].

Dumezil, Georges (1995) Les trois fonctions dans le panthéon des Kafirs. In: *Id.*, Le roman des jumeaux et autres essais. Esquisses de mythologie. Éditions Gallimard, Paris, pp. 218-30.

Dupaigne, Bernard (2002a) Le Kafiristan ou les descendants d'Alexandre. In: Bianchini, M.C., ed., Afghanistan, une histoire millénaire. Réunion des Musées Nationaux, Paris, pp. 68-77. [The extravagant Alexander fantasy seems hard to die].
———. (2002b) Le Nuristan. In: Bianchini, M.C., ed., Afghanistan, une histoire millénaire. Réunion des Musées Nationaux, Paris, pp. 182-97.

Dvorjankov, Nikolaj A. (1964) Predvaritel'noe soobŝenie o govorah gornyh tadžikov Kunara (Afganistan) [Preliminary report on the dialects of the mountain Tajiks of Kunar (Afghanistan)]. In: Dvorjankov, N.A., ed., Indijskaja i iranskaja filologija. Nauka, Moscow, pp. 40–43.

Eardley Harwood, W.S. (1902) On the Indian Frontier. Rambles on the borders of Kafiristan. Pall Mall magazine, 28: 297-305. [With very poor text, but important early photos].

Ebert, Jorinde (1994) Niches, Columns, and Figures in some Petroglyphic Stupa Depictions of the Karakorum Highway. Artibus Asiae, 54, 3-4: 268-95.

Edelberg, Lennart (1952) Afghanistan som område for fremtidige etnografiske undersøgelser [Afghanistan as an area for future ethnographic research]. Naturens Verden, 36: 97-128.
———. (1974) Kalender og økologisk balance I Hindu-Kush. Almanak Skriv- og Rejse-Kalender. Kobenhavns Observatorium. Nyt Nordisk Forlag, Arnold Busck, Copenhagen.
———. (1981) Nuristan - Skov og Folk. Om del økologisk balanse i et senter for motstandsbevegelsen. Jordens Folk, 16,3: 295-302. [This is the last work published by Edelberg before his death in November 1981].

Èdel'man Džoj I. (1980) K substratnomu naslediju central'noaziatskogo jazykovogo sojuza [On the substrate heritage of the Central Asian language union]. Voprosy jazykoznanija, 5: 21-32.
———. (1982) K perspektivam rekonstrukciji obščeiranszkogo szosztojanija [On the perspectives of reconstructing the Common Iranian stage]. Voprosy jazykoznanija, 1: 37-47.
———. ed. (1999) Dardskije i nuristanskije jazyki [Dardic and Nuristani Languages]. Indrik, Moscow.
———. (2011) On the history of non-decimal systems and their elements in numerals of Aryan languages. In: Gvozdanović, J., ed., Numeral Types and Changes Worldwide. Berlin: De Gruyter Mouton, pp. 221-42.

Eggermont, Pierre H.L. (1984) Ptolemy, the Geographer, and the People of the Dards, Alexander in Buner; the Aornus Problem and the Dards of Dyrta. JCA, 7, 1: 73-124.

Eggert, Peter (1990) Die Frühere Sozialordnung Moolkhoos und Toorkhoos. Steiner Verlag Wiesbaden Gmbh, Stuttgart.

Ehlers, Eckart & H. Kreutzmann, eds. (2000) High Mountain Pastoralism in Northern Pakistan. Franz Steiner Verlag, Stuttgart.

Elfenbein, Josef (1999) Review of Degener (1998b). JRAS, 9, 3: 442-45.

Emadi, Hafizullah (2000) Praxis of taqiyya: perseverance of Pashaye Ismaili enclave, Nangarhar, Afghanistan. Central Asian Survey, 19,2: 253-64.

Emel'janov, Aleksandr J. & S.I. Kaverin (2019) Obraz grivny v tradicionnom iskusstve Vostočnogo Prigindukuš'ja (Kohistan, Kafiristan) [The Image of the Torque in the Traditional Art of the Eastern Hindukush Area (Kohistan, Kafiristan)]. Dizajn. Materialy. Tehnologija, 2(54): 68-71.

Emerson, Richard M. (1984) Charismatic Kingship: A Study of State Formation and Authority in Baltistan. JCA, 7, 2: 95-133.

Endresen, Rolf T. & K. Kristiansen (1981) Khowar Studies. In: Duchesne-Guillemin, J. & P. Lecoq, eds., Monumentum Georg Morgenstierne 1. Brill, Leiden, pp. 211-43.

Everhard, Carol & E. Mela-Athanasopoulou (2011) Selected Papers from the International Conference on Language Documentation and Tradition; with a special interest in the Kalash of the Hindu Kush valleys, Himalayas. Aristotle University, Thessaloniki.

Faccenna, Domenico (1980) Darel Valley Survey. E&W, 30: 205-207.

Faggi, Pier Paolo & M. Ginestri (1977) La rete dei bazar nell'alta valle dell'Indo. Rivista Geografica Italiana, 84, 3/4: 315-49 & 428-50.

Faizi, Inayatullah (1996) Wakhan. A Window into Central Asia. Al-Qalam, Islamabad.

Falk, Harry (2009) Making Wine in Gandhara under Buddhist Monastic Supervision. Bulletin of the Asia Institute, N.S., 23: 65-78.

————. (2021) Two Fragmentary Kharoṣṭhī Inscriptions. Annual Report of the International Research Institute for Advanced Buddhology at Soka University, 25: 7-16. [Concerning the Palola Shahi].

Fautz, Bruno (1963) Sozialstruktur und Bodennutzung in der Kulturlandschaft des Swat (Nordwesthimalaya). Wilhelm Schmitz Verlag, Giessen.

Felmy, Sabine (1986) Märchen und Sagen aus Hunza. Diederichs, Cologne.

———. (1989) Märchen und Sagen aus der Heimat des Schnees. Zusammengestellt und übersetzt von Sabine Felmy. Insel Verlag, Frankfurt.

———. (1993) Division of Labour and Women's Work in a Mountain Society. Hunza Valley in Pakistan. In: Raju, S. & D. Bagchi, eds., Women and Work in South Asia. Regional Patterns and Perspectives. Routledge, London, pp. 196-208.

———. (1996) The Voice of the Nightingale. A Personal Account of Wakhi Culture in Hunza. Oxford U.P., Karachi.

Fentz, Mytte (1994) Kalasha kvindens røde perler. Jordens Folk - Etnografisk Tidsskrift, 2: 73-79.

———. (1996) Natural Resources and Cosmology in Changing Kalasha Society. Nordic Institute of Asian Studies Publications, Copenhagen.

———. (1999) Den etnografiske Studiesamling og Hindu Kush forskningen. In: Høiris, I.O. et al., eds., Menneskelivets mangfoldighed. Arkæologisk og antropologisk forskning på Moesgård. Moesgård, Højbjerg, pp. 287-94.

———. (2010) The Kalasha. Mountain People of the Hindu Kush. Rhodos, Humblebaek (DK).

Ferdinand, Klaus (1974/75) The Ethnographical Collection of Moesgård Museum. Folk, 16-17: 475-84.

———. (1999) Den etnografiske samling på Moesgård. In: Høiris, I.O. et al., eds., Menneskelivets mangfoldighed. Arkæologisk og antropologisk forskning på Moesgård. Moesgård, Højbjerg, pp. 33-46.

Filigenzi, Anna (2010) Le vie dello Swat [in English]. In: Kriz, K., W. Cartwright & L. Hurni, eds., Mapping Different Geographies. Springer, Berlin, pp. 183-99.

———. (2011) Post-Gandharan Swat. Late Buddhist rock sculptures and Turki Śāhis' religious centers. In: Olivieri & Rahman (2011): 186-202.

———. (2015) Art and Landscape. Buddhist Rock Sculptures of Late Antique Swat/Uḍḍiyāna. Österreichische Akademie der Wissenschaften, Wien.

————. (2016) Dionysos et son double dans l'art du Gandhāra: dieux méconnus d'Asie. In: Jouanna, J., V. Schiltz & M. Zink, eds., Colloque "La Grèce dans les profondeurs de l'Asie". Diffusion de Boccard, Paris, pp. 289-304.

————. (2017) Walled Sacred Spaces: The Myth of Yima in the Religious Imagery of Pre-Islamic Afghanistan. Trans. Izumi Ueeda. In: Miyaji, A., ed., Studies on Buddhist Art in Asia, vol. 3, Central Asia, East and West Turkestan [in Japanese]. Chuo Koron Bijyutsu Shuppan, Tokyo, pp. 199-226. [Japanese translation with original English text. With a reference to the god Imra, useful for the Yamaraja/Yima/Yama issue].

————. (2019) Non-Buddhist Customs of Buddhist People: Visual and Archaeological Evidence from North-West Pakistan. In: Kellner, B., ed., Buddhism and the Dynamics of Transculturality. New approaches. Walter De Gruyter, Berlin, pp. 53-84. [A modified translation of Filigenzi (2016), focusing on the "Kafir/Dardic" substratum in Buddhist Swat].

————. (2020) The Myth of Yima in the Religious Imagery of Pre-Islamic Afghanistan: An Enquiry into the Epistemic Space of the Unwritten. In: Tournier, V., V. Eltschinger & M. Sernesi, eds., Archaeologies of the Written: Indian, Tibetan, and Buddhist Studies in Honour of Cristina Scherrer-Schaub. Unior Press, Naples, pp. 171-204. [An extended version of Filigenzi (2017), *q.v.*].

Firasat, Sadaf, *et al.* (2007) Y-chromosomal evidence for a limited Greek contribution to the Pathan population of Pakistan. European Journal of Human Genetics, 15: 121-26.

Fischer, Reinhard (1998) The History of Settlement in Punial, Northern Areas of Pakistan, in the Nineteenth and Twentieth Centuries. In: Stellrecht (1998cI): 511-26.

Fitch, Martin & G. Cooper (1985) Report on a Language and Dialect Survey in Kohistan District. JCA, 8, 1: 39-49.

Flowerday, Julie (2018) Britain and China's 19th Century Stalemate over Hunza—Kanjut. In: Holden, L., ed. (2018): 123-60. [An important study, with new historical sources].

Forsyth, Thomas D. (1870) Trade Routes between Northern India and Central Asia. In: Report of the British Association for the Advancement of Science, 1869. William Pollard, Exeter, pp. 161-62.

———. (1875) Report of a Mission to Yarkund in 1873, under Command of Sir T.D. Forsyth [...], with historical and geographical information regarding the possessions of the Ameer of Yarkund. Foreign Department Press, Calcutta. [This is an essential source on an area that was historically a major source of external influence on northern Peristan].

Francfort, Henri-Paul (1991) Note on Some Bronze Age Petroglyphs of Upper Indus and Central Asia. Pakistan Archaeology, 26: 125-35.

Francke, August H. (1899) Wer sind die Brogpas? Nebensächliches von einer Missionsreise. Herrnhut, 32 (52): 413-15.

———. (1901a) Die vorbuddhistische Religion Tibets. Allgemeine Missions-Zeitschrift, 28: 579-84.

———. (1901b) The Ladakhi Pre-Buddhist Marriage Ritual. Indian Antiquary, 30: 131-49.

———. (1909) Ten Ancient Historical Songs from Western Tibet. Indian Antiquary, 38: 57-68. [With at least one from Dah].

Frembgen, Jürgen W. (1983) Die Nagerkuč im Licht der populären Reiseliteratur - ein Beitrag zur Vorurteilsforschung in Pakistan. In: Snoy (1983J): 147-62.

———. (1984) Einige Bemerkungen zur Bedeutung des Pferdes in der Kultur der Nagerkuts (Nord-Pakistan). In: Ozols, J. & V. Thewalt, eds., Aus dem Osten des Alexanderreiches. Völker und Kulturen zwischen Orient und Okzident. Iran, Afghanistan, Pakistan, Indien. DuMont, Cologne, pp. 219-28.

———. (1985) Zentrale Gewalt in Nager (Karakorum). Politische Organisationsformen, ideologische Begründungen des Königtums und Veränderungen in der Moderne. Franz Steiner Verlag Wiesbaden Gmbh, Stuttgart.

———. (1986a) Aspekte der Oralität und Literalität: ihre Implikationen für das Geschichtsbewusstsein der muslimischen Nagerkuts in Nordpakistan. Anthropos, 81: 567-81.

———. (1986b) Ethnographical Field Research on the History and Culture of Nager: Some Preliminary Remarks on the Process of Settlement. CAJ, 30, 1-2: 22-32.

———. (1988a) Königskronen aus Nager. Tribus, 37: 69-82.

———. (1988b) Volkstümliche Überlieferungen aus Nager. Indo-Asia, 30, 3: 39-43.

———. (1989) Bergvölker in Nordpakistan. In: Kalter (1989): 171-78.

———. (1992) Historical Rivalry and Religious Boundaries in the Karakorum: the Case of Nager and Hunza. In: Seyschab, C.-

A., A. Sievers & S. Szynkiewicz, eds., Frontiers, Boundaries, Limits: Their Notions and their Experiences in East Asia. Horlemann Verlag, Unkel & Bad Honnef, pp. 80-88.

————. (1996) Local Dignitaries as Historians: Guardians of Traditional Culture from Gilgit, Hunza, and Nager (Northern Pakistan). In: Bashir & Israr-ud-Din (1996): 97-104.

————. (1998) Zur Biographie einer Reiterstatue der Kalasha (Hindukusch). Baessler-Archiv, 46: 329-42.

————. (1999a) Indus Kohistan. An Historical and Ethnographic Outline. CAJ, 43, 1: 70-98.

————. (1999b) Musk, Bezoar and Bitumen: Materia Medica in Northern Pakistan. Hamdard Medicus, 42, 1: 24-27.

————. (2003) Review of Cacopardo & Cacopardo (2001). CAJ, 47, 2: 135-37.

————. (2005) Sayyid Shah Wali – Missionary and Miracle-worker. Notes on the Hagiography and Cult of a Muslim Saint in Nager and Hunza (Northern Pakistan). ZDMG, 155: 69-102. [With data on the Islamization of the area].

————. (2007) Traditional Art and Architecture in Hunza and Nager. In: Bianca (2007): 133-48.

————. (2008) Old Forts in Harban: Settlement and Islamization in Indus Kohistan. In: Skyhawk (2008a): 253-59.

————. (2014) The Closed Valley. With Fierce Friends in the Pakistani Himalayas. Oxford U.P., Karachi.

————. (2017) The Arts and Crafts of the Hunza Valley in Pakistan. Living Traditions in the Karakoram. Oxford U.P., Karachi.

————. (2022) At the Foot of the Fairy Mountain. The Nagerkuts of the Karakoram, Northern Pakistan. Myths - Traditions - Folklife. Reimer Verlag, Berlin. [This is a greatly re-worked English version of Frembgen (1985)]

Fremont, Annette (1984) Remarques sur l'organization des sociétés parlant le burushaski. Bulletin d'études indiennes, 2: 117-22.

Fussman, Gérard (1975) Review of Jettmar & Edelberg (1974J). Journal Asiatique, 263: 235-36.

————. (1986) La route oubliée entre l'Inde et la Chine. L'Histoire, 93: 50-60.

————. (1988) Kafiristan/Nuristan: avatars de la définition d'une ethnie. In: Digard, J.P., ed., Le fait ethnique en Iran et Afghanistan. Éditions du CNRS, Paris, pp. 55-64.

————. (1989b) Languages as a Source for History. In: Dani, A.H., History of Northern Areas of Pakistan. NIHCR, Islamabad, pp. 43-58.

————. (1989c) Les inscriptions Kharoṣṭhī de la plain de Chilas. In: Jettmar, König & Thewalt (1989): 1-39.

————. (1991) La nostalgie occidentale des paradis perdus. In: Liber (supplement au no. 90 de: Actes de la recherche en sciences sociales), pp. 25-27.

————. (1993) Chilas, Hatun et les bronzes bouddhiques du Cachemire. In: Jettmar, König & Bemmann (1993): 1-60.

————. (1994b) Chilas-Thalpan et l'art du Tibet. In: Fussman, Jettmar & König (1994): 57-72.

————. (2004) Dans quel type de bâtiment furent trouvés les manuscrits de Gilgit? Journal Asiatique, 292, 1-2: 101-50

————. (2012) Qu'y a-t-il dans un nom: Imrā au Nouristan. In: Azarnouche, S. & C. Redard, eds., Yama /Yima: variations indo-iraniennes sur la geste mythique. Édition-Diffusion de Boccard, Paris, pp. 67-82.

Fussman, G. & D. König, eds. (1997) Die Felsbildstation Shatial. MANP, Vol. 2. Philipp von Zabern, Mainz. Permalink: https://digi.hadw-bw.de/view/manp2

Fussman, G., K. Jettmar & D. König, eds. (1994) ANP. Vol. 3. Philipp von Zabern, Mainz. Permalink: https://digi.hadw-bw.de/view/anp3

Gaillard, Claire, et al. (2002) Discovery of Recent Lithic Industries with Archaic Features in the Hindu Kush Range (Chitral District, North Pakistan). Indo-Pacific Prehistory Association Bulletin, 22: 25-33.

Ghiyasoddin 'Ali di Yazd. 2009. Le gesta di Tamerlano. A cura di Michele Bernardini. [In his Italian translation of this biography of Timur, Michele Bernardini pays some attention to the emperor's abortive attempt to conquer Kafiristan in 1398. This source integrates and amends the more famous Zafar Nama of Sharif al-Din.]

Giglioli, Enrico H. (1889) Alcune notizie intorno agli ariani primitivi detti "Siah Posh" abitanti il Kafiristan. AAE, 19: 441-47.

Ginestri, Mario (1977) La regione del Kafiristan. Bollettino della Società geografica italiana, Serie 10,6: 431-68.

Girdlestone, Charles (1874) Memorandum on Cashmere and Some Adjacent Countries during 1871. Foreign Department Press,

Calcutta. [H4p., appendix. National Archives of India, New Delhi].

Gnoli, Gherardo (1980) Brief Report of the Archaeological Mission of IsMEO in Asia, Darel Valley Survey. E&W, 30: 205-207.

Godfrey, Stuart H. (1898) Report on the Gilgit Agency and Wazarat and the Countries of Chilas, Hunza-Nagar, and Yasin, including Ashkuman, Ghizr and Koh. 1896-97. Office of the Superintendent of Government Printing, Calcutta.

———. (1904) Dir, Swat and the Chitral Agency: Note on Customary Law in Swat. JASB, 73, Extra Number: 28-34.

———. (1912) A Summer Exploration in the Panjkora Kohistan. The Geographical Journal, 40,1: 45-57. [With important notes on former Kafirs in Dir and Swat].

———. (1936) In the Footsteps of Fa Hien, in Upper Swat. Journal of the Royal Central Asian Society, 23,3: 453-64.

Göhlen, Ruth (1997) The Background of Genealogical Time Structuring and Remembering: Aspects of Time in Astor Valley, Northern Pakistan. In: Stellrecht (1997a): 161-95.

Gornenskij, Ioann (2000) Legendy Pamira i Gindukuša [Legends of the Pamirs and the Hindu Kush]. Aleteja, Moscow.

Gratz, Katrin (1998) Walking on Women's Paths in Gilgit – Gendered Space, Boundaries, and Boundary Crossing. In: Stellrecht (1998cII): 489-508.

———. (2006) Verwandtschaft, Geschlecht und Raum. Aspekte weiblicher Lebenswelt in Gilgit, Nordpakistan. CAK, Vol. 11. Rüdiger Köppe Verlag, Cologne.

Graziosi, Paolo (2004) – see Ciruzzi, Mainardi & Roselli (2004).

———. (2007) – see Ciruzzi, Mainardi & Roselli (2007).

Grierson, George A. (1900a) On Pashai, Laghmani or Dehgani. ZDMG, 54: 563-98.

———. (1900b) On the Languages Spoken beyond the North-Western Frontier of India, with a Map. JRAS, 32, 2: 501-10.

———. (1911) Note on Dr. Sten Konow's article on Bashgali. The Journal of the Royal Asiatic Society of Great Britain and Ireland. 43,1: 195–97.

Griffith, William (1847) Journal of Travels in Assam, Burma, Bootan, Affghanistan and the Neighbouring Countries. Bishop's College Press, Calcutta. [With visits to Kafir villages around Chighar Serai].

Grjunberg, Aleksandr L. (1969) K izučeniju nuristanskogo fol'klora. [On the study of Nuristani folklore]. In: Iranskaja filologija.

Kratkoje izloženije dokladov naučnoj konferenciji posvjaščennoj 60-letiju prof. A.N. Boldyreva [Iranian philology. Festschrift A.N. Boldyrev]. Nauka, Moscow, pp. 52-55.

————. (1980) Putešestvija po Vostočnomu Gindukušu (1963-1968) [Travels in Eastern Hindu Kush (1963-1968)]. In: Romodin, V. A., ed., Strany i narody Vostoka. Vol. 22: Srednjaja i Central'naja Azija. Geografija, ètnografija, istorija. Kn. 2 [Countries and peoples of the East. Vol. 22: Middle and Central Asia. Book 2]. Nauka, Moscow, pp. 28-45.

————. (1981) K izučeniju kafirskih jazykov. Jazyk selenija Vama. [On the study of Kafir languages. The language of the village Wama]. In: Bogoliubov, M.N., ed., Iranskoje jazykoznanije. Ježegodnik 1980. Nauka, Moscow, pp. 228-31.

————. (=Grjunberg) (1994a) Materialy po ètnografii i mifologii Nuristana iz arhiva M. S. Andreeva [Materials on the ethnography and mythology of Nuristan from the archive of M.S. Andreev]. In: Söhnen-Thieme & Hinüber (1994): 83-107.

————. (1994b) Nuristani languages. In: Brown, K & S. Ogilvie eds., Concise Encyclopedia of Languages of the World. Elsevier, Oxford, pp. 787-88.

————. (1995a) Nuristanskie teksty iz arhiva M. S. Andreeva [Nuristani texts from the archive of M.S. Andreev]. In: Vasil'kov, Y.V. & N. V. Gurov, eds., Sthapakašraddha: Sbornik statej pamjati G. A. Zografa [Sthapakašraddha: Studies in memory of G. A. Zograf]. Centr "Peterburg Vostokovedenie", St. Petersburg, pp. 144-61.

————. (1995b) Kafirskij gimn bogu Monu (Iz arhiva M.S. Andreeva) [A Kafir hymn to the god Mon (From the archive of M.S. Andreev)]. Peterburgskoe vostokovedenie, 7: 605-20.

————. (1996) Materialy po ètnografii dardskih narodnostej Vostočnogo Gindukuša (Dolina Digal) [Materials on the ethnography of the Dardic peoples of the Eastern Hindukush (Digal Valley)]. Kunstkamera. Ètnografičeskie tetradi, 10: 310-31. [This is the area of the Ningalami-Grangali language].

Grjunberg, A.L. & I.-M. Steblin-Kamenskij (1974) Etnolingvističeskaja xarakteristika Vostočnogo Gindukusa. [An ethnolinguistic description of the Eastern Hindukush]. In: Bruk, S.I., ed., Problemy kartografirovanija v jazykoznaniji i etnografiji

[Cartography Issues in Linguistics and Ethnography]. Nauka, Leningrad [St. Petersburg], pp. 276-83.

Grombtchevsky, Bronislaw L. (n.d.) Resoconto del viaggio a Kashgar e nella Kashgaria Meridionale nel 1885 del Funzionario Anziano delle Commissioni Speciali presso il Governatore Militare della provincia di Fergana, tenente B.L. Grombtchevsky. [An account of the journey to Kashgar and southern Kashgaria in 1885]. Pinerolo (Turin), Arti Grafiche Alzani, 1994. [Italian trans. from Russian by Lionello Fogliano].

Grombtchevsky, B.L. (1889-91) Lettere scritte durante la spedizione del 1889-1890 e "Situazione politica attuale dei khanati del Pamir e della linea di confine con il Kashmir". [Letters written during the 1889-90 expedition and "Current political situation of the Pamir khanates and the Kashmir border line"]. Pinerolo (Turin), Arti Grafiche Alzani, 1996. [Italian trans. from Russian by Lionello Fogliano, includes Grombčevskij (1891a)].

————. Grombčevskij, B.L. (= Grombtchevsky) (1891a) Sovremennoe političeskoe položenie pamirskih hanstv i pograničnoj linii s Kašmirom: Voen.-polit. Očerk [The current political situation of the Pamir khanates and the Kashmir border line: A military-political study]. Novyj Margelan, Ferghana.

————. (1891b) Doklad o putešestvii v 1889-1890 dlja issledovanija gornyh dolin Gindukuša, vostočnyh sklonov Gimalaja i okrain Severo-Zapadnogo Tibeta [Report on travel in 1889-1890 for the study of the mountain valleys of the Hindu Kush, the eastern slopes of the Himalayas and the north-western end of Tibet]. St. Petersburg. [This is a narrative of G.'s unsuccessful attempt at entering Kafiristan and of his encounters with Francis Younghusband]

————. (1891c) Relazione del capitano B.L. Grombtchevsky sul viaggio negli anni 1889-1890 per l'esplorazione delle valli montane dell'Hindu Kush, dei versanti orientali dell'Himalaya e dell'estremità nord occidentale del Tibet, letta nella sessione straordinaria della Società Geografica Imperiale Russa, 10 gennaio 1891. Pinerolo (Turin), Arti Grafiche Alzani, 1993. [Italian trans. from Russian by Lionello Fogliano of Grombčevskij (1891b)].

Grötzbach, Erwin (1984) Bagrot. Beharrung und Wandel einer peripheren Talschaft Karakorum. Die Erde, 115: 305-21.

Grünberg - see Grjunberg

GSI (General Staff, India) (1928a) Military Report and Gazetteer of the
       Gilgit Agency and of the Independent Territories of Tangir and
       Darel. 1927, Second Edition. Government of India Press, Simla.
———. (1928b) Military Report and Gazetteer on Chitral. Second
       Edition. Government of India Press, Calcutta.
Guerreiro, Fernão (1930) Jahangir and the Jesuits. With an account of
       The Travels of Benedict Goes and The Mission to Pegu. From
       the relations of Father Fernão Guerreiro. Translated by C. H.
       Payne. [With useful notes by Payne on Goes's journey, see
       Ricci (1949)].
Guha, Biraja S. (1938) The racial composition of the Hindukush tribes.
       Presidential address, Section of Anthropology, 25th Indian
       Science Congress. Indian Science Congress Association,
       Calcutta.
Guillard, Jean-Michel (1974) Seul chez les Kalash. Carrefour des
       Lettres, Paris. [A young traveler's naive but extensive account
       of a stay with the Kalasha in 1974, with lots of photos].
Gul'džonov, Mamadžan (1967) Zavoevanie Kafiristana i rasprostranenie
       v nem Islama [Conquest of Kafiristan and the spread of Islam
       there]. In: Kulagina, L.M., ed., Blizhny i Sredny Vostok.
       Istorija. Ekonomika [Near and Middle East. History.
       Economics]. Nauka, Moscow, pp. 22-29.
Gurdon, Bertrand E.M. (1903) Military Report on Chitral. Part I.
       Government Central Printing Office, Simla. [An important
       source on the demography and ethnic composition of Chitral
       at the arrival of the British, by their first Political Agent there].
———. (1933) Chitral Memories. Events leading up to the Siege. The
       Himalayan Journal. 5, pp. 1-27. [With an indication on
       Kalasha Kafirs in Shishi Kuh in the 1890s].
Hackin, Joseph (1926) Les Idoles du Kāfiristān. Artibus Asiae, 1,4:
       258-62.
Haidar, Mirza M. (Dughlat) (1895) Tarikh-i-Rashidi. A History of the
       Moghuls of Central Asia. An English Version, Edited, with
       Commentary, Notes and Map by N. Elias, the Translation by
       E. Denison Ross. S. Low, Marston & Co., London. [A
       fundamental source on the "great Kafiristan" of the 16th
       century].
Hakal, Muezuddin (2014). An Ancient Settlement at Karōsingal in
       Gurunjur, Punyāl Valley, Gilgit-Baltistan, Pakistan: A
       Preliminary Study. Pakistan Heritage, 6: 141-51.

————. (2015) Origin and Development of Archaeological Studies of District Ghizer, Gilgit-Baltistan (Pakistan), Journal of Asian Civilization, 38,2: 31-48.

————. (2016) History and Archaeology of District Ghizer: A Case Study of Tehsil Punyāl, Gilgit-Baltistan (Pakistan). Lambert Academic Publishing, Riga.

————. (2019) The Mausoleums of Collective Burials in Ghizer District, Gilgit-Baltistan (Pakistan). Journal of Asian Civilizations, 42,1: 173-203.

Hale, Austin & R. Trail (1995) A rhetorical structure analysis of a Kalasha narrative. Summer Institute of Linguistics, Horsleys Green, UK.

Halfmann, Jakob (2021) Terminological Proposals for the Nuristani Languages. Himalayan Linguistics, 20, 1. [Online open access journal].

————. (2022) Advances in the historical phonology of the Nuristani languages. In: Degener & Hill (2022).

Hallet, Stanley I. & R. Samizay (1975) Nuristan's Cliff-Hangers. Afghanistan Journal, 2,2: 65-72.

Halliday, Stephen I. (1962) The Kalash Kafirs. The Geographical Magazine, 35: 75-82.

Hallier, Ulrich W. (1991) Petroglyphen in Nordpakistan: Neuentdeckungen an Gilgit und Yasin. Antike Welt: Zeitschrift für Archäologie und Urgeschichte, 22,1: 2-20.

Hamp, Eric (1966) Notes on Kafir Phonology. In: Dil, A. S., ed., Shahidullah Presentation Volume. Linguistic Research Group of Pakistan, Lahore, pp. 89-100.

————. (1968) On *R in Kafir. In: Krishnamurti, B., ed., Studies in Indian Linguistics. Prof. M. B. Emeneau ṣaṣṭipūrti volume. Centres of Advanced Study in Linguistics, Poona and Annamalainagar, pp. 121-37.

————. (1969) Two Prasun notes. Indo-Iranian Journal, 12,1: 24–26.

————. (1977) The quality of nasal clusters in Prasun. Acta Orientalia, 38: 41–42.

————. (1993) K metodike analiza istoriko-fonetičeskih anomalij. Indra, ego luk i vinogradnaja gvozd'. [On the method of analysing historical phonetic anomalies. Indra, his bow and grapes]. Voprosy jazykoznanija, 2: 80-82.

————. (2002) Indic-Nuristani sakth-i/an-, cupti- and Albanian sup. Linguistica, 42, 1: 3-4.

Hansen, Roland (1997) Demonic Sabotage - Corruption - Natural Hazard: Channel Breaks and the Manipulation of "Myth" in Astor Valley, Northern Pakistan. In: Stellrecht (1997a): 197-234.

Harrison, John (1995) Himalayan Buildings. Recording Vernacular Architecture, Mustang and the Kalash. The British Council, Islamabad.

———. (1996) Kalash Buildings. In: Bashir & Israr-ud-din (1996): 345-58.

———. (1998) A Brief Introduction to the Architecture of the Kalasha, Chitral. In: Stellrecht (1998cI): 595-602.

Haserodt, Klaus (1989) Hochgebirgsräume Nordpakistans im Hindukusch, Karakorum und Westhimalaya. Beiträge zur Natur- und Kulturgeographie. Institut für Geographie der Technischen Universität Berlin, Berlin.

Hashmatullah Khan, A.-H.M. (1987) History of Baltistan. Translated by Adam Nayyar. Lok Virsa (NIFTH), Islamabad 1987. [Original Urdu edition 1939. The chronology is conjectural].

Hasrat, Gul M.K. (1996) Some Ancient Customs of Chitral. In: Bashir & Israr-ud-Din (1996): 181-92.

Hauptmann, Harald (2007) Pre-Islamic Heritage in the Northern Areas of Pakistan. In: Bianca (2007): 21-39.

———. (2008) Rock Art in the Upper Indus Region. In: Luczanits, C., ed., Gandhara, the Buddhist Heritage of Pakistan. Philipp von Zabern, Mainz, pp. 352-57.

———. (2013) Die Felsbildstation Thalpan: 6. Kataloge Ba Das, Ba Das Ost, Gali, Gukona, Mostar Nala, Ke Ges, Ame Ges und Drang Das. MANP, Vol. 11. Philipp von Zabern, Mainz. Permalink: https://digi.hadw-bw.de/view/manp11

Hauptmann, H. & M. Bemmann (1993) Rockcarvings and Inscriptions along the Karakorum Highway. Field Campaign 1990. Preliminary Report. In: Gail, A.J. & G. Merissen, eds., South Asian Archaeology 1991. Franz Steiner Verlag, Stuttgart, pp. 313-22.

Hayward, George W. (1871) Letters from Mr. G.W. Hayward on his explorations in Gilgit and Yassin. JRAS, 41: 1-46.

Hayward, G.S.W. & Mahomed Amin (1869) Route from Jellalabad to Yarkand through Chitral, Badakhshan and Pamir Steppe, given by Mahomed Amin of Yarkand, with Remarks by G.S.W. Hayward. Proceedings of the Royal Geographical Society, 13: 122-30.

Heegård Petersen, J., (2012a) How to put and take in Kalasha. In:
    Kopecka, A. & B. Narasimhan, eds., Events of Putting and
    Taking: A crosslinguistic perspective. John Benjamins
    Publishing Company, Amsterdam & Philadelphia, pp. 349-
    61.
————. (2012b) Animacy, Vedic accent and Kalasha Case Allomorphy.
    MSS, 66, 1: 55-64.
————. (2014) Local case semantics in Kalasha. Journal of South
    Asian Languages and Linguistics, 1, 2: 187-215.
————. (2015) Kalasha Texts – With introductory grammar. Acta
    Linguistica Hafniensia, 47, 1: 1-275.
Heegård Petersen, J. & H. Liljegren (2018) Geomorphic coding in
    Palula and Kalasha. Acta Linguistica Hafniensia, 50, 2: 129-
    60.
Heegård Petersen, J. & I.E. Mørch (2004) Retroflex vowels and other
    peculiarities in the Kalasha sound system. In: Saxena, A., ed.,
    Himalayan Languages. Past and Present. Mouton de Gruyter,
    Berlin, pp. 57-76.
————. Kalasha dialects and a glimpse into the history of the Kalasha
    language. In: Simmelkjær, B. et al., eds., Usque ad radices:
    Indo-European studies in honour of Birgit Anette Olsen.
    Museum Tusculanum Press, Copenhagen, pp. 233-48.
Heegård [Petersen], J. & Nabaig (2022) Ek akhabir sher ais-- There
    was an Old Lion: A Linguistic Analysis of a Kalasha Narrative
    as told by Sher John of Kraka, Mumoret. In: Baart, Liljegren
    & Payne (2022): 198-241.
Hegedűs, Irén (2002) Proto-Nuristani *kur-ak 'offspring'. In: Cavoro,
    F., ed., The Linguist's Linguist. A Collection of Papers in
    Honour of Alexis Manaster-Ramer. Lincom Europa, Munich,
    pp. 189-96.
————. (2005) Review of Èdel'man (1999). Indogermanische
    Forschungen, 110: 319-27.
————. (2011) A nurisztáni nyelvek genetikus osztályozásának
    alternatívái. [Alternatives in the genetic classification of
    Nuristani languages] In: Fekete, M., ed., "...eleitől fogva"
    Régész – Tanár – Ember. A 75 éves Makkay János köszöntése
    [Festschrift J. Makkai]. BTK- Genianet, Pécs, pp. 137-54.
————. (2012) The RUKI-rule in Nuristani. In: Nielsen, B. et al., eds.,
    The Sound of Indo-European. Museum Tusculanum Press,
    Copenhagen, pp. 199-21.

————. (2017) The etymology of Prasun *at'əg* 'one, once, a (little)'. In: Simmelkjær, B. *et al.*, eds., Usque ad radices: Indo-European studies in honour of Birgit Anette Olsen. Museum Tusculanum Press, Copenhagen, pp. 249-60.

————. (2018) Progress in Prasun Linguistic Studies. Review article of Buddruss & Degener (2015) & (2017). Archiv Orientální, 86, 1: 177-88.

————. (2020a) A Hindukus kincsei. A nurisztáni népek és nyelvek történeti kutatása. [Treasures of the Hindukush. The historical investigation of Nuristani peoples and their languages]. In: Böhm G., D. Czeferner & T. Fedeles, eds., Pécsi Tudományegyetem, Bölcsész Akadémia, 4. [University of Pécs, Academy of Humanities, 4.]. A Pécsi Tudományegyetem Bölcsészet- és Társadalomtudományi Kar - Tudományos Diákköri Tanácsának Kiadványa, Pécs, pp. 295-328.

————. (2020b) The etymology of Prasun *ü'pün*. In: Bichlmeier, H., R. Sukač & O. Šefčík, eds., Etymologus. Festschrift for Václav Blažek. Baar Verlag, Hamburg, pp. 211-24.

————. (forthcoming in 2022) Towards reconstructing Proto-Nuristani: State of the art and prospects for progress. In: Degener & Hill (2022).

Hellenthal, Garrett, *et al.* (2016) The Kalash genetic Isolate? The evidence for recent admixture. AJHG, 98: 396-97.

Hemphill, Brian E. (2009) Bioanthropology of the Hindu Kush High Lands: A Dental Morphology Investigation. Pakistan Heritage, 1: 19-36.

————. (2020) Origins and Interactions of the Ethnic Groups of Greater Dardistan I: A Tooth Size Allocation Analysis of the Khow of Chitral District. Ancient Pakistan, 19: 23-99. [This study investigates "Khow biological origins in light of three models offered for the population history of Greater Dardistan": the "Aryan invasion", the "Indo-Iranian" and the "Indigenous" model].

Hemphill, B.E., I. Ali, S. Blaylock & N. Willits (2013) Are the Kho an Indigenous Population of the Hindu Kush? A Dental Morphometric Approach. In: M. Tosi & D. Frenez, eds., South Asian Archaeology 2008, Vol. I. Archaeopress-BAR, Oxford, pp. 127-37.

Hemphill, B.E., M. Zahir & I. Ali (2017) Skeletal Analysis of Gandharan Graves at Shah Mirandeh, Singoor, Chitral. Ancient Pakistan, 28: 1-60.

Herbers, Hiltrud (1998) Arbeit und Ernährung in Yasin. Aspekte des Produktions-Reproduktions-Zusammenhangs in einem Hochgebirgstal Nordpakistans. Mit 40 Abbildungen und 45 Tabellen. Franz Steiner Verlag, Stuttgart.

Herbordt, Oskar (1926) Eine Reise nach 'Där-i-Nur' im Nordosten Afganistans [sic]. Petermanns Mitteilungen, 72: 206-208.

Herrlich, Albert (1939-40) A Contribution to Anthropology of the Hindu Kush Kafirs. Rendered into English by A.K. Mitra. Journal of the Indian Anthropological Institute, 2, 3-4: 51-99. [This long-forgotten article seems to be the only publication in English from the "Deutsche in Hindukusch" Expedition 1935].

Hill, John E. (2003) The Western Regions According to the Hou Han-shu. The Xiyu Juan ("Chapter on the Western Regions") from Hou Hanshu 88. Translated by J.E. Hill. Second Edition, extensively revised with additional notes and appendices. Silk Road Seattle Project, Seattle.

Hinüber, Oskar von (1983) Zu Einigen Felsinschriften in Brāhmī aus Nordpakistan. In: Snoy (1983J): 272-79.

———. (1989) Brāhmī Inscriptions on the History and Culture of the Upper Indus Valley. In: Jettmar, König & Thewalt (1989): 41-72.

———. (2004) Die Palola Ṣāhis. Ihre Steininschriften, Inschriften auf Bronzen, Handschriftenkolophone und Schutzzauber. Materialien für Geschichte von Gilgit und Chilas. ANP, Vol. 5. Philipp von Zabern, Mainz. [A landmark study on the Buddhist period in Peristan]. Permalink: https://digi.hadw-bw.de/view/anp5

———. (2007) Three New Bronzes from Gilgit. Annual Report of the International Research Institute for Advanced Buddhology at Soka University, 10: 39–44.

———. (2009) More on Gilgit Bronzes and Some Additions to "Die Palola Ṣāhis". Annual Report of the International Research Institute for Advanced Buddhology at Soka University, 12: 3-6.

———. (2014) The Gilgit Manuscripts: An Ancient Buddhist Library in Modern Research. In: Harrison, P. & J.U. Hartmann, eds., From Birch Bark to Digital Data. Österreichische Akademie der Wissenschaften, Wien, pp. 79-135.

———. (2021) Vaiśramaṇavarman, King of the Dards. Annual Report of the International Research Institute for Advanced Buddhology at Soka University, 25: 3-5.

Hock, H. Heinrich (2015) The Northwest of South Asia and Beyond: the issue of Indo-Aryan retroflection yet again. Journal of South Asian Languages and Linguistics, 2, 1: 111-35.

Hock, H.H. & E. Bashir, eds. (2016) The Languages and Linguistics of South Asia. A Comprehensive Guide. De Gruyter, Berlin. [With several contributions by E. Bashir discussing aspects of Dardic languages].

Holden, Livia, ed. (2018) Law, Culture, and Governance in Hunza. Department of Cross-Cultural and Regional Studies at University of Copenhagen. Copenhagen = NAVEIÑ REET: Nordic Journal of Law and Social Research, 8. [A collection of essays focused mainly on change, development and socio-political issues, but with valuable data on pre-colonial history and traditions].

Holdich, T.H. (1896) The Origin of the Kafir of the Hindu Kush. The Geographical Journal, 7: 42-49.

Holdschlag, Arnd (2005) "...a curious and intricate ethnological puzzle": Diversität und rezente interkulturelle Interaktionsprozesse im Hochgebirge Nordwestpakistans. Südasien, 25, 2-4: 17-21.

Holzwarth, Wolfgang (1980) Segmentation und Staatsbildung in Afghanistan: Traditionale sozio-politische Organisation in Badakhshan, Wakhan und Sheghnan. In: Greussing, K. & J-H. Grevemeyer, eds., Revolution in Iran und Afghanistan. Syndicat, Frankfurt am Main, pp. 177-233.

———. (1993) Auguste Court's Questionnaire on the Kafir Way of Life Answered by Tak and Shamlar from Kamdesh. Paper presented at the European Conference of Kalasha Researchers, Moesgård 1993. Berlin. Unpublished manuscript.

———. (1994a) Die Ismailiten in Nordpakistan. Zur Entwicklung einer Religiösen Minderheit im Kontext neuer Aussenbeziehungen. Verlag Das Arabische Buch, Berlin.

———. (1994b) Sich verständlich machen. Tak und Shamlar aus Kamdesh beantworten einen Fragebogen des Generals Auguste Court zum "kafirischen Lebensstil". In: Elsas, C. et al., eds., Tradition und Translation. Zum Problem der interkulturellen Übersetzbarkeit religiöser Phänomene. [Festschrift C. Colpe]. De Gruyter, Berlin, pp. 179-99.

———. (1996) Chitral History, 1540-1660: Comments on Sources and Historiography. In: Bashir & Israr-ud-Din (1996): 117-34.

————. (1997) Islam in Baltistan: Problems of Research on the Formative Period. In: Stellrecht (1997a): 1-40.

————. (1998a) Ein Kriegszug in das Bashgal-Tal (um 1790) und sein regionalpolitischer Kontext. In: Kushev *et al.* (1998): 369-84.

————. (1998b) Change in Pre-Colonial Times – An Evaluation of Sources on the Karakorum and Eastern Hindukush Regions (from 1500 to 1800). In: Stellrecht (1998cII): 297-336.

————. (1999) Materialien zur Geschichte des Karakorum und östliches Hindukusch 1500-1800. Anlage 4 zum Abschlussbericht des Projekts "Wandel im vorkolonialen Gebirgsraum [...]" im Schwerpunktprogramm "Kulturraum Karakorum" der Deutschen Forschungsgemeinschaft. Unpublished.

————. (2006) Sources of Gilgit, Hunza and Nager History (1500-1800) and Comments on the Oral Roots of Local Historiography. In: Kreutzmann (2006a): 171-90.

————. (2008) Der persische Feenprinz besiegt den Kannibalenkönig von Gilgit: ein Kapitel aus der Kulturgeschichte Nordpakistans. In: Markus Ritter, ed., Iran und iranisch geprägte Kulturen: Studien zum 65. Geburtstag von Bert G. Fragner. Reichert, Wiesbaden, pp. 174–86.

Hook, Peter Edwin (2005) Searching for the Goddess: A Study of Sensory and Other Impersonal Causative Expressions in the Shina of Gilgit. In: Singh, R. & T. Bhattacharya, eds., The Year book of South Asian Languages and Linguistics 2005. Special Issue on South Asian Syntax. Mouton de Gruyter, Berlin, pp. 165-88.

Howard, J.E. (1889) Memoir of William Watts Mcnair, [...]. The First European Explorer of Kafiristan. Keymer & Co., London.

Howell, Evelyn B. (1908) Some Songs of Chitral. JASB (N.S.), 4: 381-89.

Humbach, Helmut. (1980a) Hybrid Sanskrit in the Gilgit Brāhmī Inscriptions. SII, 5-6: 99–121.

————. (1980b) Die Kharoṣṭhī-Inschriften aus Gilgit. MSS, 39: 53–58.

————. (1985) The Sogdian Inscriptions at Thor-Shatial. JCA, 8: 51-57.

————. (1994) Review of Sims-Williams (1992). ZDMG, 144: 177-85.

Hussain, Qandeel (2021a) Fundamental Frequency and Phonation Differences in the Production of Stop Laryngeal Contrasts of Endangered Shina. Languages, 6: 139(1-17).[Online publication].

————. (2021b) Phonetic correlates of laryngeal and place contrasts of
    Burushaski. Speech Communication, 126: 71–89.
Hussain, Q. & J. Mielke (2020a) An acoustic and articulatory study of
    laryngeal and place contrasts of Kalasha (Indo-Aryan,
    Dardic). Journal of the Acoustical Society of America (Special
    Issue: Phonetics of Under-Documented Languages), 147,4:
    2873-90.
————. (2020b) Kalasha (Pakistan) – Language Snapshot. In: Austin,
    P.K., ed., Language Documentation and Description 17. EL
    Publishing, London, pp. 66-75.
Hussain, Shafqat (2015) Remoteness and Modernity. Transformation
    and Continuity in Northern Pakistan. Yale U.P., New Haven
    and London. [An ethnography of Hunza].
Illi, Dieter W. (1988) Die Laterne über dem Wohnraum. Eine
    Sonderform seiner Überdeckung in den Gebirgstälern des
    Hindukush. In: Bucherer-Dietschi (1988): 93-107.
————. (1991) Das Hindukush-Haus. Zum symbolischen Prinzip der
    Sonderstellung von Raummitte und Raumhintergrund. Franz
    Steiner Verlag, Stuttgart.
Inaytur-Rahman (1969) Ethnological Wealth of Swat. Pakistan
    Archaeology, 6: 285-300.
Inayat-ur-Rahman (1984) Folk Tales of Swat, Collected and Translated
    by Inayat-ur-Rahman, Part 2. IsMEO, Rome. [Printed in
    Peshawar. Part 1 was published by IsMEO in 1968 and is
    listed in Jettmar (2018)].
————. (1989) Wooden Mosques of Swat and Dir and List of
    Monuments. JCA, 12, 1: 131-208.
Inostrancev, K. A. (1909) Venec indo-skifskogo carja, tjurban indijcev
    v vostočnom iskusstve i ženskij golovnoj ubor Kafiristana
    [The Crown of the Indo-Scythian King, the Turban of the
    Indians in Oriental Art, and the Female Headdress of
    Kafiristan]. Izvestija Instituta istorii Akademii Nauk, 2: 135-
    38.
Irgens-Møller, Christer (2005) Remnants of the Kafir music of Nuristan
    – a historical documentation. The Danish Society for Central
    Asia Journal, 2: 57–68.
————. (2009) Music in Nuristan: traditional music from Afghanistan:
    an investigation of the field recordings of Lennart Edelberg
    and Klaus Ferdinand, 1953-54, 1964, 1970. Moesgaard
    Museum, Moesgaard & Aarhus U.P., Aarhus.

———. (2021) Choir music and polyphony in Nuristan. In: Johnsen *et al.* (2021): 49-67.

Israr-ud-Din (1979) Chitral. A Historical Sketch. Central Asia, 3, 4: 1-13. Peshawar.

———. (1984) House Types and Structures in Chitral District. In: Miller, K.J., ed., The International Karakorum Project, Vol. 1. Cambridge U.P., Cambridge, pp. 265-89.

———. (1992) Irrigation and Society in Chitral District: A Case Study of Khot Valley in Upper Chitral. Pakistan Journal of Geography, 2: 113-43.

———. (1996) Irrigation and Society in Chitral District. In: Bashir, E. & Israr-ud-Din (1996): 19-42.

———. ed. (2008) Proceedings of the 3rd International Hindukush Cultural Conference (Chitral 1995). Oxford U.P., Karachi.

Ivanow, Wladimir (1932) A Specimen of Bashgali from Kamdesh. AO, 10: 154-57.

———. (1938) A Forgotten Branch of the Ismailis. JRAS, 12: 57-79.

Izzatullah, Mir (1872) [=Izzet Ullah] Safar Nama-i-Izzatullah. Travels in Central Asia in the years 1812-21. Translated into English from Persian by Capt. Henderson. Calcutta: Foreign Dept. Press. [This is one of the early "pandits", who was dispatched beyond the frontier by William Moorcroft].

———. Izzet Ullah, Mir (1842) [=Izzatullah] Travels beyond the Himalayas. Translated by H.H. Wilson. JRAS, 7: 283-342. [Originally published in Calcutta Oriental Quarterly Magazine, 1825].

Jacobsen, Jens-Peter (1995) 14C Findings Relating to the Settlement History of Yasin Valley in Northeastern Hindukush, Northern Pakistan. In: Stellrecht, I., ed., Pak-German Workshop on Problems of Comparative High Mountain Research with Regard to the Karakorum, Tübingen, October 12-14, 1992 (Culture Area Karakorum Occasional Papers, 2). University of Tübingen, Tübingen, pp. 93-99.

Janjua, Zahid J. (1998) Tradition and Change in the Darel and Tangir Valleys. In: Stellrecht (1998cI): 415-27.

Jansari, Sushma (2014) Making myth a reality: Funerary carvings of Kalasha people. British Museum Magazine, 78: 48-51.

———. (2017) The Great Game & Alexander the Great: 19th century transformation in Kalasha material culture. The Wonder House. [Online blog – This documents the British Museum

collection of Kalasha/Kati "model gandau" more extensively
than the previous article].

Jensen, Adolf E. (1956) Adolf Friedrich †, 22. April 1914 - † 25. April
1956. Paideuma, 6,4: 189-93. [This is the extensive obituary
of the leader of the 1955-56 German Hindukush Expedition,
written by his mentor Adolf Jensen, the successor in Frankfurt
of Jettmar's first teacher Leo Frobenius].

Jettmar, Karl (1977) Fragment einer Balti-Version der Kesar-Sage.
ZAS, 11: 277–286.

———. (1985a) Addenda et Corrigenda zum Artikel "Felsbilder am
Indus: Die nachbuddhistische Periode", Central Asiatic
Journal 28/3-4. CAJ, 29, 1-2: 158-59.

———. (1985b) Non-Buddhist Traditions in the Petroglyphs of the
Indus Valley. In: Schotsmans, J. & M. Taddei, eds., South
Asian Archaeology 1983. Istituto Universitario Orientale,
Naples, pp. 751-77.

———. (1986a) Religii Gindukuša. Nauka, Moscow. [Russian edition
of "Die Religionen des Hindukusch", entirely revised by
Jettmar and Grjunberg and translated by K.D. Tsivin].

———. (1986b) The Religions of the Hindukush. Vol. 1 The Religion
of the Kafirs. The pre-Islamic heritage of Afghan Nuristan.
Aris & Phillips, Warminster (UK). [Translation of the
Nuristan section of Jettmar (1975J)].

———. (1989a) Northern Areas of Pakistan, an Ethnographic Sketch.
In: Dani (1989a): 59-87.

———. (1989b) Documentation and Exploration in Northern Areas of
Pakistan. Preliminary Report, 1988. Pakistan Archaeology,
24: 177-94.

———. (1990a) Exploration in Baltistan. In: Taddei, M. & P. Callieri,
eds., South Asian Archaeology 1987, vol. 2. IsMEO, Rome,
pp. 801–13.

———. (1990b) The Gilgit Manuscripts and the Political History of
Gilgit. Pakistan Archaeology, 24: 305-14.

———. (1991) Sogdians in the Indus Valley. In: Bernard, P. & F.
Grenet, eds., Histoire et cultes de l'Asie Centrale préislamique.
Éditions du CNRS, Paris, pp. 251-53.

———. (1992) Jenseits bekannter Ikonographien. Graffiti am
Karakorum Highway. Akademie-Journal. Mitteilungsblatt
der Konferenz der Deutschen Akademien der Wissenschaften,
92, 1: 18-28.

————. (1993a) Voraussetzungen, Verlauf und Erfolg menschlicher Anpassung im nordwestlichen Himalaya mit Karakorum. In: Schweinfurth, U., ed., Neue Forschungen im Himalaya. Franz Steiner Verlag, Stuttgart, pp. 31-47.

————. (1993b) The Paṭolas, their Governors and their Successors. In: Jettmar, König & Bemmann (1993): 77-122.

————. (1993c) The area around the Nanga Parbat. A focus of Pakistani-German collaboration. In: Zingel-Avé Lallemant, S. & W.-P. Zingel, eds., Neuere deutsche Beiträge zu Geschichte und Kultur Pakistans. Deutsch-Pakistanisches Forum e.V., Bonn, pp. 64-72. [An overview of German work in northern Pakistan, in social sciences, archaeology and mountaineering].

————. (1994) Prähistorische Wanderrouten in den zentralasiatischen Hochgebirgen. Voraussetzungen und frühe Nachweise. In: Söhnen-Thieme & Hinüber (1994): 157-72.

————. (1995) The Dards and Connected Problems: Giuseppe Tucci's Last Contribution. In: Melasecchi, B., ed., Giuseppe Tucci. Nel centenario della nascita. IsMEO, Rome, pp. 35-54.

————. (1996) Approaches to the History of North Pakistan. In: Bashir & Israr-ud-Din (1996): 77-96.

————. (2002) Beyond the Gorges of the Indus: Archaeology before excavation. Edited by Ellen Kattner. Oxford U.P., Karachi.

————. (2003a) Die Religion der Alttürken. In: Jettmar & Kattner (2003): 219-28.

————. (2003b) Die Aussage der Archäologie zur Religionsgeschichte Innerasiens. In: Jettmar & Kattner (2003): 229-310.

————. (2008) Petroglyphs as Evidence of Religious Configurations? Journal of Asian Civilizations, 31, 65-146. [This is now included as "Part VI. Epilogue", in Jettmar (2022/2018)].

————. (forthcoming in 2022 [2018]) The Religions of the Hindukush. With contributions by Georg Buddruss, Schuyler Jones, Max Klimburg and Peter S.C. Parkes. Translated by Adam Nayyar and colleagues. Orchid Press, Bangkok. [Translation of Jettmar (1975J), second edition, after the first of 2018].

Jettmar, K. & E. Kattner, eds. (2003) Die vorislamischen Religionen Mittelasiens. Verlag W. Kohlhammer, Stuttgart.

Jettmar, K. & V. Thewalt (1985) Zwischen Gandhāra und den Seidenstrassen. Felsbilder am Karakorum Highway. Entdeckungen deutsch-pakistanischer Expeditionen 1979-

1984. Katalog zur Ausstellung. Philipp von Zabern, Mainz. [= Between Gandhāra and the Silk Road, parallel English version]

Jettmar, K., D. König & M. Bemmann (1993) ANP. Vol. 2. Philipp von Zabern, Mainz. Permalink: https://digi.hadw-bw.de/view/anp2

Jettmar, K., D. König & V. Thewalt, eds. (1989) Rock Inscriptions in the Indus Valley. ANP. Vol. 1. Philipp von Zabern, Mainz. Permalink: https://digi.hadw-bw.de/view/anp1text

Johansen, Ulla (2002) Karl Jettmar, 1918-2002. Zeitschrift für Ethnologie, 127: 133-38. [Jettmar's obituary].

Johnsen, Ulrik H. (2016) On Collections and Collectors – The Double Gaze of Museum Collections. In: Johnsen et al. (2016): 207-20. [On Siiger's collection at Moesgaard Museum].

Johnsen, U.H., A.W. Geertz, S. Castenfeldt & P.B. Andersen, eds. (2016) In the Footsteps of Halfdan Siiger. Danish Research in Central Asia. Moesgaard Museum, Moesgaard.

Johnsen, U.H., T. Funder, S. Jones & Taj K. Kalash (2021) Toward the horizon: Lennart Edelberg and the Danish Hindukush research. Aarhus University Press, Aarhus.

Joldan, Eliezer (1985) Harvest Festival of Buddhist Dards of Ladakh and Other Essays. Kapoor Bros, Srinagar.

Jones, Schuyler (1978) Nuristan: Mountain Communities in the Hindu Kush. Afghan Studies, 1: 79-92.

———. (1979) Opnåelse af rang og symboler på status hos Kalashaerne i Nuristan [Achieving rank and symbols of status among the Kalasha in Nuristan]. Hikuin, 5: 7-20.

———. (1981) Institutionalised Inequalities in Nuristan. In: Berreman, G.D., ed., Social Inequality: Comparative and Developmental Approaches. Academic Press, New York, pp. 151-62.

———. (1983) In Search of the Horned Head-Dress. In: Snoy (1983J): 343-50.

———. (1984) On the function of KK32: An Ethnographic Specimen from Nuristan in the Kabul Museum. Folk, 26: 179-89.

———. (2003) Lost Horizon – A Glimpse of Nuristan. SAALG [South Asia Archive & Library Group] Newsletter, 1: 16-18.

———. (2021) Lennart Edelberg and Nuristan. In: Johnsen et al. (2021): 175-83.

Kakar, Hasan (1971) Afghanistan, a Study in Internal Political Developments, 1880-1896. Punjab Educational Press, Kabul.

———. (1981) International Significance of the Conquest of Former Kafiristan in 1896. Afghanistan, 34, 2: 47-54.

Kalash, Taj Khan (2021a) Jinn Pinn Dance in the Floods: Perceptions of Flood Disasters Among the Kalasha of Pakistan. In: Riboli D., P.J. Stewart, A.J. Strathern, D. Torri, eds, Dealing with Disasters. Palgrave Macmillan, Cham, pp. 101-27.

———. (2021b) Kafiristan revisited. In: Johnsen *et al.* (2021): 131-55.

Kalash, Taj Khan & J. Heegård (2016) Dynamics of Cultural Survival of Kalasha. In: Johnsen *et al.* (2016): 115-36.

Kalter, Johannes (1982) Die Sammlungen des Linden-Museums aus Afghanistan und den Nachbargebieten. Afghanistan Journal, 9, 3: 76-85.

———. ed. (1989) Swat. Bauern und Baumeister im Hindukush. Edition Hansjörg Mayer & Linden-Museum, Stuttgart. [English transl.: The Arts and Crafts of the Swat Valley. Living Traditions in the Hindu Kush. Thames and Hudson, New York, 1991].

Katz, David (1980) Review of: Edelberg, L. & S. Jones, Nuristan, Graz, 1979. Middle East Studies Association bulletin, 14,2: 65-67.

Katz, David J. (1982) Kafir to Afghan: religious conversion, political incorporation and ethnicity in the Vaygal Valley, Nuristan. PhD Dissertation. University of California, Los Angeles.

———. (1984) Responses to Central Authority in Nuristan: the case of the Vaygal Valley Kalasha. In: Sharani, M.N. & R.L. Canfield, eds., Revolutions and Rebellions in Afghanistan. Anthropological Perspectives. University of California, Berkeley, pp. 94–118.

Kaverin, Sviatoslav I. (2019) Perspektivy izučenija iskusstva Central'nogo Gindukuša v Rossii [Prospects for Russian Research on the Arts and Crafts of Central Hindukush]. In: Karlova, E., ed., Problemy izučenija vostočnyh kollekcij. Materialy naučnoj konferencii / Naučnye soobŝenija Gosudarstvennogo Muzeja Vostoka, Vol. 28 [Issues in the study of Oriental Collections: National Oriental Museum Conference, Proceedings]. Gosudarstvennyj Muzej Vostoka, Moscow, pp. 66-77.

———. (2020) Perspektivy izučenija dardov i nuristancev v Rossii [Prospects for the study of the Dards and Nuristanis in Russia]. In: Kogan, A., ed., Trudy Instituta vostokovedenija RAN.

Vyp. 27. Problemy obŝej i vostokovednoj lingvistiki. Jazyki
    Azii i Afriki. [Papers of the Institute of Oriental Studies of the
    Russian Academy of Sciences. Issue 27. Studies in General
    and Oriental Linguistics. Languages of Asia and Africa].
    Institut vostokovedenija RAN [Institute of Oriental Studies
    of the Russian Academy of Sciences], Moscow, pp. 56-61.
Keay, John (1977) Where Men and Mountains Meet. The explorers of
    the Western Himalayas 1820-75. John Murray, London.
————. (1979) The Gilgit Game. The explorers of the Western
    Himalayas 1865-95. John Murray, London.
Keiser, R. Lincoln (1973) Genealogical Beliefs and Social Structure
    among the Sum of Afghanistan. The Afghanistan Council of
    the Asia Society, Occasional Paper 5, New York. [Ethnography
    of a Pashai group].
————. (1981) The Relevancy of Structural Principles in the Study of
    Political Organization. Anthropos, 76, 3/4: 430-40. [Based on
    Pashai ethnography].
————. (1986) Death Enmity in Thull: Organized Vengeance and
    Social Change in a Kohistani Community. American
    Ethnologist, 13: 489-505.
————. (1991) Friend by Day, Enemy by Night. Organized Vengeance
    in a Kohistani Community. Holt, Rinehart and Winston, Fort
    Worth. [An ethnography of Dir Kohistan]
Khan, Fawad (2013) Recent Discovery of Petroglyphs at Parwak,
    District Chitral, Pakistan. JAC, 36, 2: 101-13.
Khan, Husain (1984) Mughal Relations with Baltistan and the Northern
    Region, from Akbar to Aurangzeb. JCA, 7, 1: 179-89.
————. (1991) The Genesis of the Royal Title 'Shah Kaṭur'. JCA,
    14,1: 111-14.
Khan, M. Afzal (1975) Chitral and Kafiristan. A Personal Study.
    Printing Corporation of Frontier, Peshawar.
Khan, M. Hayat (1874) The Siah Posh Kafirs. In: Afghanistan and Its
    Inhabitants. Translated from the "Hayat-i-Afghan" of
    Muhamad Hayat Khan, C.S.I. by Henry Priestly, Bengal Civil
    Service. Printed at the "Indian Public Opinion" Press, by
    Rookun-ud-Din, Lahore, pp. 314-24. [This little-known
    native account of the Kafirs is partly copied verbatim from
    Elphinstone and others, but has also apparently original
    information, possibly based on the author's mission to
    Afghanistan in 1864].

Khan, M. Nasim (2000) Archaeological Discoveries in Darel Muzot: An Iron Period Grave Culture Site. Ancient Pakistan, 13: 109-19.

―――. (2002) A Short Note on Archaeological Discoveries in Chitral, Pakistan. Ancient Pakistan, 15: 179-85.

―――. (2020) A Proto Śāradā Inscription in the Chitral Museum, Pakistan. Online at: https://www.academia.edu/42382007 (acc. July, 30, 2021) [A brief note with photo, transcription and translation of one of the very rare ancient inscriptions found in Chitral, announcing future publication of a study in Gandhāran Studies, vol. 14].

Khan, Nazim (1936) The Autobiography of Sir Mohomed Nazim Khan, K.C.I.E. Mir of Hunza. Karimabad, Hunza. [This is a rare English translation of the original Persian manuscript kept at the Baltit Research Library in Baltit fort at Karimabad, Hunza. An English translation dated 1931 is catalogued in "Lorimer Collection 1962" at School of Oriental and African Studies, London].

Khan, Raja (1845) Account of the Panjkora Valley, and of Lower and Upper Kashkar, by Rajah Khan, of Cabool. Translated by Major R. Leech, at whose request it was drawn up in 1840. JASB, 14: 812-17.

Khan, Rafiullah & I. Shaheen (2015) Ahmad Hasan Dani's popularization of history/archaeology. Its praxes, context and outcomes. JAC, 38, 1: 107-30.

Kahn, Sarfraz, Z.A. Kalhoro & Zia-ur-Rehman (2015) Marriage Ceremonies and Rituals in Astore Valley, Gilgit-Baltistan, Pakistan. JAC, 38, 2: 153-63.

Khan, Taleem & E. Mela-Athanasopoulou (2011) How many are we? A demographic survey on the Kalash of the Hindu Kush valleys, Himalayas. In: Everhard & Mela-Athanasopoulou (2011): 247-56.

Khan, Yar M. (1985) The Political Relations of the Mughuls with the Rulers of Northern Pakistan. JCA, 8, 1: 161-69.

Kisljakov, Nikolaj A. (1957) Kafiry (nuristancy) [Kafirs (Nuristanis)]. In: Kisljakov, N.A. & A.I. Perschits, eds., Narody Perednej Azii [Peoples of Western Asia]. Izd-vo Akademii Nauk SSSR, Moscow, pp. 133-48.

―――. (1963) Novaja nuristanskaja kollekcija v Muzee antropologii i ètnografii AN SSSR [New Nuristan Collection at the Museum

of Anthropology and Ethnography of the USSR Academy of
Sciences]. Sovetskaja Ètnografija, 2: 120-25.

Klimburg, Maximilian (1982) The Western Trans-Himalayan
Crossroads. In: Klimburg-Salter, D.E., ed., The Silk Route
and the Diamond Path. UCLA Art Council, Los Angeles, pp.
24-37.

―――. (1983) The Monumental Art of Status among the Kafirs of the
Hindu Kush. In: Snoy (1983J): 351-57.

―――. (1987) Notes on the Architecture of Nuristan. Archiv für
Völkerkunde, 41: 41-52.

―――. (1990) Kulturformen bei den Kafiren des Hindukusch.
Mitteilungen der Berliner Gesellschaft für Anthropologie,
Ethnologie und Urgeschichte, 11: 47-60.

―――. (1993) Das Nuristan-Haus und die 'Architektonik'. Archiv für
Völkerkunde, 47: 127-39.

―――. (1997) The Wooden Mosques in the Northern Areas of
Pakistan. In: Austrian Scholarship in Pakistan. A Symposium
Dedicated to the Memory of Aloys Sprenger. PanGraphics,
Islamabad, pp. 148-74.

―――. (1999) The Kafirs of the Hindukush. Art and Society of the
Waigal and Ashkun Kafirs (2 vols). Franz Steiner Verlag,
Stuttgart.

―――. (2001) The Situation in Nuristan. Central Asian Survey, 20(3):
383-90.

―――. (2002a) Afghanistan: The Culture of the Kafirs. german
research: Magazine of the Deutsche Forschungsgemeinschaft,
1: 20-25.

―――. (2002b) The Arts and Culture of Parun, Kafiristan's "Sacred
Valley". Arts Asiatiques, 56: 51-68.

―――. (2004) The Arts and Societies of the Kafirs of the Hindu Kush.
Asian Affairs, 35: 365-86.

―――. (2005) Review article of Cacopardo & Cacopardo (2001).
E&W, 55, 1-4: 502-507

―――. (2007a) The 'Enclaved' Culture of Parun in Former Kafiristan.
Asien. The German Journal on Contemporary Asia, 104: 65-
87.

―――. (2007b) Traditional Art and Architecture in Baltistan. In:
Bianca (2007): 149-64.

―――. (2007c) Hölzerne Moscheen und Grabmäler in Nordpakistan.
In: Pich, W.J. & M. Leonhard, eds., EOTHEN IV. Gesellschaft

der Freunde Islamischer Kunst und Kultur. Scaneg Verlag, Munich, pp 125-48.

————. (2008a) Status Imagery of the Kalasha: Some Notes on Social Change. In: Israr-ud-Din (2008): 129-34.

————. (2008b) A Former Kafir Tells His 'Tragic Story'. Notes on the Kati Kafirs of Northern Bashgal (Afghanistan). E&W, 58: 391-402. [Review article of Cacopardo & Schmidt (2006)].

————. (2008c) Status Culture of the Kalasha Kafirs. In: Skyhawk (2008a): 168-94.

————. (2008d) Karl Jettmar - Experiences and Reminiscences. In: Skyhawk (2008a): 195-209.

————. (2014) Viticulture in Kafiristan. In: Fragner, B.G., R. Kauz & F. Schwarz, eds., Wine Culture in Iran and Beyond. Österreichische Akademie der Wissenschaften, Vienna, pp. 53-70, 331-39.

————. (2016) Transregional Intoxications. Wine in Buddhist Gandhara and Kafiristan. In: Pellò, S., ed., Borders. Itineraries on the Edges of Iran. Edizioni Ca' Foscari, Venice, pp. 271-302.

————. (2019) Traditional Construction in Nuristan. In: Schittich, C., ed., Vernacular Architecture: Atlas for Living throughout the World. Birkhäuser Verlag, Basel, pp. 149-59. [Parallel German version: Traditionelles Bauen in Nuristan. In: Schittich, C., ed., Traditionelle Bauweisen: Ein Atlas zum Wohnen auf fünf Kontinenten].

Kochetov, Alexei, P. Arsenault, J. Heegård Petersen, S. Kalas & T. K. Kalash (2020) Kalasha (Bumburet Variety). Journal of the International Phonetic Association, 51,3: 468-89.

Kohzad, Ahmad Ali (1948) La statuaire au Nouristan et le travail sur bois. Afghanistan, 3,3: 1-4.

————. (1954) The Nuristanis are Aryans and not Greek Remnants. Afghanistan, 9,2: 36-40.

Kogan, Anton I. (2003) Indo-European Gutturals in Dardic. In: International Conference on South-Asian Literatures and Languages (ICOSAL 5). Moscow State University, Moscow, pp. 22-24.

————. (2005) Dardskie jazyki. Genetičeskaja harakteristika [Dardic languages. Genetic characterization]. Vostočnaja literatura & Institut vostokovedenija, Moscow.

————. (2007) Dardskie i nuristanskie elementy v jazyke dameli [Dardic and Nuristani elements in the Dameli language]. In:

V.A. Dybo, O.A. Mudrak, & G.S. Starostin, eds., Orientalia et Classica: Trudy Instituta vostočnyh kul'tur i antičnosti. Vyp. 11. Aspekty komparativistiki vyp.2 [Orientalia et Classica: Papers of the Institute of Oriental and Classical Studies, Vol. 11, 2]. RGGU, Moscow, pp. 310-27.

————. (2008) O statuse i proishoždenii zvonkoj pridyhatel'noj serii v rjade dardskih jazykov [On the status and origin of the voiced aspirated series in a number of Dardic languages]. In: Kulikov, L. & M. Rusanov, Indologica. Pamjati T.Ja. Elizarenkovoj. (Orientalia et Classica, Vol. 20, 1). RGGU, Moscow, pp. 197-227.

————. (2009) Perspektivy issledovanija ètničeskoj istorii Kašmira [Prospects for the study of the ethnic history of Kashmir]. Vostok (Oriens), 3: 115-24.

————. (2012) Dardy i strana dardov v «Radžatarangini» Kal'hany [The Dards and the country of Dards in the "Rajatarangini" of Kalhana]. In: Vertogradova V.V., ed., Indija-Tibet: tekst i fenomeny kul'tury: Rerihovskie čtenija 2006-2010 v Institute vostokovedenija RAN [India-Tibet: Texts and Cultural Phenomena]. Jazyki slavjanskoj kul'tury, Moscow, pp. 107-15.

————. (2014) Kašmir i ego sosedi v XII-XIII vekah [Kashmir and its neighbors in the XII-XIII centuries]. Vostok, 4: 37-47.

————. (2015) Nekotorye voprosy genetičeskoj klassifikacii dardskih jazykov po dannym istoričeskoj fonetiki [Some Issues of the Genetic Classification of Dardic Languages According to Historical Phonetics]. Journal of Language Relationship - Voprosy Jazykovogo Rodstva, 13,1: 1-21.

————. (2016) Genealogical classification of New Indo-Aryan languages and lexicostatistics. Journal of Language Relationship - Voprosy Jazykovogo Rodstva, 14,4: 227-58.

————. (2019) On possible Dardic and Burushaski influence on some Northwestern Tibetan dialects. Journal of Language Relationship, 17,4: 263-84.

————. (2021) Novoye v issledovanii kontaktov severozapadnykh tibetskikh dialektov s dardskimi yazykami i yazykom burushaski [Update on the study of contact between Northwestern Tibetan dialects, Dardic languages, and Burushaski]. Rodnoy yazyk. Linguistic Journal, 1. [Online journal].

Kogan, A.I. & D.I. Èdel'man (2004) Review of Skyhawk (2003). Voprosy jazykoznanija, 1: 151-56.

Kohzad, Ahmad A. (1955) Sefat Nama ou Djang Nama. Les exploits guerriers de Darwish Mohammad Khan Ghazi, Commandant en chef. Afghanistan, 10, 2: 1-6. [On the discovery of the 16th century chronicle of a *jihad* against the Kafirs, cf. Scarcia 1965J]

König, Ditte (= Bandini-König) (1994) Zu den Tierdarstellungen auf den Felsen am Oberen Indus. Versuch einer zoologischen Bestimmung. In: Fussman, Jettmar & König (1994): 73-171.

Konow, Sten (1911) Notes on the Classification of Bashgali. JRAS, 43,1: 1-47.

Konow, S. (1913) Bashgali Dictionary: An analysis of Colonel J. Davidson's Notes on the Bashgali Language. JASB (N.S.) 9, Extra No.

Kreutzmann, Hermann (1986) A Note on Yak-keeping in Hunza (Northern Areas of Pakistan). Production Pastorale et Société, 19: 99-106.

———. (1988) Oases of the Karakoram: The Evolution of Irrigation and Social Organization in Hunza (North-Pakistan). In: Allan, N.J.R., G.W. Knapp & C. Stadel, eds., Human Impact on Mountains. Rowman & Littlefield, Totowa, pp. 243-54.

———. (1993) Zur Kulturgeographie des Hunza-Tales/Cultural Geography of the Hunza Valley. In: Zingel-Avé Lallemant, S. & W.-P. Zingel, eds., Neuere deutsche Beiträge zu Geschichte und Kultur Pakistans. Deutsch-Pakistanisches Forum e.V., Bonn, pp. 144-58.

———. (1994) Habitat Conditions and Settlement Processes in the Hindukush-Karakoram. Petermanns Geographische Mitteilungen, 138, 6: 337-56.

———. (1995) Sprachenvielfalt und regionale Differenzierung von Glaubensgemeinschaften im Hindukusch-Karakorum. Die Rolle von Minderheiten im Konfliktfeld Nordpakistans. Erdkunde, 49: 106-22.

———. (1996a) Ethnizität im Entwicklungsprozeß. Die Wakhi in Hochasien. Dietrich Reimer Verlag, Berlin.

———. (1996b) Marathon im Karakorum. Beobachtungen über vergangene und gegenwärtige Wettkampf-praktiken in Hunza. Kleine Beiträge. Aus dem Staatlichen Museum für Völkerkunde, 15: 2-8.

———. (1998a) Trans-montane Exchange Patterns prior to the Karakoram Highway. In: Stellrecht (1998cII): 21-43.

————. (1998b) The Chitral Triangle: Rise and Decline of Trans-montane Central Asian Trade, 1895-1935. Asien-Afrika-Lateinamerika, 26, 3: 289-327.

————. (1999) The Origin of Our Belief: How the Ismailiya came to Ghojal in Hunza. European Bulletin of Himalayan Research, 15/16: 39-40.

————. ed., (2000) Sharing Water - Irrigation and Water Management in the Hindukush-Karakoram-Himalaya. Oxford U.P., Oxford.

————. (2002) Un système irrigué à Hunza, Nord-Pakistan. ASAinfo, 1: 9; ASAinfo, 2: 9.

————. (2003) Yak-keeping in Western High Asia: Tajikistan, Afghanistan, Southern Xinjiang, Pakistan. In: Wiener, G., H. Jianlin & L. Ruijun, eds., The Yak. RAP Publication, Bangkok, pp. 323-36.

————. (2004a) Pastoral practices and their transformation in the North-Western Karakoram. Nomadic Peoples, 8, 2: 54-88.

————. (2004b) Der weiße Fleck auf der Landkarte - geographische Forschungsreisen entlang der chinesischen Seidenstraße im Umfeld des 'Great Game'. In: Plappert, R., ed., Reise zur verbotenen Stadt. Europäer unterwegs nach China. Universitätsbibliothek, Erlangen-Nürnberg, pp. 75-94.

————. ed. (2006a) Karakoram in Transition. Culture, Development and Ecology in the Hunza Valley. Oxford U.P., Karachi.

————. (2006b) Settlement History of the Hunza Valley and Linguistic Variegations in Space and Time. In: Kreutzmann (2006a): 251-72.

————. (2007) The Karakoram Landscape and the Recent History of the Northern Areas. In: Bianca (2007): 41-76.

————. (2008a) Die chinesische Seidenstraße – Kreuzweg der Kulturen und Jahrhunderte altes Handelsnetzwerk. HGG-Journal, 22: 5-15.

————. (2008b) Trade links in the Eastern Hindukush: The Chitral Route. In: Israr-ud-din (2008): 305-16.

————. ed., (2013) Preservation of built environment and its impact on community development in Gilgit-Baltistan. Freie Universität Berlin, Berlin.

————. (2015a) Pamirian Crossroads. Kirghiz and Wakhi of High Asia. Harrassowitz Verlag, Wiesbaden.

————. (2015b) Boundaries and Space in Gilgit-Baltistan. Contemporary South Asia, 23, 3: 276-91.

————. (2017a) Language variegation across the Pamir-Hindukush-Karakoram: Perceptions and mobilities. Südasien-Chronik, 7: 251-73.

————. (2017b) Historical geography of the Pamirs. In: Ludden, D., ed., Oxford Research Encyclopedia of Asian History. Oxford U.P., New York. [Online publication]

————. (2017c) Wakhan quadrangle. Exploration and espionage during and after the Great Game. Harrassowitz Verlag, Wiesbaden.

Kristiansen, Knut (1986) A Káfir on the Káfir Life Cycle. In: Kars, E., ed., Kalyānamitrārāganam. Essays in Honour of Nils Simonnson. Oslo, pp. 145-58.

————. (2008) Shaikh Abdullah Khan, a Most Remarkable Man from Bumburet Shaikhanande. In: Israr ud-Din (2008): 449-52.

Kristiansen, K. & I. Ross (1973) Georg Morgenstierne. A Bibliography, compiled at the Indo-Iranian Institute, University of Oslo. In: Morgenstierne (1973bJ): 241-54.

Kristiansen, K. & W. Witek, eds., (2001) Georg Morgenstierne. Database for pictures, moving images and audio. The Languages and Culture of South Asia. National Library of Norway. Online open access: https://www.nb.no/baser/morgenstierne/english/index.html (acc. Jan. 15, 2019).

Kuiper, Franciscus B.J. (1978) Review of Morgenstierne (1973aJ) [Irano-Dardica]. Indo-Iranian Journal, 20, 1-2: 99-102.

Kushev, V.V. (1971) Pervyj nuristanskij učenyj i poèt [The First Nuristani Scholar and Poet]. In: Pis'mennye pamjatniki i problemy istorii kul'tury narodov Vostoka. VII godičnaja naučnaja sessija LO IV AN SSSR (kratkie soobŝenija) [Written documents and problems in the cultural history of the peoples of the East]. GRVL, Moscow, pp. 88-90.

Kushev, Vladimir V., N.L. Luzhetskaia, L. Rzehak & I.M. Steblin-Kamensky, eds. (1998) Central Asia. Eastern Hindukush (= Strany i Narody Vostoka 30 [= Countries and Peoples of the East Vol. 30]). St. Petersburg for Oriental Studies, St. Petersburg.

Kussmaul, Friedrich & P. Snoy (1972) Bergvölker im Hindukusch. Eine Dokumentation des Instituts für Auslandsbeziehungen und des Linden-Museums. Stuttgart. [This booklet features 135 valuable B&W photos by Friedrich, Kussmaul, Schlenker and Snoy of parts of Peristan, including Kalasha and Chitral, and surroundings, including Minjan, Sanglech, Badakhshan].

Kuwayama, Shōshin (2002). Across the Hindukush of the First Millenium: A Collection of the Papers. Institute for Research in Humanities, Kyoto University, Kyoto.

Kvaerne, Per (1986) Review of Jettmar (1986). Journal of the Tibet Society, 6: 87-88.

Lal, Mohan (1834) Further Information regarding the Siah Posh Tribe, or reputed descendants of the Macedonians. JASB, 3: 76-79

―――. (1846) Travels in the Panjab, Afghanistan and Turkistan, to Balkh, Bokhara, and Herat; and a Visit to Great Britain and Germany. W.H. Allen & Co., London.

Lavan, Spencer (1988) Review of Jettmar (1986). Journal of Asian Studies, 47, 1: 181-82.

L'Homme, Erik (1999) Parlons Khowar. L'Harmattan. Paris.

Le Sidaner, Yves (1979) Les Relations sociales chez les Kafir Kalash du Nord-Pakistan (minorité indo-européenne et polythéiste de l'Himalaya). Thèse de doctorat sous la direction de M. Duvignaud. Université François Rabelais, Tours.

Lehr, Rachel (2014) A descriptive grammar of Pashai: The language and speech community of Darrai Nur. PhD Dissertation. University of Chicago, Chicago.

Leitner, Gottlieb W. (1872a) Manners and Customs of the Dards. Indian Antiquary, 1: 7-14.

―――. (1872b) Dardu Legends. Dardu Riddles, Proverbs and Fables. Indian Antiquary, 1: 84-92.

―――. (1874) Siah Posh Kafirs. Journal of the Anthropological Institute of Great Britain and Ireland, 3: 341-69.

―――. (1950) The Future of Chitrál and Neighbouring Countries. Reprinted from the Asiatic Quarterly Review, July 1895, with the addition of an Appendix, Routes, etc. In: Lasker, B., Human Bondage in Southeast Asia. University of North Carolina Press, Chapel Hill, pp. 1-28.

Lentz, Sabine (2000) Rechtspluralismus in den Northern Areas/ Pakistan. CAK, Vol. 9. Rüdiger Köppe Verlag, Cologne.

Lessar, Pavel M. (1888) Svedenija o Kafaristane (po anglijskim istočnikam) [Information on Kafaristan (on the basis of English sources)]. (Sbornik geografičeskih, topografičeskih i statističeskih materialov po Azii [Collection of geographic, topographical and statistical materials on Asia]. Vol. 29). Voenno-učebnyj komitet Glavnogo štaba, St. Petersburg.

Levy, Peter (1973) The Light Garden of the Angel King. Journeys in Afghanistan. Newton Abbot, Devon. [With a visit to Nuristan in the company of Bruce Chatwin].

Lièvre, Viviane (1983a) Ethno-médecine au Nord Pakistan. Santé païenne, médecine islamique. Tribune Médicale, 80: 20-31.

———. (1983b) Pratiques médicales avec intervention de guérisseurs liés au sacré, étiologie de la maladie, chez les Kalash du Pakistan. Bulletin d'Ethnomédecine, 23: 25-48.

———. (1996) The Status of Kalasha Women in the Religious Sphere. In: Bashir & Israr-ud-Din (1996): 337-43.

Lièvre, V. & J.-Y. Loude (1990) Le chamanisme des Kalash du Pakistan. Des montagnards polythéistes face à l'islam. CNRS – Presses Universitaires de Lyon, Lyon.

———. (1991) Vendanges en Asie: le vin du ciel. L'univers du vivant, 34: 16-37.

Liljegren, Henrik (2008): Towards a Grammatical Description of Palula. An Indo-Aryan Language of the Hindu Kush. Stockholm University, Stockholm.

———. (2009) The Dangari Tongue of Choke and Machoke: Tracing the Proto-Language of Shina Enclaves in the Hindu Kush. Acta Orientalia, 70: 7–62.

———. (2013) Notes on Kalkoti: A Shina Language with Strong Kohistani Influences. Linguistic Discovery, 11, 1: 129–60.

———. (2014) A Survey of Alignment Features in the Greater Hindukush with Special References to Indo-Aryan. In: Suihkonen, P. & L.J. Whaley, eds., On Diversity and Complexity of Languages Spoken in Europe and North and Central Asia. John Benjamins Publishing Company, Amsterdam, pp. 133–74.

———. (2016) A Grammar of Palula. Studies in Diversity Linguistics 8. Language Science Press, Berlin.

———. (2017) Profiling Indo-Aryan in the Hindukush-Karakoram: A Preliminary Study of Micro-Typological Patterns. Journal of South Asian Languages and Linguistics, 4,1: 107–56.

———. (2019) Gender typology and gender (in)stability in Hindu Kush Indo-Aryan languages. In: Di Garbo, F., B. Olsson & B. Wälchli, eds., Grammatical gender and linguistic complexity: Volume I: General issues and specific studies. Language Science Press, Berlin, pp. 279–328.

———. (forthcoming in 2022) Nuristani in its areal and typological context. In: Degener & Hill (2022)

Liljegren, H. & A. Ali Khan (2017) Khowar. Journal of the International Phonetic Association, 47, 02: 219–29.

Liljegren, H. & F. Akhunzada (2017) Linguistic diversity, vitality and maintenance: a case study on the language situation in northern Pakistan. multiethnica, 36/37: 61-79.

Liljegren, H., R. Forkel, N. Knobloch & N. Lange (2021) Hindu Kush Areal Typology (Version v1.0) [Data set]. Zenodo. Online at: https://hindukush.clld.org/ (acc. July 28, 2021) [A most valuable database of features and vocabulary of 64 languages and dialects of Peristan and surroundings].

Liljegren, H. & N. Haider (2009) Palula. Journal of the International Phonetic Association, 39: 381–86.

————. (2011) Palula vocabulary. Forum for Language Initiatives, Islamabad.

————. (2015a) Facts, Feelings and Temperature Expressions in the Hindukush. In: Koptjevskaja-Tamm, M., ed., The Linguistics of Temperature. John Benjamins Publishing Company, Amsterdam & Philadelphia, pp. 440-70.

————. (2015b) Palula Texts. Forum for Language Initiatives, Islamabad.

Liljegren, H. & E. Svärd (2017) Bisyndetic contrast marking in the Hindukush: Additional evidence of a historical contact zone. Journal of Language Contact, 10,3: 450–84.

Lines, Maureen (1988) Beyond the North-West Frontier. Travels in the Hindu Kush and Karakorams. Haynes Publishing Group, Sparkford.

————. (1996) The Kalasha people of North-Western Pakistan. Emjay Books International, Peshawar.

————. (2014) The Kalasha of the Hindu Kush. Lé Topical Printers, Lahore.

Litvinskij, Boris. A. (1968) Kangjujsko-sarmatskij farn (k istoriko-kul'turnym svjazjam plemën južnoj Rossii i Srednej Azii) [Kangju-Sarmatian "farn" (On the historical and cultural ties of the tribes of southern Russia and Central Asia)]. Doniš, Dushanbe.

————. (1983) Schaf und Ziege in der Glaubenswelt der Pamir-Tadschiken. In: Snoy (1983J): 389-98.

————. (1993) Pamir und Gilgit - Kulturhistorische Verbindungen. In: Jettmar, König & Bemmann (1993): 141-49.

————. (2002) Copper Cauldrons from Gilgit and Central Asia: More about Saka and Dards and Related Problems. E&W, 52: 127-49.

————. (2003) Relikte vorislamischer Religionsvorstellungen der Pamirbevölkerung (Ende des 19. und Anfang des 20. Jahrhunderts). In: Jettmar & Kattner (2003): 15-93.

Löffler, Reinhold (1983) Lur Huntinglore and the Culture-History of the Shin. In: Snoy (1983J): 399-409.

Löhr, Johannes (1994) Social Organization in Yasin. Culture Area Karakorum Newsletter, Department of Anthropology, University of Tübingen, 3: 68-70.

————. (1997a) Gender, Power, and Public Identity: Maintaining the Masculine Past in Yasin Valley. In: Stellrecht (1997a): 111-34.

————. (1997b) History as a Social Practice: An Example from Northern Pakistan. In: Stellrecht & Winiger (1997): 135-56.

Lorimer, David L.R. (1927) A Burushaski text from Hunza. Bulletin of the School of Oriental Studies, 4: 505-31.

————. (1937) Burushaski and its Alien Neighbours: Problems in Linguistic Contagion. Transactions of the Philological Society, 36,1: 63–98.

————. (1962) Werchikwar English Vocabulary. With a Few Werchikwar Texts. Norwegian Universities Press, Oslo.

————. (1981) Folk Tales of Hunza. Institute of Folk Heritage (=Lok Virsa), Islamabad. [These are the texts from Lorimer 1935-38J, Vol. II, re-printed without the Burushaski text. Repr. in 1987 with new front cover. Both prints have "of Hunza" on the frontispiece and "from Hunza" on the front cover].

Lorimer, Emily O. (1936a) Road to Hunza. The Geographical Magazine, 3,3: 161-78.

————. (1936b) Peasant Life in Hunza. The Geographical Magazine, 3,4: 235-54.

————. (1938) The Burusho of Hunza. Antiquity, 12,45: 5-15.

Loude, Jean-Yves (1980) Kalash. Berger-Levrault, Paris.

————. (1982) Les statues funeraires des Kalash-Kafirs du Chitral. Object et Monde, 22,1: 7-18.

————. (1996) The Kalash Shamans' Practice of Exorcism. In: Bashir & Israr-ud-Din (1996): 329-35.

————. (2007) Lait et camouflage chez les Kalash du Pakistan. In: Colloque international sur les masques et arts tribaux de l'Himalaya. Musée Cernuschi, Paris, pp. 37-44.

Loude, J.-Y. & V. Lièvre (1984) Solstice païen. Presse de la Renaissance, Paris. [English transl.: Kalash Solstice. Lok Virsa (NIFTH), Islamabad, 1987].

————. (1988) Fêtes d'été chez les Kalash du Nord-Pakistan: cascades de lait, vin de jambes et berger géniteur. L'Ethnographie, 83, 100/101: 191-220.

————. (1997) Men between fairies and women. The bipolarity of the environment of the kalash mountaineers of the Hindu Kush. In: McDonald, A.W., ed., Mandala and Landscape. D.K. Printworld, New Delhi, pp. 407-33.

Lumsden, Harry B. (1860) A description of Kaffiristan and its inhabitants compiled from the accounts by Mr. Elphinstone and Sir A. Burnes, as well as from information gathered from Kaffir slaves in the service of different Affghan Sirdars. In: Id., The Mission to Kandahar, with Appendices. C. B. Lewis, Baptist Mission Press, Calcutta, pp. 113-23. [With a large sketch map of Kafiristan].

Lurje, Pavel B. (2021) Boginya Khshum – Kshumaĭ ot Khorezma do Kafiristana [Goddess Khshum – Kshumai from Khorezm to Kafiristan]. Rodnoy yazyk. Linguistic Journal, 1. [Online journal. This study analyzes correspondences between names of goddesses in Soghdian, Khorezmian and Bactrian, and the Kati/Kalasha theonym Kshumai, Kushumai]

Lushina, Aleksandra V. (2009) Ob odnom nuristanskom obyčae [On a Nuristani custom]. In: Istoriko-arheologičeskie zapiski, I [Historical and Archaeological Notes, I]. Zimovnikovskij kraevedčeskij muzej, Zimovniki, pp. 169-70.

Lužeckaja, Nina L. = Bartasheva, Nina L., see also.

Lužeckaja, N.L. (1986) Očerki istorii Vostočnogo Gindukuša vo vtoroj polovine XIX v [Essays on the history of the Eastern Hindu Kush in the second half of the nineteenth century]. Nauka, Moscow.

————. (1998) «Rodoslovnaja pravitelej Hunzy, Nagara i Gilgita» Muhammada Gani-hana ["Genealogy of the rulers of Hunza, Nagar and Gilgit" by Muhammad Ghani Khan. Text. Translation]. In: Kushev *et al.* (1998): 300-40.

Maev, Nikolay A. (1874) Kjafiry ili Sijagpuši. (Narody strany, ležaŝej na sev. granice Britanskoj Indii) [Kafirs or Siyahposhes. (Peoples of the country lying on the northern border of British India)]. In: Materialy dlja statistiki Turkestanskogo kraja [Materials for statistics of the Turkestan region], Vol. 3. Turkestanskij statističeskij komitet, St. Petersburg, pp. 342-52.

Maggi, Wynne (2001) Our Women Are Free. Gender and Ethnicity in the Hindu Kush. The University of Michigan Press, Ann Arbour. [An ethnography of Kalasha women].

———. (2006) "Heart-Stuck": Love Marriage as a Marker of Ethnic Identity among the Kalasha of Northwest Pakistan. In: Hirsch, J.S. & H. Wardlow, eds., Modern Loves: The Anthropology of Romantic Courtship and Companionate Marriage. University of Michigan Press, Ann Arbor, pp.78–91.

———. (2008) Don't Cry My Daughter: Lullabies as a Keyhole into Kalasha Culture. In: Israr-ud-Din (2008): 146-51.

Mankiralay, Abd al-Haq (Jashni) (1987) A political history of Kalam Swat, Part I. Translated from Pashto by A.R. Palwal. ZAS, 20: 282-357.

———. (1992) A political History of Kalam Swat. Part II: The Recent History. Translated from Pashto by A.R. Palwal. ZAS, 23: 152-201.

Mansoor, Atika, et al. (2004) Investigation of the Greek ancestry of populations from Northern Pakistan. Human Genetics, 114, 5: 484-90.

Maraini, Fosco (1963) Sulle tracce di Dioniso in Asia. Visita agli ultimi kafiri Kalash. In: Maraini, F., Paropamiso. Leonardo da Vinci Editore, Bari, pp. 357-96. [English transl.: Where Four Worlds Meet: Hindu Kush, 1959. Hamish Hamilton, London, 1964].

Marhoffer-Wolff, Maria (1997) Family History as Legitimizing Strategy: The Thui Khalīfa. In: Stellrecht (1997a): 135-60. [On a lineage of healers from Yasin, specialized in illnesses caused by demons and fairies].

———. (2002) Frauen und Feen. Entwicklung und Wandel einer Beziehung (Besessenheit in Yasin / Nordpakistan). CAK, Vol. 10. Rüdiger Köppe Verlag, Cologne.

Marx, Edward (1999) How we lost Kafiristan. Representations, 67: 44-66. [An essay on context and sources of Kipling's "The Man Who Would Be King"].

Massari-Mariottini, Claudia (1974) Resti scheletrici dei Kalash e dei Kati (Chitral, Pakistan). Materiali raccolti dal Prof. Paolo Graziosi 1955, 1960. IsMEO, Roma.

Matveev, Pavel P. (1883) Poezdka po Buharskim i Afganskim vladenijam (1877 g.) [A Journey to the Bukhara and Afghan Possessions (1877)]. In: Sbornik geografičeskih, topografičeskih i statističeskih materialov po Azii [Collection of geographic, topographical and statistical materials on Asia], Vol. 5. Voennaja tipografija, St. Petersburg, pp. 1-57. [With interviews to Kafirs met in Faizabad].

Mayrhofer, Manfred (1967) Review of Jones (1966J). Sprache, 13: 133.

Mazumdar, S.K. (1976) A Biometric Study on the Tribes of North-Western Himalayan Region. Anthropological Survey of India, Government of India, Calcutta. [Presents the data recorded by Guha when with Morgenstierne in Chitral, 1929].

McCoy Owens, Bruce, Th. Riccardi Jr. & T.T. Lewis (n.d. [1987]) Bibliography of the History and Culture of the Himalayan Region. Vol. 1: History. Anthropology and Related Social Sciences. Vol. 2: Art. Development. Language and Linguistics. Travel Accounts. Bibliographies. No publ., no place. [This unpublished work lists over 7000 titles on the whole Himalayan area, including sections on "Pakistan Himalayan Region", with many little-known items, also on Nuristan. Compiled at Columbia University. Available in two files at: http://www.digitalhimalaya.com/collections/ rarebooks/].

Mela-Athanasopoulou, Elizabeth (2012) The Kalasha Woman Today. International Journal of Humanities and Social Science, 2, 17: 88-94.

———. (2014) Kalasha Grammar Based on Fieldwork Research. University Studio Press, Thessaloniki.

Meyendorff, Egor K. de (1826) Voyage d'Orenbourg à Boukhara, fait en 1820: à travers les steppes qui s'étendent à l'est de la mer d'Aral et au-delà de l'ancien Jaxartes. Librairie Orientale de Dondey-Dupré Père et fils, Paris. [With a brief note on Kafiristan].

Miloserdov, Dmitry Y. (2019) Holodnoe oružie Afganistana XIX – načala XX vekov., XIX – nachala XX vekov [Edged Weapons of Afghanistan, 19th – Early 20th Century]. Atlant, St. Petersburg. [With a section on Kafir daggers, pp. 294-99]].

Mit'ko, Oleg A. (2011) Dvulezvijnye kresala iz arheologičeskih pamjatnikov Sibiri i Dal'nego Vostoka i ih analogii iz Nuristana [Double-edged flints from the archaeological sites of Siberia and the Far East and their analogies from Nuristan]. Vestnik Novosibirskij Gosudarstvennyj Universitet. Serija: istorija, filologija, 10, 7: 246-55.

Mock, John (1998a) The Discursive Construction of Reality in the Wakhi Community of Northern Pakistan. PhD Dissertation. University of California, Berkeley. [With much data on affinities of Wakhi traditions with Peristani cultures].

———. (1998b) Shri Badat the Cannibal King: A Buddhist Jataka from Gilgit. In: Stellrecht (1998cII): 653-62.

———. (2011) Shrine Traditions of Wakhan Afghanistan. Journal of Persianate Studies, 4: 117-45.

———. (2013a) Darkot Revisited: New Information on a Tibetan Inscription and mchod-rten. Revue d'Études Tibétaines, 27: 11–19.

———. (2013b) New Discoveries of Rock Art in Afghanistan's Wakhan Corridor and Pamir: A Preliminary Study. The Silk Road, 11: 36–53 + Plates III-IV.

———. (2013c) A Tibetan Toponym from Afghanistan. Revue d'Études Tibétaines, 27: 5–9.

———. (2016a) Tibetans in Wakhan: New Information on Inscriptions and Rock Art. Revue d'Études Tibétaines, 3: 121-41.

———. (2016b) Snow Leopards in Art and Legend of the Pamir. In: McCarthy, T. & D. Mallon, eds., Snow Leopards, Biodiversity of the World: Conservation from Genes to Landscapes. Academic Press, London & San Diego, pp. 210-13.

———. (2017) Raising the Alarm: Defensive Communication Networks and the Silk Roads through Wakhan and Chitral. The Silk Road, 15: 1-12.

———. (2018a) Khandut Revisited: Shrines, Monuments, Rock Art and Indigenous Traditions of Wakhan in Afghanistan. The Journal of the American Institute of Afghanistan Studies, 1, 2: 282-301.

———. (2018b) The Red Buddha Hall Road Revisited: New Information about the Tibetan and Tang Empires in Afghanistan Wakhan. Revue d'Études Tibétaines, 45: 89-109.

Mohyuddin, Aisha, et al. (2002) HLA polymorphism in six ethnic groups from Pakistan. Tissue Antigens, July 2002: 492-501.

Mohyuddin, Aanwar, I. Sheikh & H.R. Chaudhry (2015a) Bashalini a Place for Biological Gender Impurities Segregating Women During Menstruation in Kalsah. Sci.Int.(Lahore), 27,1: 549-54. [Though not always factually accurate, this study stems from fieldwork and informs on non-Western researchers' perceptions of Kalasha culture. "Bashalini" is the Khowar word for bashali and Khalsa is a misprint for "Kalash"].

————. (2015b) Kalash Dress Adornment as Space for Identity: A Case Study of Bumburet Valley in District Chitral, Pakistan. Sci.Int.(Lahore), 27,1: 591-96. [Data from field work are largely reliable, though transcriptions are often imaginative].

Moorcroft, William & George Trebeck (1841) Travels in India. Himalayan Provinces of Hindustan and the Punjab; in Ladakh and Kashmir, in Peshawar, Kabul, Kunduz and Bokhara from 1819 to 1825 (2 vols). John Murray, London.

Mørch, Ida, E. & J., Hegård (2008) Some Observations on the Variation in the Pronunciation of Kalashamon as Spoken Inside and Outside Present-day Kalasha Society. In: Israr-ud-Din (2008): 288-95.

Morgenstierne, Georg (1927) The Linguistic Classification of Dardic and Kafiri. In: Oosters Genootschap in Nederland, Verslag van het 5. congres. Leiden, pp. 31-32.

————. (1932) The Kafirs of the Hindukush. Man, 32: 167-8.

————. (1935a) Die Wörter für 'Lüge' und 'Wahrheit' in den Dard- und Kafirsprachen. Göteborgs Högskolas Årsskrift, 41: 35-39.

————. (1935b) The Personal Pronouns First and Second Plural in the Dardic and Kafir Languages. Indian Linguistics, vol. 5 (Grierson Commemoration volume, pt.4.): 357-62.

————. (1942) Notes on Dameli, a Kafir-Dardic Language of Chitral. NTS, 12: 115-98.

————. (1945a) Indo-European k' in Kafir. NTS, 13: 225-38.

————. (1945b) Notes on Shumashti. A Dardic Dialect of the Gawar-Bati type. NTS, 13: 239-81.

————. (1947) Notes on Burushaski phonology. NTS, 14: 61–95.

————. (1952) Linguistic Gleanings from Nuristan. NTS, 16: 117-35.

————. (1973) Genealogical traditions among the Kati Kafirs. In: Morgenstierne (1973aJ): 307-16.

————. (1992) På Sprogjakt i Hindu Kush. Dagboksnotater fra Chitral 1929. Utgitt ved Eva M. Loerentsen, I samarbeide met Knut Kristiansen og Fridrik Thorardson. Indo-iransk bibliotek, Universitetet i Oslo. Oslo. [Field diary of the 1929 expedition to Chitral].

————. (2001). See: Kristiansen & Witek (2001).

Morin, Yves-Charles, J. Presot & E. Tiffou (1979) Complément au lexique du bourouchaski. Journal asiatique, 267, 1-2: 137-53.

Motamedi, Ahmad A. (1957) Some notes on the mythology of the Kafirs of the Hindu Kush (before 1898). Afghanistan, 12, 3: 9-15 and 12, 4: 7-12.

———. (1983) L'importance socio-économique et socio-religieuse de la chèvre au Nuristan. In: Snoy (1983J): 418-22.

Müller-Stellrecht, Irmtraud = Stellrecht, Irmtraud, see also.

Müller-Stellrecht, Irmtraud (1978) Hunza und China (1761-1891). 130 Jahre einer Beziehung und ihre Bedeutung für die Wirtschaftliche und politische Entwicklung Hunzas im 18. und 19. Jahrhunderten. Franz Steiner Verlag, Wiesbaden.

———. (1981) Menschenhandeln und Machtpolitik im westlichen Himalaya. Ein Kapitel aus der Geschichte Dardistans (Nordpakistan). ZAS, 15: 391-472.

———. (1983) Der Thronantritt König Muhammad Nazim Khans von Hunza (Nordpakistan): Ein Beispiel 'indirekter Herrschaft' im kolonialen Indien. In: Snoy (1983J): 423-37.

———. (1984) Tribute Relationship Between Hunza and China (1761 – 1947). JCA, 7, 1: 125-32.

Mumtaz, Mah Noor, H. Ihsan, S. Aziz, Hizbullah, S.G. Afridi, S. Shams & A. Khan (2019) The genetic composition of Shina population from Gilgit-Baltistan, Pakistan based on mtDNA analyses. Mitochondrial DNA Part B, Resources, 4,2: 3802-3808. [An online open access journal].

Munphool Meer (1869) On Gilgit and Chitral. Proceedings of the Royal Geographical Society, 13: 130-33.

———. (1872) Badakhshan and the Countries around it. JRAS, 42: 440-48.

Munphool Pundit [= Munphool Meer] (1870) Relations between Gilgit, Chitral, and Kashmir. The Journal of the Ethnological Society of London (1869-1870), 2, 1: 35-39.

Munshi, Sadaf (2016) Burushaski Language Resource. A digital collection of Burushaski oral literature. Online at: https:// digital.library.unt.edu/explore/collections/BURUS/ (acc. July 26, 2021). [A valuable collection of 390 Burushaski texts in digital recording, including stories, proverbs, personal narratives, poems and songs, etc. No transcription, no English translation].

Murtaza, M. Ghulam (1982) New History of Chitral (Nai Tarikh Chitral). Translated from the Urdu Version into English by Wazir Ali Shah. Chitral. Unpublished Manuscript.

Mustafa, Mehreen (2019) The Kalasha Art of Dwelling: Built Heritage of Kalasha Valley. In: Pir *et al.* (2019): 23-71.

Narasimhan, Vagheesh, N. Patterson, P. Moorjani, *et al.* (2019) The formation of human populations in South and Central Asia. Science, 365, eaat7487. [A landmark genetic study of ancient population movements in Eurasia, including samples from 117 inviduals from Swat and Chitral. Online open access].

Nasr-ul-Mulk (1935) The Ismailis or Maulais of the Hindu Kush. Journal of the Royal Central Asian Society, 22: 641-45.

Nayyar, Adam (1983) The Chili-Gari-Ai Ceremony. In: Snoy (1983J): 438-39. [A pastoral rite in Astor].

———. (1984) Cosmology and Colour Perception in the Astore Valley. JCA, 7: 269-75.

Neelis, Jason (2000) Kharoṣṭhī and Brāhmī Inscriptions from Hunza-Haldeikish: Sources for the Study of Long-Distance Trade and Transmission of Buddhism. In: Taddei, M. & G. De Marco, eds., South Asian Archaeology 1997. IsIAO, Rome, pp. 903-23.

———. (2002) La Vieille Route Reconsidered: Alternative Paths for Early Transmission of Buddhism Beyond the Borderlands of South Asia. Bulletin of the Asia Institute, 16: 143–64.

———. (2006) Hunza-Haldeikish Revisited: Epigraphic Evidence for Trans-regional History. In: Kreutzmann (2006a): 159-70.

———. (2011) Early Buddhist Transmission and Trade Networks. Mobility and Exchange within and beyond the Northwestern Borderlands of South Asia. Brill, Leiden & Boston.

———. (2012a) Overland Shortcuts for the Transmission of Buddhism. In: Alcock, S.E., J. Bodel & R. Talbert, eds., Highways, Byways, and Road Systems in the Pre-Modern World. Wiley-Blackwell, Chichester, pp. 12-32.

———. (2012b) Central Asian Silk Routes and Early South Asian Trade Networks. In: Parker, P. , ed., Great Trade Routes. Anova, London, pp. 71-79.

———. (2013) Localizing the Buddha's Presence at Wayside Shrines in Northern Pakistan. In: Wick, P. & V. Rabens, Religion and Trade. Religious Formation, Transformation and Cross-Cultural Exchange between East and West. Brill, Leiden, pp. 43-64.

———. (2014) Networks for Long-distance Transmission of Buddhism in South Asian Transit Zones. In: Tansen, Sen, ed., Buddhism across Asia. Networks of Material, Intellectual and Cultural

Exchange. Institute of Southeast Asian Studies, Singapore, pp. 3-18.

―――. (2017) Endangered Signposts: Upper Indus Petroglyphs and Inscriptions in Northern Pakistan. TAASA Review, 26, 3: 12-13.

Nelson, David N. (1986) The Historical Development of the Nuristani Languages. PhD Dissertation. University of Minnesota, Minneapolis.

―――. (1993) OIA kumbakurïra – 'horned headdress". Acta Orientalia, 54: 62-67.

―――. (2018) Nuristani Studies. Department of Linguistics, University of Tokyo, Tokyo.

―――. (2020) Vedic *kílbiṣa* 'obligation'. Tōkyōdaigaku gengo-gaku ronshū [The University of Tokyo Linguistics], 42 (9): e231-e253. [Discusses the similarities in beliefs surrounding oaths between the Kalasha and the Vedic 'Aryans'.]

Neubauer, Hans Franz (1974a) Die Nuristanrebe und ihre Kulturhistorische Bedeutung. Angewandte Botanik, 49, 3/4: 123-30.

―――. (1974b) Die Nuristanrebe, Herkunft der Edelrebe und Ursprung des Weinbaues. Afghanistan Journal, 1, 2: 32-36.

Neve, Arthur (1913) Thirty Years in Kashmir. Edward Arnold, London.

Newby, Eric (1958) A Short Walk in the Hindu Kush. Secker & Warburg, London. [The last sixty pages narrate a trek through Ramgul, Nuristan in 1956].

Nicolaus, Peter (2015a) Residues of Ancient Beliefs among the Shin in the Gilgit-Division and Western Ladakh. Iran and the Caucasus, 19: 201-64.

―――. (2015b) The Taming of the Fairies. In: Bläsing, U., V. Arakelova & M. Weinreich, eds., Studies on Iran and The Caucasus. In Honour of Garnik Asatrian. Brill, Leiden, pp. 205-27.

Nicoletti, Martino (2014) Cantare tra le mani. Un viaggio tra gli Ismailiti dell'Hindu Kush. Lindau, Torino.

Nizam, Muhammad Huzaifa (2020) Chitrali Mythology. World History Encyclopedia. [An online resource. This entry affords a useful comparison with Jettmar's treatment of the matter, being independent of it].

Nizam-ul-Mulk & G.W. Leitner (1891) Fables, Legends and Songs of Chitral. The Imperial Asiatic Quarterly Review, 1, 1: 145-58.

Noci, Francesco (2006) Beyond the Swat Valley. Research on Wooden Architecture to Other Areas of Northern Pakistan. E&W

(Special Issue for the 50th Anniversary of the IsIAO Italian Archaeological Mission in Pakistan, edited by L.M. Olivieri), 56, 1-3: 263-74.

Nuristani, Ahmad Yusuf (1973) The Palae of Nuristan (A Type of Cooperative Dairy and Cattle Farming). In: Rathjens, C., C. Troll & H. Uhlig, eds., Vergleichende Kulturgeographie der Hochgebirge des südlichen Asien. Franz Steiner Verlag, Wiesbaden, pp. 177-81.

————. (1994a) Emergence of *ulama* as political leaders in the Waigal Valley: The intensification of Islamic identity. PhD Dissertation. The University of Arizona, Tucson.

————. (1994b) Traditional Use of Nuristani Forests. In: Asian Study Group (Afghanistan Circle), The Destruction of the Forests and Wooden Architecture of Eastern Afghanistan and Northern Pakistan: Nuristan to Baltistan. Islamabad 30 October 1993. Asian Study Group, Islamabad, pp. 25-31.

Nüsser Marcus, A. Holdschlag & Fazlur-Rahman (2012) Herding on High Grounds: Diversity and Typology of Pastoral Systems in the Eastern Hindukush (Chitral, Northwest Pakistan). In: Kreutzmann H., ed., Pastoral practices in High Asia. Agency of 'development' effected by modernisation, resettlement and transformation. Springer, Dordrecht, pp. 31-52.

Olivieri, Luca Maria (1998) The Rock-Carvings of Gogdara I. Documentation and Preliminary Analysis. E&W, 48: 57-91.

————. (2008) Hanging Rocks and 'Intoxicating Drinks': The Rock Art Sequence of the Swat Valley. South Asian Studies, 24: 15-26.

————. (2009) Swat. Storia di una frontiera. IsIAO, Roma.

————. (2010a) Late Historic Cultural landscape in Swat. New data for a tentative Historical Reassessment. In: Allram M., D. Klimburg-Salter, M. Pfisterer, & Minoru Inaba, eds., Coins, Art and Chronology II. The First Millennium CE in the Indo-Iranian Borderlands, Vol. 1. Österreichische Akademie der Wissenschaften, Vienna, pp. 357-69.

————. ed. (2010b) Picture in Transformation. Rock Art Research from Central Asia to the Subcontinent. Papers presented at the 19th EASAA Conference (Special Session and Thematic Symposia), Ravenna 2-6 July 2007. Hadrian Books, Oxford.

————. (2011) Behind the Buddhist Communities: Subalternity and Dominancy in Ancient Swat. JAC, 34, 1: 123-151.

————. (2013) Rock shelters of the Swat-Malakand from the bronze age to Buddhism. Materials for a tentative reconstruction of the religious and cultural stratigraphy of ancient Swat. Freie Universität, Berlin. [On a complex of petroglyphs with possible "Kafir"-like connections].

————. (2015a) Bibliography [of the Italian Archaeological Mission on Buddhist Archaeology 1955-2015]. In: Callieri P., A. Filigenzi & L.M. Olivieri, eds., At the Origin of Gandharan Art. vol. 1. Shanghai Classics Publishing House, Shanghai, pp. 181-97.

————. (2015b) Sir Aurel Stein and the 'Lords of the Marches': New Archival Materials. Sang-e-Meel Publications, Lahore.

————. (2015c) Talking Stones. Painted Rock Shelters of the Swat Valley. Sang-e-Meel Publications, Lahore.

————. (2016a) Behind the Buddhist Communities. A Revised Note on Subalternity and Dominancy in Ancient Swat. Pakistan Archaeology, 31: 45-67.

————. (2016b) Guru Padmasambhava in Context: Archaeological and Historical Evidence from Swat/Uddiyana (c. 8th century CE). Journal of Bhutan Studies, 34: 20-42.

————. (2016c) The Last Phases at Barikot: Urban Cults and Sacred Architecture. Data from the Spring 2013 Excavation Campaign in Swat. Journal of Inner Asia Art and Archaeology, 7: 7-30.

————. (2017) Decline or Transformations: Patterns of Change in Swat at and after the end of the Kushan Era (3rd-6th Century AD). JAC, 40: 41-59.

————. (2018) Vajirasthana/Bazira and Beyond: foundation and current status of the archaeological work in Swat. In: Ray, H.P., ed., Buddhism and Gandhara: An Archaeology of Museum Collections. Vol. 1. Routledge India, New Delhi, pp. 173-212.

Olivieri, L.M. & A. Filigenzi (2018) On Gandharan sculptural production from Swat: recent archaeological and chronological data. In: Wannaporn, R. & P. Stewart, eds., Problems of Chronology in Gandharan Art. Proceedings of the First International Workshop of the Gandhara Connections Project, University of Oxford, 23rd-24th March, 2017. Vol. 1. Archaeopress Publishing, Oxford, pp. 71-92.

Olivieri, L.M. & Ghani-ur-Rahman, eds. (2011) Italian Archaeology and Anthropology in Northern Pakistan (1955-2011). JAC, 34: 1-360.

Olivieri, L.M. & M. Vidale (2004) Beyond Gogdara I. New Evidence of Rock Carvings and Rock Artefacts from the Kandak Valley and Adjacent Areas (Swat, Pakistan). E&W, 54: 121-80.

———. (2006) Archaeology and Settlement History in a Test Area of the Swat Valley. Preliminary Report on the AMSV Project. E&W, 56: 73-150.

Ottley, J.F.S. (1936) A Journey in Western Chitral. The Himalayan Journal, 8: 44-52. [With a short visit to the Kalasha valleys].

Ovesen, Jan (1978) Ethnographic Field Research among the Pashai People of Darrah-i Nur. Afghanistan, Historical and Cultural Quarterly, 32, 1: 87–98.

———. (1979) An Annotated Bibliography of Sources relating to the Pashai People of Afghanistan. Afghanistan Quarterly, 32, i: 87-98.

———. (1981) The continuity of Pashai Society. Folk, 23: 221-34.

———. (1982a) Marriage and Social Groupings among the Pashai. Folk, 24: 143-56.

———. (1982b) A Note on the Relation between Language and Culture: the Pashai Case. In: Monumentum Georg Morgenstierne 2 (= Acta Iranica 22). Brill, Leiden, pp. 131-40.

———. (1983) Environment and History in Pashai World-View. Folk, 25: 167-84.

———. (1984) On the Cultural Heritage of the Pashai. Anthropos, 79, 4/6: 397-407.

———. (1986) The construction of ethnic identities: the Nurestani and Pashai. In: Orywal, E., ed., Die ethnischen Gruppen Afghanistans: Fallstudien zu Gruppenidentität und Intergruppenbeziehungen. Ludwig Reichert, Wiesbaden, pp. 239-53.

Pallarés, Juan G. (1978) Viaje al país de los Kafires. EDAF, Madrid. [A young traveler's account of a land trip from Spain to the Kalasha in 1976, with lots of misunderstandings and several colour photos].

Parker, Edward H. (1897a) A Few Chinese Observations about Chitral, Hunza, etc. The China Review, 22, 6: 787-89.

———. (1897b) China and the Pamirs. The Contemporary Review, 72: 867-79.

Parkes, Peter (1987) Review of Jettmar (1986). Man (N.S.), 22, 3: 581-82.

————. (1990) Kalasha Rites of Spring. Anthropology Today, 6, 5: 11-13.

————. (1991) Temple of Imra, Temple of Mahandeu: A Kafir sanctuary in Kalasha cosmology. Bulletin of the SOAS, 54, 1: 75-103.

————. (1992) Reciprocity and Redistribution in Kalasha Prestige Feasts. Anthropozoologica, 16: 37-46.

————. (1994) Personal and Collective Identity in Kalasha Song Performance: The Significance of Music-Making in a Minority Enclave. In: Stokes, M., ed., Ethnicity, Identity and Music. Berg Publishers, Oxford, pp. 157-87.

————. (1996a) Indigenous Polo and the Politics of Regional Identity in Northern Pakistan. In: MacClancy, J., ed., Sport, Identity and Ethnicity. Berg Publishers, Oxford, pp. 43-67.

————. (1996b) Kalasha Oral Literature and Praise Songs. In: Bashir & Israr-ud-Din (1996): 315-28.

————. (1997) Kalasha Domestic Society: Practice, Ceremony and Domain. In: Donnan, H. & F. Selier, eds., Family and Gender in Pakistan: Domestic Organization in a Muslim Society. Hindustan Publishing Co., Delhi, pp. 25-63.

————. (2000) Enclaved Knowledge: Indigent and Indignant Representations of Environmental Management and Development among the Kalasha of Pakistan. In: Ellen, R., P. Parkes & A. Bricker, Indigenous Environmental Knowledge and its Transformations: Critical Anthropological Perspectives. Harwood Academics, Amsterdam, pp. 253–91.

————. (2001a) Alternative Social Structures and Foster Relations in the Hindu Kush. Milk Kinship Allegiance in Former Mountain Kingdoms of Northern Pakistan. Comparative Studies in Society and History, 43: 4-36.

————. (2001b) Unwrapping Rudeness. Inverted Etiquette in an Egalitarian Enclave. In: Hendry, J. & C.W. Watson, eds., An Anthropology of Indirect Communication. Routledge, London, pp. 232-51.

————. (2003) Fostering Fealty. A Comparative Analysis of Tributary Allegiances of Adoptive Kinship. Comparative Studies in Society and History, 45: 741-82.

————. (2004) Fosterage, kinship, and legend. When milk was thicker than blood? Comparative Studies in Society and History, 46: 587-615.

————. (2005) Milk Kinship in Islam: Substance, Structure, History. Social Anthropology, 13: 307-29.

————. (2008) A Minority Perspective on the History of Chitral: Katore Rule in Kalasha Tradition. In: Israr-ud-Din (2008): 349-77.

Parkin, Robert (1987a) Tibeto-Burman and Indo-European loans in Burushaski kinship terminology. Bulletin of the School of Oriental and African Studies, 50, 2: 325-29.

————. (1987b) Kin Classification in the Karakorum. Man (N.S.) 22, 1: 157-70.

Parpola, Asko (1988) The Coming of the Aryans to Iran and India and the Cultural and Ethnic Identity of the Dāsas. Studia Orientalia Electronica, 64: 196-302.

————. (2002a) Pre-Proto-Iranians of Afghanistan as initiators of Śākta Tantrism: on the Scythian/Saka affiliation of the Dāsas, Nuristanis and Magadhans. Iranica Antiqua, 37: 233-324.

————. (2002b) From the dialects of Old Indo-Aryan to Proto-Indo-Aryan and Proto-Iranian. In: Sims-Williams, N., ed. Indo-Iranian Languages and Peoples. Oxford U.P., Oxford, pp. 43-102.

————. (2012) The Dāsas of the Ṛgveda as Proto-Sakas of the Yaz I-related Cultures. With a revised model for the protohistory of Indo-Iranian speakers. In: Huld, M.E., K. Jones-Bley & D. Miller, eds., Archaeology and Language: Indo-European Studies Presented to James P. Mallory. Institute for the Study of Man, Washington DC, pp. 221-64.

————. (2015) The Roots of Hinduism. The Early Aryans and the Indus Civilization. Oxford U.P., New Delhi.

Pellò, Stefano (2009) Massoni o manichei? Immaginario etnografico sui Kafiri dell'Hindu Kush. Hiram. Rivista del Grande Oriente d'Italia, 2: 95-104. [On the Persian manuscript by Allahdad commissioned by Court, ca. 1840].

Perder, Emil (2013) A grammatical description of Dameli. PhD dissertation. Universitetsservice AB, Stockholm.

Pfeffer, Georg (1984) Kin-Classification in Hunza. JCA, 7, 2: 57-67.

Pir, Ghiasuddin (2019a) Suri Jagek: Meteorological and Astronomical Practice of Observing the Sun, Moon, Stars, and Shadows. In: Pir et al. (2019): 173-85.

————. (2019b) Chaumos: The Winter Solstice Festival. In: Pir et al. (2019): 115-41.

Pir. G., *et al.* (2019) From Tsiam to the Hindu Kush: Kalasha People and their Culture. UNESCO, Islamabad & THAAP [Trust for History Arts & Architecture, Pakistan], Lahore.

Pisowicz, Andrzej (2008) Review of Pstrusińska (1999). Zeitschrift für celtische Philologie, 53, 1: 341–48.

Planhol, Xavier de (1977) Le vin de l'Afghanistan et de l'Himalaya occidental. Revue Géographique de l'Est, 17,1-2: 3-26.

Plattner, Stewart (2002) Review of Cacopardo & Cacopardo (2001). American Anthropologist, 104: 973.

Pott, Janet (1965) Houses in Chitral, West Pakistan. Architectural Association Journal, 80: 245-49.

Potts, Daniel T. (2016) The Bronze Age roots of the Nuristani *urei*. In: Dubova, N.A., ed., Transactions of Margiana Archaeological Expedition, Vol. 6. To the Memory of Professor Victor Sarianidi. N.N. Miklukho-Maklay Institute of Ethnology and Anthropology of Russian Academy of Sciences, Moscow, pp. 418-21.

Preller, Charles du Riche (1924) The Racial and Economic Conditions of Trans-Himalaya Upper Indus Basin: Ladak and Baltistan. Scottish Geographical Journal, 40: 334-44.

Prontera, Francesco (2017) The Indian Caucasus from Alexander to Eratosthenes. In: Antonietti, C. & P. Biagi, eds., With Alexander in India and Central Asia: Moving East and Back to West. Oxbow Books, Oxford, pp. 212-21.

Pstrusińska, Jadwiga (1999) Old Celtic Cultures from the Hindukush perspective. Towarzystwo Autorów i Wydawców Prac Naukowych Universitas, Kraków.

————. (2003) Eurasiatic Context of the Old Celtic Cultural Phenomena. In: Bellingeri, G. & G. Pedrini, eds., Central Asia: a Decade of Reforms, Centuries of Memories. Leo S. Olschki, Florence, pp. 123-31. [With a reference to Nuristan and Kalasha].

Qamar, Raheel, *et al.* (2002) Y-chromosomal DNA variation in Pakistan. AJHG, 70: 1107-24.

Qasim, Ayub, *et al.* (2015) The Kalash Genetic Isolate: Ancient Divergence, Drift and Selection. AJHG, 96: 775-83.

Radloff, Carla F. (1999) Aspects of the Sound System of Gilgiti Shina. NIPS & SIL, Islamabad.

Radloff, C.F. & H. Liljegren (2022) Ergativity in Gilgiti Shina. In: Baart, Liljegren & Payne (2022): 248-76.

Radloff, C.F. & S.A. Shakil (1998) Folk Tales in the Shina of Gilgit. NIPS & SIL, Islamabad.

Rahman, Fazlur- (2007) Persistence and Transformation in the Eastern Hindu Kush. A Study of Resource Management Systems in Mehlp Valley, Chitral, North Pakistan. Asgard-Verlag, Sankt Augustin.

Rahman, Ghani-ur- (2011) Persistence of Pre-Islamic Decorative Patterns in Swat: A Wooden Mosque from Shangla District. In: Olivieri & Rahman (2011): 277-302.

Rahman, Hidayat ur (2010) The Genealogical History of the Last Royal Families of Chitral and Yasin: A Preliminary Study. Journal of Persianate Studies, 4: 208-32. [This paper discusses the relations between the Katur dynasty and the Kafirs, arguing in favour of the hypothesis that the Chitral rulers were of Kafir descent].

Rapin, Claude (2005) L'Afghanistan et l'Asie Centrale dans la géographie mythique des historiens d'Alexandre et dans la toponymie des géographes gréco-romains. In: Bopearachchi, O. & M-F. Boussac, eds., Afghanistan: Ancien carrefour entre l'est et l'ouest. Brepols, Turnhout, pp. 143–72.

Raverty, Henry G. (1862) An Account of Upper and Lower Suwát, and the Kohistán, to the source of the Suwát River; with an account of the tribes inhabiting those valleys. JASB, 31: 227-81.

———. (1864a) An Account of Upper Kash-Kar and Chitral or Lower Kash-Kar. JASB, 33, 2: 125-51.

———. (1864b) On the Language of the Siah Posh Kafirs. JASB, 33, 3: 267-78.

Rawlinson, Henry C. (1869) On Trade Routes between Turkestan and India. Proceedings of the Royal Geographical Society, 13: 10-23.

Rehman, Saeed ur (1990) Unique Find of Gold Ornaments from Pattan/ Kohistan. JCA, 13, 1: 5–17.

Reichert, Pierre (1983) Review of Grünberg (1980). Bulletin de la Société de Linguistique de Paris, 78, 2: 81-85.

———. (1986) Notes sur les structures élémentaires de la phrase en kati occidental. Bulletin de la Société de Linguistique de Paris, 81, 1: 205-16.

———. (1990/91) Un fossile linguistique: la labiovélaire de l'ashkun et du kati. Bulletin de la Société de Linguistique de Paris, 85, 1: 353-57.

————. (1998) Anmerkungen zur Dialektologie des Kati (Lautlehre). In: Kushev *et al.* (1998): 123-36.

Rennell, James (1792) Memoir of a Map of Hindoostan; or the Mogul Empire. The Second Edition. With very considerable additions, and many corrections. W. Bulmer & Co., London. [With the earliest British geographical inquiry on Kafiristan].

Rensch, Calvin R., S.J. Decker & D.G. Hallberg (1992) Languages of Kohistan. SSNP (5 vols). Vol. 1. NIPS & SIL, Islamabad.

Ricci, Matteo (1949) Del viaggio del Fratello Benedetto di Góis della nostra Compagnia che fece per terra dall'India verso Ponente mandato da' suoi superiori per scoprire il Gran Cataio fino alla città regia del regno di Cascar. In: D'Elia, P., ed., Fonti ricciane. Documenti originali concernenti Matteo Ricci e la storia delle prime relazioni tra l'Europa e la Cina (1579-1615), Vol. 2. Libreria dello Stato, Roma, pp. 391-445. [The primary source on Goes, author of the earliest European notice about Kafiristan].

Rieck, Andreas (1997a) From Mountain Refuge to "Model Area": Transformation of Shi'i Communities in Northern Pakistan. In: Stellrecht & Winiger (1997): 215-31.

————. (1997b) Who Are the Nurbakshis? Controversy about the Identity of a Beleaguered Community in Baltistan. In: Stellrecht (1997a): 41-60.

Ringdal, Nils J. (2008) Georg Valentin von Munthe af Morgenstiernes forunderlige liv og reiser [The marvelous Life and Travels of Georg Valentin von Munthe of Morgenstierne]. Aschenhoug, Oslo. [A 900-page biography of G. Morgenstierne].

Ritter Carl & V.V. Grigorjev (1867) Zemlevedenie: Kabulistan i Kafiristan [Geography: Kabulistan and Kafiristan]. St. Petersburg.

Rizvi, Janet (1994) The Trans-Karakoram Trade in Nineteenth and Twentieth Centuries. Indian Economics and Social History Review, 31: 27-64.

Robertson, George S. (1894a) Report on Journey to Kafiristan Confidential. Eyre and Spottiswoode Printers to the Queen, London. [This earliest, secret version of Robertson's classic includes passages later removed from the published volume].

————. (1894b) Kafiristan. The Geographical Journal, 3: 193-218.

————. (1897) Kafiristan: Its Manners and Customs. The Journal of the Society of Arts, 45: 573-81.

————. (1898) Kafiristan and Its People. The Journal of the Anthro-
pological Institute of Great Britain and Ireland, 27: 75-89.
————. (1914) Kafiristan. In: Hastings, J., ed., Encyclopaedia of
Religion and Ethics, Vol. 7. T. & T. Clark, Edinburgh, pp.
634-36.
Rose, Horace A. & E.B. Howell (1908) North West Frontier Province
(Imperial   Gazetteer   of   India.   Provincial   Series).
Superintendent of Government Printing, Calcutta. [Includes
Dir, Swat and Chitral].
Roselli, Maria Gloria (2012) Kafiri, gli infedeli. Il leggendario popolo
delle valli dell'Hindukush tra Afghanistan e Pakistan
attraverso i racconti di Paolo Graziosi. Bollettino della
Società Italiana dei Viaggiatori, Vol. 0: 31-39.
————. (2016) I popoli delle valli kalash raccontati dagli oggetti
raccolti da Paolo Graziosi. In: Chelazzi et al. (2016): 21-67.
Rousselet, Louis-Théophil M. (1885) Le Kafiristan et les Kafirs. Revue
d'ethnographie, 3: 218-26.
Russell, Gerard (2014) Heirs to Forgotten Kingdoms. Journeys into the
Disappearing Religions of the Middle East. Simon &
Schuster, London. [With a chapter on the Kalasha].
Rustamov, Uzbek A. (1956) Kolonial'naja politika Anglii na severe
Indii i zahvat knjažestva Čitral v 1892-1895 gg [The colonial
policy of England in the north of India and the seizure of the
principality of Chitral in 1892-1895]. Trudy IVAN UzSSR,
Tashkent, 4: 55-67.
Rybatzki, Volker (2013a) Vocabularies from the Middle of the 20th
Century from Afghanistan. Part One: Iranian, Nuristani and
Dardic Materials I collected by A. F. Mackenzie, edited and
explained by Volker Rybatzki. Acta Orientalia Academiae
Scientiarum Hungaricae, 66, 3: 297–348. [Includes a list of
21 words in Pashai and Western Kati recorded in 1951].
————. (2013b) Vocabularies from the Middle of the 20th Century
from Afghanistan. Part One: Iranian, Nuristani and Dardic
Materials II collected by A. F. Mackenzie, edited and
explained by Volker Rybatzki. Acta Orientalia Academiae
Scientiarum Hungaricae, 66, 4: 443–69. [Includes an
extensive comparative inquiry on the Pashai/Kati word list
presented in the previous article].
Rysiewicz, Zygmunt (1956) Zgadnienie palatalnych w jezykach
dardyjskich [Palatal issues in the Dardic languages]. In:

Rysiewicz, Z., Studia Językoznawcze. Zakład Narodowy imienia Ossolińskich, Wroclaw, pp. 285-92.

Rzehak, Lutz (2013) Recalling the Past to Assert Ethnic Rights in the Present: The Case of the Gawars in Afghanistan. Asien, 129: 22-37.

Sagaster, Klaus (1984) The Kings of Baltistan and Other Kings: Some Remarks on Balti Folk Literature. JCA, 7, 2: 49-55.

―――. ed. (1989) Die Baltis: Ein Bergvolk in Norden Pakistans. Museum für Völkerkunde (= Roter Faden zu Ausstellung, 16), Frankfurt, pp. 7-181.

―――. (1993) Tales from Northern Pakistan: The Discovery of the Folk Literature of Baltistan. In: Zingel-Avé Lallemant, S. & W.-P. Zingel, eds., Neuere deutsche Beiträge zu Geschichte und Kultur Pakistans. Deutsch-Pakistanisches Forum e.V., Bonn, pp. 83-92.

―――. (1995) Mündliche Epische Traditionen in Westtibet (Baltistan). In: Heissig, W., ed., Formen und Funktion mündlicher Tradition. Vorträge eines Akademiesymposiums in Bonn, Juli 1993. Westdeutscher Verlag, Opladen, pp. 121-31.

Samad, Abdul, et al. (2012) Archaeology in Chitral, Khyber Pakhtunkhwa, Pakistan. Placing New Results in Context. Pakistan Heritage, 4: 33-76.

Samreen, Akita (2013) Folksongs: The Real Portrayal of Baltistan's Culture. Pakistan Journal of History and Culture, 34, 2: 121-38.

Samrin, Farah (2008) The 'Kafirs' of Afghanistan. Proceedings of the Indian History Congress, 69: 915-20. [A review of early Eastern and colonial sources].

Shahab, Qudratullah (1952) The Strange Valley of Kafiristan. Pakistan Quarterly, 2, 1: 7-11. [An enthusiastic and rather confused description of the Kalasha valleys as "an oasis of pastoral bliss", with some precious old-time photographs].

Scarcia, Gianroberto (1967) Dal ms. persiano "Egerton 1104" del "British Museum" (Rieu. 1, 212b-213b) e altre "addenda" al "Şifat-nāma". Annali dell'Istituto Universitario Orientale di Napoli, N.S., 17: 227-50.

Scerrato, Ilaria E. (2003) Motivi decorativi convenzionali e figure naturalistiche: note su alcuni oggetti lignei kafiri. In: Fontana, V. & B. Genito eds. Studi in onore di Umberto Scerrato per il suo settantacinquesimo compleanno. Università degli Studi di Napoli "L'Orientale", IsIAO, Napoli, pp. 769-80, CXVII-CXX.

————. (2005) Arte lignea nel Pakistan del Nord Ovest/Wooden craft of North Western Pakistan, DecArt, 4: 95-105 [Italian and English text, with comparisons of Swat woodcraft with pre-Islamic motifs from surrounding areas].

————. (2006) Wood Carvers in Swat Valley. Fieldwork Documentation and Preliminary Analysis. E&W, 56, 1-3: 275-99.

————. (2009) Wood Art from the Swat Valley. The Ethnographic Activity of the IsIAO Italian Archeologicаl Mission in Pakistan. Scienze e lettere, Rome.

————. (2010) Dwellings in the Snow. Living Traditions in the Braldu Valley (Baltistan). In: Callieri, P. & L. Collica, eds., South Asian Archaeology 2007. Proceedings of the 19th Meeting of the European Association of South Asian Archaeology in Ravenna, Italy, July 2007. Vol. II, Historic Periods. Archaeopress, Oxford, pp. 307-14.

————. (2011) The ethnographic activity of the IsIAO Italian Archaeological Mission in Swat and Gilgit Baltistan. In: Olivieri & Rahman (2011): 242-76.

————. (2017) Attraverso le antiche vie del Karakorum. Architettura lignea e miti di fondazione in Baltistan. In: Genito, B. & L. Caterina, eds., Archeologie delle Vie della Seta: Percorsi, Immagini e Cultura Materiale. Vol. 3. Scienze e Lettere editore, Rome, pp. 31-50, Figs. 1-23. [Foundation myths with pre-Islamic elements in Baltistan].

Scerrato, Umberto (1980) Darel Valley Survey. IsMEO Activities: Pakistan. E&W, 31: 205-207.

————. (1981) Survey of Wooden Mosques and Related Wood-Carvings in the Swat Valley. E&W, 31: 178-81.

————. (1983a) Labyrinths in the Wooden Mosques of North Pakistan: A Problematic Presence. E&W, 33: 21-29.

————. (1983b) Survey of Wooden Mosques and Related Wood-Carvings in North-West Frontier Province, 3rd Report – 1982. E&W, 33: 325-28.

————. (1984) The Wooden Architecture of Swat and the Northern Areas of Pakistan: A Report on the Research Carried Out in 1984. E&W, 34: 501-15.

————. (1985) More on Wooden Mosques in North Pakistan. JCA, 8, 1: 105-109.

————. (1997) Ricerche di archeologia, storia dell'arte e architettura islamica. In: Ministero degli affari esteri, Direzione generale delle relazioni culturali, Missioni archeologiche italiane: la ricerca archeologica, antropologica, etnologica. L'erma di Bretschneider, Rome, pp. 243-48.

Schmid, Anna (1997) Die Dom zwischen sozialer Ohnmacht und kultureller Macht. Interethnische Beziehungen in Nordpakistan. Franz Steiner Verlag, Stuttgart.

———. (2002) Review of Cacopardo & Cacopardo (2001). Anthropos, 97: 568-70.

———. (2007) The Dom of Hunza (Northern Areas of Pakistan). In: Brower, B. & B. Rose Johnston, eds., Disappearing Peoples? Indigenous Groups and Ethnic Minorities in South and Central Asia. Left Coast Press, Walnut Creek, Cal., pp. 107–27.

Schmidt, Ruth Laila (1981) Report on a Survey of Dardic Dialects of Kashmir. Indian Linguistics, 42: 17-21.

———. (1985) Where Have the Shina Speakers Come from? Some Linguistic Clues. JCA, 8, 1: 17-26.

———. (2002) Review of Cacopardo & Cacopardo (2001). Acta Orientalia, 63: 277-84.

———. (2003) Converbs in a Kohistani Shina Narrative. Acta Orientalia, 64: 137-52.

———. (2004) A Grammatical Comparison of Shina Dialects. In: Saxena, A., ed., Himalayan Languages Past and Present. Mouton de Gruyter, Berlin/New York, pp. 33-55.

———. (2003-2004) The Oral History of the Darmá Lineages of Indus Kohistan. European Bulletin of Himalayan Research, 25/26: 61-79.

———. (2006) A Nāga-Prince Tale in Kohistan. Acta Orientalia, 67: 159-88.

———. (2013) The Transformation of a Naga Prince Tale. Oriental Archive, 81, 1: 1-15.

Schmidt, R.L. & R. Kohistani (2008) A Grammar of the Shina Language of Indus Kohistan. Harrassowitz Verlag, Wiesbaden.

Schmidt, R.L. & O.N. Koul (1983) Dardistan Revisited: an Examination of the Relationship between Kashmiri and Shina. In: Koul, O.N. & P.E. Hook, eds., Aspects of Kashmiri Linguistics. Bahri Publications, New Delhi, pp. 1-26.

Schmidt, R.L., O.N. Koul & V.K. Kaul (1984) Kohistani to Kashmiri: An Annotated Bibliography of Dardic Languages. Indian Institute of Language Studies, Patiala.

Schmidt, R.L. & M.M. Zarin (2008) Narratives of Blood Enmity in Indus Kohistan. In: Skyhawk (2008a): 260-95.

Schneid, Monika (1997) Identity, Power, and Recollection: Inside and
        Outside Perspectives on the History of Bagrot Valley
        (Northern Pakistan). In: Stellrecht (1997a): 83-110.
Schomberg, Reginald C.F. (1934) The Yarkhun Valley of Upper Chitral.
        Scottish Geographical Magazine, 50: 209-12.
————. (1936) Lotkuh and Hunza. The Alpine Journal, 48: 124-33.
————. (1947) The Expeditions – The Bagrot Valley, Gilgit. The
        Himalayan Journal, 14: 72-75.
Schwartz, Martin (1990) Viiāmburas and Kafirs. Bulletin of the Asia
        Institute (In honor of Richard Nelson Frye: Aspects of Iranian
        Culture), NS, 4: 251-255.
Schweinfurth, Ulrich (1983) Mensch und Umwelt im Indus-Durchbruch
        am Nanga Parbat (NW-Himalaya). In: Snoy (1983J): 536-59.
Scott, David (1988) Review of Jettmar (1986). JRAS, 120, 1: 200–202.
Scott, Ian Dixon (1937) Notes on Chitral. Government of India Press,
        Simla. [An important source on the mehtarship of Chitral].
Semino, Ornella, et al. (2004) Where West Meets East: the complex
        mtDNA landscape of the southwest and Central Asian
        corridor. AJHG, 74: 827-45.
Shah, Wazir Ali & G. Morgenstierne (1959) Some Khowar Songs. Acta
        Orientalia, 24, 1/2: 29-58.
Shaw, Robert B. (1871) Visits to High Tartary, Yârkand, and Kâshghar
        (formerly Chinese Tartary) and Return Journey over the
        Karakoram Pass. John Murray, London.
Sheikh, Abdul G. (1998) Ladakh and Baltistan through the Ages. In:
        Stellrecht (1998cII): 337-50.
Sheikh, Irum, Hafeez-ur-Rehman & A. Naz (2013) An Ethnographic
        Study of Marriage System and the Runaway Brides of Kalash.
        Middle-East Journal of Scientific Research, 16, 10: 1393-
        1402. [Though not always factually accurate, this study stems
        from fieldwork and informs on non-Western researchers'
        perceptions of Kalasha culture].
Sheikh, I., A. Mohyuddin, H.R. Chaudhry & S. Iqbal (2014) Identity
        and Self Image in Adolescence: A case study of Bumburet
        Valley in District Chitral Pakistan. World Applied Sciences
        Journal, 29, 1: 96-105. [Though not always factually accurate,
        this study stems from fieldwork and informs on non-Western
        researchers' perceptions of Kalasha culture].
Sher, Hassan, R.W. Bussman, R. Hart & H.J. de Boer (2016) Traditional
        use of medicinal plants among Kalasha, Ismaeli and Sunni

groups in Chitral District, Khyber Pakhtunkhwa province, Pakistan. Journal of Ethnopharmacology, 188: 57-69.

Siddiqi, M. Idris (1965) Kafir Gods & Shrines. Museums Journal of Pakistan, 17: 30-42.

Sidky, M. Homayun (1994) Shamans and Mountain Spirits in Hunza. Asian Folklore Studies, 53,1: 67-96.

———. (1996) Irrigation and State Formation in Hunza: The Anthropology of a Hydraulic Kingdom. University Press of America, Lanham.

———. (1997) Irrigation and the Rise of the State in Hunza: A Case for the Hydraulic Hypothesis. Modern Asia Studies, 31, 4: 995-1017.

———. (1999) Alexander the Great, the Graeco-Bactrians, and Hunza: Greek descent in Central Asia. CAJ: 43, 2. [On the evergreen Alexander fantasy].

———. (2003) Verticality, Multiple Resource Utilization and Subsistence Economy in the Karakoram Mountains: The Case of the Transhumant Hunzakutz. In: Rao, A. & M. Casimir, eds., Nomadism in South Asia. Oxford U.P., New Delhi, pp. 307-41.

———. (2004) Hunza, an Ethnographic Outline. ABD Publishers, Jaipur.

———. (2015) Agropastoralism and Transhumance in Hunza. In: Kardulias, P.N., ed., The Ecology of Pastoralism. University Press of Colorado, Boulder, pp. 71-96.

Sidky, M.H. & J. Subedi (2000) Bitan, Oracles, and Healers in the Karakorams. Illustrated Book Publishers, Jaipur.

Sihler, Andrew L. & J. Greppin (1997) The Myth of Direct Reflexes of the PIE Palatal Series in Kati. In: Disterheft, D., J. Greppin & M. Huld, eds., Studies in Honor of Jaan Puhvel. Institute for the Study of Man, Washington D.C., pp. 187-94.

Siiger, Halfdan (1950): Som etnograf blandt de sorte kafirer. Erfaringer fra den 3. danske centralasiatiske ekspedition. [As an Ethnographer among the Black Kafirs. Experiences from the 3rd Danish Central Asian expedition]. Offprint No. 295 Folkeuniversitetsudvalget, Copenhagen.

———. (1951) Statuer af træ hos Kalash-kafirerne i Chitral. Materiale fra den 3. Danske Centralasiatiske Ekspedition. [Wooden statues of the Kalash Kafirs in Chitral. Materials from the 3rd Danish Central Asian Expedition]. Offprint from Nationalmuseets Arbejdsmark, Copenhagen, pp. 29-38.

————. (1976) Two Indigenous Peoples of the Hindukush-Himalayan
        Regions. Temenos, Nordic Journal of Comparative Religion,
        12: 39-99.
————. (1977) Review of Snoy (1975J). Afghanistan Journal, 4, 1, S:
        38.
Siiger, H., S. Castenfeldt & M. Fentz (1991) Small Functional Items
        and Regeneration of Society. Dough Figurines from the
        Kalash People of Chitral, Northern Pakistan. Folk, 33: 37-66.
Simpson, William (1879) On the Dara Nur, or Dara Nuh, in Afghanistan.
        Proceedings of the Royal Geographical Society, 1: 802-803.
Sims-Williams, Nicholas (1989) Sogdian and Other Iranian Inscriptions
        of the Upper Indus. I. Corpus Inscriptionum Iranicarum: Part
        II, Inscriptions of the Seleucid and Parthian Periods and of
        Eastern Iran and Central Asia. SOAS, London.
————. (1992) Sogdian and Other Iranian Inscriptions of the Upper
        Indus. II. Corpus Inscriptionum Iranicarum: Part II,
        Inscriptions of the Seleucid and Parthian Periods and of
        Eastern Iran and Central Asia. SOAS, London.
Sindhi, Hysar (1992) Nasalo: A Famous Festival of Shin and Yeshkun
        Tribes. Culture Area Karakorum Newsletter, Department of
        Anthropology, University of Tübingen, 2: 54-55.
Singh, Thakur (1917) Assessment Report of the Gilgit Tahsil. Khosla
        Bros., Lahore. [With data on traditional land tenure and
        irrigation systems].
Skinner, Joseph (2013) Imperial Visions, Imagined Past: Ethnography
        and Identity on India's North-Western Frontier. In: Almagor,
        E. & J. Skinner, eds., Ancient Ethnography: New Approaches.
        Bloomsbury Academic, London, pp. 203-21. [On the colonial
        view of Kafiristan].
Sköld, Hannes (1927) Die sprachliche Stellung der Kāfirsprachen.
        ZDMG, 81: lxxiv.
Skrine, Clarmont P. (1925) The Roads to Kashgar. JRAS, 12: 226-50.
Skyhawk, Hugh van (2003) Burushaski-Texte aus Hispar. Materialien
        zum   Verständnis   einer   archaischen   Bergkultur   in
        Nordpakistan. Harrassowitz Verlag, Wiesbaden.
————. (2006) Zawaar Mayun Ali of the Clan of Yabon: Hispare
        Sajira. In: Kreutzmann (2006): 225-35.
————. ed. (2008a) Masters of Understanding: German Scholars in the
        Hindu Kush and Karakoram, 1955-2005. JAC, Special
        Tribute Edition, 31, 1-2.

————. (2008b) Goat-Sacrifice to a Dardic Genius Loci. In: Skyhawk (2008a): 296-306.

————. (2021) Nur Qhatún Ćórokuć on Blessedness (barkát). Rodnoy yazyk,. Linguistic Journal, 1. [Online journal. Burushaski text and translation of a tale of abduction by spirits from Nagar].

Skyhawk, H. van, H. Berger & K. Jettmar (1996) Libi Kisar; Ein Volksepos im Burushaski von Nager. Harrassowitz Verlag, Wiesbaden.

Snoy, Peter (1969) Ethnologische Feldforschungen in Afghanistan. In: Jahrbuch des Südasien Instituts der Universität Heidelberg, Vol. 3, 1968/69: Problems of Land Use in the South Asia. Harrassowitz Verlag, Wiesbaden, pp. 127-30.

————. (1983) Thronfolge in den Fürstentümern der grossen Scharungszone. In: Snoy (1983J): 573-81.

————. (1993) Alpwirtschaft im Hindukusch und Karakorum. In: Schweinfurth, U., ed., Neue Forschungen im Himalaya. Franz Steiner Verlag, Stuttgart., pp. 49-73.

————. (1994) Von der Umwelt der Kalasch. In: Söhnen-Thieme & Hinüber (1994a): 287-304.

————. (2008) The Rites of the Winter Solstice among the Kalash of Bumburet. In: Skyhawk (2008a): 36-64.

Söhnen, Renate (= Söhnen-Thieme) (1983) On Reflections of Historical Events in Balti Folk-Songs. In: Snoy (1983J): 582-601.

Söhnen-Thieme, Renate & O. von Hinüber, eds. (1994a) Festschrift Georg Buddruss zur Vollendung des 65. Lebensjahres und zu seiner Emeritierung. SII, 19.

————. (1994b) Bibliographie der Schriften von Georg Buddruss [1954-1994]. In: Söhnen-Thieme & Hinüber (1994a): IX-XX.

Sökefeld, Martin (1988) Stereotypes and Boundaries: Paṭhān in Gilgit, Northern Pakistan. In: Kushev et al. (1998): 280-99.

————. (1994) Shin und Yeshkun in Gilgit: Die Abgrenzung zwischen zwei Identitätsgruppen in Gilgit und das Problem ethnografischen Schreiben. Petermanns Geographische Mitteilungen, 138: 357-69.

————. (1997a) Ein Labyrinth von Identitäten in Nordpakistan. Zwischen Landbesitz, Religion, und Kaschmir-Konflikt. CAK, Vol. 8. Rüdiger Köppe Verlag, Cologne.

————. (1997b) Migration and Society in Gilgit, Northern Areas of Pakistan. Anthropos, 92: 83-90.

————. (1998) "The People Who Really Belong to Gilgit"–Theoretical and Ethnographical Perspectives on Identity and Conflict. In: Stellrecht & Bohle (1998): 93-224.

————. (2003) Selves and Others: Representing Multiplicities of Difference in Gilgit and Northern Areas of Pakistan. In: Lecomte-Tilouine, M. & P. Dollfus, eds., Ethnic Revival and Religious Turmoil: Identities and Representations in the Himalayas. Oxford U.P., Delhi, pp. 309-36.

Sperber, Birgitte Glavind (1990) Kalash. Dresses, Body Decorations, Textile Techniques. Paper presented at the 2nd International Hindukush Cultural Conference, 19-23 September 1990. [Full version of Sperber 1996, available online on academia.edu].

————. (1992) Nature in the Kalasha Perception of Life and Ecological Problems. In: Bruun, O. & A. Kalland, eds., Asian Perceptions of Nature: papers presented at a Workshop, NIAS, Copenhagen, Denmark, October 1991. Nordic Proceedings in Asian Studies, Copenhagen, pp. 110-30.

————. (1995) Nature in the Kalasha Perception of life. In: Bruun, O. & A. Kalland, eds., Asian Perceptions of Nature. A Critical Approach. Curzon Press, Richmond, pp. 126-47.

————. (1996) Dresses and Textile Techniques. In: Bashir & Israr-ud-Din (1996): 377-408.

————. (2008) No People is an Island. In: Israr-ud-din (2008): 135-43.

————. (2017) Balanguru. Mennesker og myter I en kalashalandsby I Hindukush. Mellemgaard Forlaget, Odense.

————. (2021) Nuristan in Kalasha myth, history and life. In: Johnsen et al. (2021): 157-73.

Stacul, Giorgio (1987) Prehistoric and Protohistoric Swat, Pakistan (3000-1400 B.C.). IsIAO, Rome.

————. (2001) The Swāt in the Late 2nd and Early 1st Millennium B.C. In: Eichmann, R. & H. Parzinger, eds., Migration und Kulturtransfer. Der Wandel vorder- und zentralasiatischer Kulturen im Umbruch von 2. zum 1. vorchristlichen Jahrtausend. Habelt, Bonn, pp. 237-46.

Staley, Elizabeth (1966) Arid Mountain Agriculture in Northern West Pakistan (A Geographical Study). Thesis submitted for PhD at the University of the Punjab, Lahore.

Staley, John (1966) Economy and Society in Dardistan. Traditional Systems and the Impact of Change. Thesis submitted for PhD at the University of the Punjab, Lahore.

————. (1982) Words for My Brother. Oxford U.P., Karachi.

Stein, M. Aurel (1930) An Archaeological Tour in Upper Swat and Adjacent Hill Tracts. Memoirs of the Archaeological Survey of India, 42: 1-104.

————. (1934) Review of De Filippi (1932). JRAS, 66, 1: 165-69.

Steinmann, Alfred (1959-60) Die Holzfiguren von Kafiristan. Bulletin der Schweizerischen Gesellschaft für Anthropologie und Ethnologie, 36: 14-20.

Stellrecht, Irmtraud = Müller-Stellrecht, Irmtraud

Stellrecht, Irmtraud (1991) Protective Spirit Belief in Hunza, Northern Areas of Pakistan. Pakistan Archaeology, 26, 2: 124-35.

————. (1992) Umweltwahrnehmung und verticale Klassifikation im Hunza-Tal (Karakorum). Geographische Rundschau, 44: 426-34.

————. ed., (1997a) The Past in the Present. Horizons of Remembering in the Pakistan Himalaya. CAK, Vol. 2. Rüdiger Köppe Verlag, Cologne.

————. (1997b) Writings Concerning the Past in Northern Pakistan - A Short Introduction. In: Stellrecht (1997a): vii-xx.

————. (1997c) Dynamics of Highland-Lowland Interaction in Northern Pakistan since the 19th Century. In: Stellrecht & Winiger (1997): 3-22.

————. ed., (1998a) Bibliography – Northern Pakistan. CAK, Vol. 1. Rüdiger Köppe Verlag, Cologne.

————. (1998b) Trade and Politics. The High-Mountain Region of Pakistan in the 19th and 20th Century. In: Stellrecht & Bohle (1998): 7-92.

————. ed., (1998c) Karakorum – Hindukush – Himalaya. Dynamics of Change. CAK, Vols. 4.I. & 4.II. Rüdiger Köppe Verlag, Cologne.

————. (1998d) Economic and Political Relationships between Northern Pakistan and Central as well as South Asia in the Nineteenth and Twentieth Centuries. In: Stellrecht (1998cII): 3-20.

————. (2006a) Feldforschung als Erfahrung. Adolf Friedrich und Karl Jettmar in Nordpakistan. In: Brandstetter, A.-M. & C. Lentz, eds., 60 Jahre Institut für Ethnologie und Afrikastudien. Ein Geburtstag. Rüdiger Köppe Verlag, Köln, pp. 23-47. [This is the essay translated in the present volume].

————. (2006b) Passage to Hunza: Route Nets and Political Process in a Mountain State. In: Kreutzmann (2006): 191-216.

————. (2007a) Entwicklung als Identitätsprozess. In: Boeckh, A. &
R. Sevilla, eds., Kultur und Entwicklung: vier Weltregionen
im Vergleich. Nomos Verlagsgesellschaft, Baden-Baden, pp.
165-95. [With notes on historical and pre-Islamic roots of
present identity configurations in Hunza/Nagar].

————. (2007b) "Gemischte" Grenzgängerinnen. Schamaninnen in
Hunza/Nordpakistan. In: Eschbach-Szabo, V. & H. Buck-
Albulet, eds., Kulturwissenschaften und Frauenstudien.
Aktuelle Arbeiten und Vorträge an der Fakultät für
Kulturwissenschaften der Universität Tübingen, Bd. 2.
Eberhard Karls Universität Tübingen, Tübingen, pp. 49-112.
[A most valuable study on women shamans in Hunza].

Stellrecht, I. & H.G. Bohle, eds. (1998) Transformation of Social and
Economic Relationships in Northern Pakistan. CAK, Vol. 5.
Rüdiger Köppe Verlag. Cologne.

Stellrecht, I. & M. Winiger, eds. (1997) Perspectives on History and
Change in the Karakorum, Hindukush, and Himalaya. CAK,
Vol. 3. Rüdiger Köppe Verlag. Cologne.

Strand, Richard F. (1975) The Changing Herding Economy of the Kom
Nuristani. Afghanistan Journal, 2, 4: 123-34.

————. (1976) Review of Schuyler Jones (1974aJ). Journal of Asian
Studies, 3, 4: 712-13.

————. (1978) Ethnic Competition and Tribal Schism in Eastern Nuristan.
In: Anderson, J.W. & R.F. Strand, eds., Ethnic Processes and
Intergroup Relations in Contemporary Afghanistan. Afghanistan
Council of the Asia Society, New York, pp. 9-14.

————. (1985) Locality and Nominal Relationships in Kamviri. In: Zide,
A., D. Magier & E. Schiller, eds. Proceedings of the Conference
on Participant Roles: South Asian and Adjacent Areas. Indiana
University Linguistics Club, Bloomington, pp. 48-57.

————. (1997-2021) Nuristan. Hidden Land of the Hindu-Kush.
https://nuristan.info/ (acc. Aug. 4, 2021) [A very large and
fundamental source on Nuristani and Dardic languages].

————. (1999) Review of Degener (1998b). Acta Orientalia, 60: 236-
44.

————. (2001) The Tongues of Peristan. In: Cacopardo & Cacopardo
(2001): 251-59.

————. (2016) Nûristânî. In: Hock, H.H. & E. Bashir, eds., The
Languages and Linguistics of South Asia. A Comprehensive
Guide. De Gruyter Mouton, Berlin, pp. 66-72.

————. (2022) Phonatory Location in Far North-Western Indo-Âryan Languages. In: Baart, Liljegren & Payne (2022): 446-95.

————. (forthcoming in 2022) Ethnolinguistic and genetic clues to Nûristânî origins. In: Degener & Hill (2022).

Streefland, Pieter H., S.H. Khan & O. van Lieshout (1995) A contextual Study of Northern Areas and Chitral. AKRSP, Gilgit.

Susumu, Nejima (1998) Diversity of Lineages in Ghizer, Northern Areas, Pakistan. In: Stellrecht (1998cII): 405-16.

Syama, Adikarla, V.S. Arun, G. ArunKumar, *et al.* (2019) Origin and identity of the Brokpa of Dah-Hanu, Himalayas – an NRY-HG L1a2 (M357) legacy. Annals of Human Biology, 46, 7-8: 562-73.

Szabo, Albert & T.J. Barfield (1991) Afghanistan. An Atlas of Indigenous Domestic Architecture. University of Texas Press, Austin. [With a good architectural study of the Mum (Mandugal) village of Sasco (Saskü) in Bashgal, pp. 149-51, 229-43].

Taj, Aamer & S. Ali (2018) Erosion of Kalasha's Religio-Cultural Identity in Northern Pakistan: Context, Causes and Implications. FWU Journal of Social Sciences, 12,2: 35-47. [A study based on fieldwork, with little knowledge of existing literature. Focused on present causes of conversion, it presents responses to questionnaires on the subject and can be useful to compare present-day processes with the historical factors in the Islamization of Peristan].

Tanner, Henry C.B. (1891) Notes on the Inhabitants of the Himalayas. Scottish Geographical Magazine, 7: 581-85.

Thesiger, Wilfred (1957) A Journey in Nuristan. The Geographical Journal, 123: 457-64.

Thewalt, Volker (1983) Jātaka-Darstellungen bei Chilas und Shatial am Indus. In: Snoy (1983J): 622-35.

————. (1985) Rock Carvings and Inscriptions along the Indus. The Buddhist Tradition. In: Schotsmans, J. & M. Taddei, eds., South Asian Archaeology 1983. Istituto Universitario Orientale, Naples, pp. 779-800.

————. (1998-2000) Stupas, Tempel und verwandte Bauwerke aus drei Felsbildstationen bei Chilas am oberen Indus (Nordpakistan). Volker Thewalt Verlag. Web publication: http://thewalt.de/stupa.htm (acc. Aug. 4, 2021).

Thornton, Edward (1844) A Gazetteer of the Countries Adjacent to India on the North-West; Including Sinde, Afghanistan,

Beloochistan, the Punjab, and the Neighbouring States. 2 vols. W.H. Allen, London.

Thuillier, Henry R. (1898) Obituary. Colonel Henry C. B. Tanner, Indian Staff Corps. The Geographical Journal, 11, 5: 556-58.

Thurley, Matty & Jonathan Thurley (2019) Voices from the Hindu Kush. Echoes of Life in Western Nuristan. SIL, n.p. ["Printed in Afghanistan" - English translation of texts recorded in Kati from the "valley of Mondul" (probably Mandol district of Nuristan province, i.e Ramgal) - available online].

Tiffou, Étienne (1993) Hunza Proverbs. With collaboration of Y.-C. Morin, H. Berger, D.L.R. Lorimer & N.U. Hunzai. University of Calgary Press, Calgary.

———. ed. (2004) Bourouchaskiana. Actes du Colloque sur le Bourouchaski organisé à l'occasion du XXXVIème Congrès International sur les Études Asiatiques et Nord-Africaines (ICANAS), Montréal (27.8.–7.9.2000). Peeters, Louvain-la-Neuve.

———. (2014) Dictionnaire du bourouchaski du Yasin. Bourouchaski–Français et Français–Bourouchaski. Peeters, Louvain-la-Neuve.

Tiffou, É. & J. Pesot (1989) Contes du Yasin. Introduction au Bourouchaski du Yasin avec grammaire et dictionnaire analytique. Peeters & Seelaf, Paris.

Tikkanen, Bertil (1988) On Burushaski and Other Ancient Substrata in Northwestern South Asia. Studia Orientalia, 64: 303-25.

———. (1991) A Burushaski Folktale, Transcribed and Translated: The Frog as a Bride, or, The Three Princes and the Fairy Princess Salaasír. Studia Orientalia, 67: 65-125.

———. (1999) Archaeological-linguistic correlations in the formation of retroflex typologies and correlating areal features in South Asia. In: Blench, R. & M. Spriggs, eds., Archaeology and Language IV: Language Change and Cultural Transformation. Routledge, London, pp. 138–48.

———. (2007) Burushaski hurútas and Domaki beeśiná "to sit, stay, dwell" as Aspectual Auxiliaries and Their Regional Parallels. Acta Orientalia, 68: 135-60.

———. (2008) Some Areal Phonological Isoglosses in the Transit Zone between South and Central Asia. In: Israr-ud-Din (2008): 250-62.

———. (2022) Tonogenesis in Burushaski and Domaki. In: Baart, Liljegren & Payne (2022): 496-512.

Toporov, Vladimir N. (1970) About the Phonological Typology of Burushaski. In: Jakobson, R. & S. Kawamoto, eds., Studies in General and Oriental Linguistics Presented to Shiro Hattori on the Occasion of His Sixtieth Birthday. TEC Corporation for Language and Educational Research, Tokyo, pp. 632–47.

Topper, Uwe (1977) Beobachtungen zur Kultur der Kalasch (Hindukusch). Zeitschrift für Ethnologie, 102: 216-96. [An important source, based on extensive field stays in early times].

———. (2000) Grabstelen in Kohistan (Nordpakistan). Münchner Beiträge zur Völkerkunde, 6: 313–53. [An English version is available at: https://wemountains.com/06/02/1317/]

Torwali, Zubair (2014) Vestiges of Torwali Culture. How Torwali Culture Changed in Past Sixty Years. Idara Baraye Taleem-o-Taraqi, Bahrain Swat.

———. (2021) My Dardistan and its linguistic tapestry. Criterion Quarterly, 16,2: 1-14.

Trail, Ronald L. (1996) Kalasha Case-Marking System. In: Bashir & Israr-ud-Din (1996): 149-58.

Trail R.L. & G.R. Cooper (1999) Kalasha Dictionary: with English and Urdu. NIPS & SIL, Islamabad.

Trail, R.L. & A. Hale (1995) A Rhetorical Structure Analysis of a Kalasha Narrative. (=South Asia Work Papers I). SIL South Asia Group, Horsleys Green, UK.

Tribulato, Olga & L.M. Olivieri (2017) Writing Greek in the Swat Region: A New Graffito From Barikot (Pakistan). Zeitschrift für Papyrologie und Epigraphik, 204: 128-35.

Trumpp, Ernst (1866) Über die Sprache der sogenannten Kāfirs im indischen Caucasus (Hindū Kūsch). Zeitschrift der Deutschen Morgenländischen Gesellschaft, 20,2/3: 377–418. [A modified version of Trumpp 1862J, including a German translation of Fazl Huq & Nurulla 1878J].

Tsuchiya, Haruko (1998) Field Research Along the Ancient Routes in the Northern Areas of Pakistan (1991-1995). In: Stellrecht (1998cII): 45-70.

———. (1999) Tracing Ancient Routes in Northern Pakistan. Field research (1991–1996) (Preliminary report). In: Alram, M. & D. Klimburg-Salter, eds., Coins, Art, and Chronology: Essays on the Pre-Islamic History of the Indo-Iranian Borderlands.

Österreichischen Akademie der Wissenschaften, Vienna, pp. 353-90.

Tucci, Giuseppe (1997) On Swāt. Historical and Archaeological Notes. IsIAO, Rome. [A collection of nine important essays 1940-1977, including Tucci (1977J)].

Tuite, Kevin (1998) Evidence for Prehistoric Links between the Caucasus and Central Asia: The Case of the Burushos. In: Mair V., ed., The Bronze Age and Early Iron Age Peoples of Eastern Central Asia (2 Vols.). The Institute for the Study of Man, Washington DC, pp. 448-75.

Turner, Ralph L. (1926-28) Notes on Dardic. Bulletin of the SOAS, 4: 533-41.

———. (1931-32) A Note on IE *k'* in 'Ancient Illyrian' and 'Kafiri'. Transactions of the Philological Society, 31, 1: 15.

———. (1932) Review of Morgenstierne (1929J). JRAS, 1932: 173-75.

———. (1966) A Comparative Dictionary of the Indo-Aryan Languages. Oxford U.P., London.

Tusa, Sebastiano (1985) An Archaeological Survey in Darel. JCA, 8, 1: 179-91.

Twist, Rebecca L. (2011) The Patola Shahi Dynasty. A Buddhological Study of their Patronage, Devotion and Politics. VDM Verlag, Saarbrücken.

Ujfalvy, Charles E. de (1883) Les traces des religions anciennes en Asie Centrale et au sud de l'Hindou Kouch. Bulletin de la Société d'Anthropologie de Paris, 6: 278-91.

———. (1884) Aus dem westlichem Himalaja. Erlebnisse und Forschungen. F.A. Brockhaus, Leipzig.

———. (1887) Quelques observations sur les peuples du Dardistan. L'Homme: Journal illustré de sciences anthropologiques, 4, 6: 161-69.

———. (1896) Les Aryens au nord et au sud de l'Hindou Kouch. G. Masson, Paris.

Vakil, Safar (1948) Le Nouristan. Afghanistan, 3,4: 3-7.

Vasil'ev, Mihail E. & A.I. Kogan (2013) K voprosu o vostočnodardskoj jazykovoj obŝnosti [On the question of the Eastern Dardic linguistic community]. Vestnik RGGU. Naučnyj žurnal. Serija «Filologičeskie nauykoznanie». Voprosy jazykovogo rodstva, 10: 149-78.

Vernier, Martin (2007) Exploration et documentation des pétroglyphes du Ladakh: 1996-2006. Nodo Libri, Como.

Vigne, Godfrey T. (1842) Travels in Kashmir, Ladak, Iskardu, the Countries Adjoining the Mountain-Course of the Indus, and the Himalaya, North of the Panjab. Henry Colburn, London.

Villa, Luca (2016a) Tra le selve del Paropamiso. In: Chelazzi et al. (2016): 151-71.

———. (2016b) Di kupàs, soh'olyak e bashali: Chitral 1970. In Chelazzi et al. (2016): 197-227.

Vohra, Rohit (1983) History of the Dards and the concept of Minaro traditions among the Buddhist Dards of Ladakh. In: Kantowsky, D. & R. Sander, eds., Recent Research in Ladakh. History, culture, sociology, ecology. Weltforum Verlag, Munich, pp. 51-82.

———. (1985) Ethno Historical Notes on Nubra in Ladakh. In: Dendaletche, C., ed., Ladakh, Himalaya Occidental: ethnologie, ecologie. Acta biologica montana. Centre Pyrénéen de Biologie et Anthropologie des Montagnes, Pau, pp. 247-56.

———. (1988) Ethno-Historicity of the Dards in Ladakh: Observations and Analysis. In: Uebach, H. & J.L. Panglung, eds., Studia Tibetica, Vol. 2, Proceedings of the 4th Seminar of the International Association for Tibetan Studies, Schloss Hohenkammer, Munich 1985. Bayerische Akademie der Wissenschaften, Munich, pp. 1-24.

———. (1989a) An Ethnography: The Buddhist Dards of Ladakh. Mythic Lore, Household, Alliance System, Kinship. Ettelbrück, Luxemburg.

———. (1989b) The Religion of the Dards in Ladakh: investigations into their pre-Buddhist 'Brog-pa traditions. Ettelbrück, Luxemburg.

———. (1993) Antiquities on the Southern Arteries of the Silk Route: Ethnic movements and new discoveries. In: Ramble C. & M. Brauen, eds., Anthropology of Tibet and Himalaya. Ethnological Museum of the University of Zurich, Zurich, pp. 386-405.

———. (1995) Early History of Ladakh: Mythic Lore and Fabulation. A preliminary note on the conjectural history of the 1st millennium A.D. In: Osmaston, H. & P. Denwood, Recent Research on Ladakh, 4 & 5: Proceedings of the Fourth and Fifth International Colloquia on Ladakh. SOAS, London, pp. 215-34.

Wada, Akiko (2003) Kalasha: Their Life and Tradition. Sang-e-Meel Publications, Lahore.

Wade, Claude M. (1835) Notes Taken in 1829, Relative to the Territory and Government of Iskardoh. JASB, 4: 589-620.

Walter, Anna-Maria (2022) Intimate Connection: Love and Marriage in Pakistan's High Mountains. Rutgers University Press, New Brunswick, N.J. [An inquiry into contemporary attitudes and practices, with much attention to the weight of traditions, particularly related to fairies].

Weidert, Alfons (1973) Review of Fussman (1972J). Erasmus, 26: 729-34.

Weinreich, Matthias (2008) Two Varieties of Ḍomaaki. ZDMG, 158, 2: 299-316. [With full reference to previous studies on this language by Lorimer, Buddruss and Tikkanen, not listed here].

———. (2010) Language Shift in Northern Pakistan: The Case of Ḍomaakí and Pashtu. Iran and the Caucasus, 14: 43-56.

———. (2015) Ethno-linguistic Diversity on the Roof of the World. In: Bläsing, U., V. Arakelova, & M. Weinreich, eds., Studies on Iran and the Caucasus. In Honor of Garnik Asatrian. Brill, Leiden, pp. 455-71.

Werba, Chlodwig (2016) Ur(indo)arisches im Nūristāni. Zur historisches Phonologie des Indoiranischen. In: Byrd, A.M., J. DeLisi & M. Wenthe, eds., Tavet Tat Satyam. Studies in Honor of Jared S. Klein on the Occasion of his Seventieth birthday. Beech Stave Press, Ann Arbor, pp. 341-59.

Wiegand, Jahn (2009) Freundschaft und Macht. Eine Fallstudien aus Indus Kohistan / Nordpakistan. CAK, Vol. 7. Rüdiger Köppe Verlag, Cologne.

Willson, Stephen R. (1999a) A Look at Hunza Culture. NIPS and SIL, Islamabad.

———. (1999b) Basic Burushaski vocabulary. NIPS and SIL, Islamabad.

Witek, Wlodek (2005a) The Eyes and Ears of an Explorer: Database for Audiovisual Archives of a Norwegian Linguist from his Journeys to Afghanistan and South Asia, 1923-1975. Visual Resources, 21, 1: 25-39. [On the online Morgenstierne database, in Kristiansen & Witek (2001)].

———. (2005b) With Camera to India, Iran and Afghanistan: Access to Multimedia Sources of the Explorer Professor Dr Morgenstierne (1892–1975). In: Bentkowska-Kafel, A., T. Cashen & H. Gardiner, eds., Digital Art History: A Subject in

Transition. Intellect Books, Bristol/Portland, pp. 45–56. [The book was reprinted in 2009 by the same publishers, under the new title "Digital Visual Culture: Theory and Practice"].

Witzel, Michael, E.J. (2004a) The R̥gvedic Religious System and its Central-Asian and Hindu Kush Antecedents. In: Griffiths, A. & J.E.M. Houben, eds., The Vedas, Texts, Language & Ritual. Proceedings of the Third International Vedic Workshop, Leiden 2002. Egbert Forsten, Groningen, pp. 581-636.

———. (2004b) Central Asian roots and acculturation in South Asia: Linguistic and archaeological evidence from western Central Asia, the Hindukush and northwestern South Asia for early Indo-Aryan language and religion. In: Osada, T., ed., Linguistics, Archaeology and the Human Past. Indus Project, Research Institute for Humanity and Nature, Kyoto, pp. 87-211.

———. (2019) Early 'Aryans' and their neighbours outside and inside India. Journal of Biosciences, 44, 3: (ID 58) 1-10. [doi: 10.1007/s12038-019-9881-7]

Wutt, Karl (1976) Über Zeichen und Ornamente der Kalash in Chitral. Archiv für Völkerkunde, 30: 137-73.

———. (1977) Zur Bausubstanz des Darrah-e Nur. Afghanistan Journal, 4, 2: 54-65.

———. (1978) Über Herkunft und Kulturelle Merkmale einiger Pashai-Gruppen. Afghanistan Journal, 5, 2: 43-58.

———. (1983) Chaumos = "Vier Mal Fleisch": Notizen zum Winterlichen Festkalender der Kalash von Bumburet, Chitral. Archiv für Völkerkunde, 37: 107-48.

———. (1986) The Pashai in Darra-i Mazar and Wamagal. In: Orywal, E., ed., Die ethnischen Gruppen Afghanistans. Fallstudien zu Gruppenidentität und Intergruppenbeziehungen. Dr. Ludwig Reichert, Wiesbaden, pp. 304-308.

———. (1997) Kalasha Drawings and Pakistani Sign Systems. In: Austrian Scholarship in Pakistan. A Symposium Dedicated to the Memory of Aloys Sprenger. PanGraphics, Islamabad, pp. 52-79.

———. (2010) Afghanistan von innen und außen. Welten des Hindukusch, Springer, Vienna.

———. (2017) At the second glance /Afghanistan/ Auf den zweiten blick. edition tethys, Potsdam.

———. (2020) Die Zeichenbücher der Kalascha / The Kalasha Drawing Books (1973-1997). edition-tethys, Potsdam. [This

collection of drawings made for the author by Kalasha people
starting from the Seventies is not only of ethnographic
interest, but can be useful to archaeologists for comparison
with Peristan petroglyphs.]

Young, Ruth (2003) Agriculture and Pastoralism in the Late Bronze
and Iron Age, North-West Frontier Province Pakistan. BAR
International Series, Oxford. [Dir and Swat compared with
Charsadda in the 2nd millennium BCE, with support of
ethnographic evidence].

Young, R., R. Coningham, C. Batt & I. Ali (2000) A Comparison of
Kalasha and Kho Subsistence Patterns in Chitral, NWFP,
Pakistan. South Asian Studies, 16: 133-42.

Young, R., M. Zahir, A. Samad, I. Ali & I. Shah (2012) Archaeology
and Heritage in Chitral, Pakistan. Journal of British
Archaeology, 124: 42-47.

Younghusband, Francis E. (1890) Report of a Mission to the Northern
Frontier of Kashmir in 1889. Superintendent of Government
Printing India, Calcutta. [Reprinted as: The Northern Frontier
of Kashmir, Oriental Publishers, Delhi, 1973].

———. (1895) Chitral, Hunza and the Hindukush. The Geographical
Journal, 5: 409-26.

Yule, Henry (1872a) Papers connected with the Upper Oxus Regions.
JRAS, 42: 438-40.

———. (1872b) Notes regarding Bolor, and some other Names in the
Apocryphal Geography of the Upper Oxus. JRAS, 42: 473-
81.

Yule, H. & H. Cordier (1913-16) Cathay and the Way thither. Being a
collection of medieval notices on China translated and edited
by Sir Henry Yule. New edition revised in the light of recent
discoveries by Henry Cordier. Hakluyt Society, London.
[Includes much on ancient, medieval and later sources for
Peristan and surroundings].

Zaheer-ud-Din (2015) Muslim Impact on Religion and Culture of the
Kalash. Al-Adwa, 30, 43: 13-22.

Zahir, Muhammad (2016a) Unique Terracotta Figurine from Singoor,
District Chitral, Pakistan: Contextualizing Possible Hariti
Figurine in the Buddhist Wilderness? Ancient Pakistan, 27: 1-26.

———. (2016b) The "Gandhara Grave Culture": New Perspectives on
Protohistoric Cemeteries in Northern and Northwestern
Pakistan. In: Robbins, S.G. & S.R. Walimbe, eds., A

Companion to South Asia in the Past. Wiley Blackwell, Hoboken, pp. 274-93.

———. (2017) The Geographical Distribution of Gandhara Grave Culture or Protohistoric Cemeteries in Northern and North-Western South Asia. Gandhāran Studies, 10: 1-30.

———. (2019) Discovery and Contextualization of a Possible Buddhist Monastic Complex at Thalpan, District Diamer, Gilgit-Baltistan Province, Pakistan. Gandhāran Studies, 13: 37-52.

———. (2020) Analysis and contextualization of potential protohistoric petroglyphs at the Kalasha valley of Birir in Chitral. The Journal of Humanities and Social Sciences, 28,2: 35-60.

Zarin, Mohammad Manzar & R.L. Schmidt (1984) Discussions with Hariq. Land Tenure and Transhumance in Indus Kohistan. Berkeley Working Papers on South and Southeast Asia, Islamabad.

Zavattaro, Monica (2016) La collezione Eleonora Dall'Omo e Verena Blenkle realizzata in Afghanistan da Gabriele Romiti. In: Chelazzi et al. (2016): 229-51. [A Nuristan collection in Florence].

Zeisler, Bettina (2010) East of the moon and west of the sun: Approaches to a land with many names, north of ancient India and south of Khotan. In: Roberto Vitali (ed.) The Earth Ox Papers. Proceedings of the International Seminar on Tibetan and Himalayan Studies, Held at the Library of Tibetan Works and Archives, September 2009 on the Occasion of the 'Thankyou India' Year. The Tibet Journal, Special Issue, 34,3-4/35,1-2: 371-463. [On Bolor and neighbouring areas in Buddhist times, with vast research on sources].

Zimmer, Stefan (1984) Iran. baga- ein Gottesname? MSS, 44: 187-215. [With reference to the god Bagisht].

Zoller, Claus Peter (2005) A grammar and dictionary of Indus Kohistani. Volume 1: Dictionary. Mouton de Gruyter, Berlin & New York.

———. (2007) Himalayan Heroes. In: Brückner, H., H. van Skyhawk and C.P. Zoller, eds., The Concept of Hero in Indian Culture. New Delhi, pp. 237–74.

———. (2010) Love and vengeance in Indus Kohistan. In: Lecomte-Tiloine, M., ed., Nature, Culture and Religion at the Crossroads of Asia. Social Science Press, New Delhi, pp. 244–59.

————. (2014) A South Asian perspective on the Burushaski controversy. Indian Linguistics, 75, 3-4: 101-32.

————. (2016a) Proto Indo-European – Indo-Aryan – Himalayan Aryan languages: New perspectives on some old questions. Bishen Singh Mahendra Pal Singh, Dehradun.

————. (2016b) Outer and Inner Indo-Aryan, and northern India as an ancient linguistic area. Acta Orientalia, 77: 71-132.

————. (2017) Northern India before and after the arrival of Indo-Aryan. In: Joshi, V. & P. Maheshwar Joshi, eds., Unfolding Central Himalaya: The Cradle of Culture. Doon Library and Research Centre, Dehradun and Almora, pp. 1-45.

————. (2018) "Pagan Christmas. Winter Feasts of the Kalasha of the Hindu Kush" and the True Frontiers of 'Greater Peristan'. Acta Orientalia, 79: 163-377. [A vast review article of Cacopardo (2016b)].

————. (2022) On Synonym Compounds in Indo-Aryan. In: Baart, Liljegren & Payne (2022): 513-40.

AFTERWORD

FIELD RESEARCH AS EXPERIENCE: ADOLPH FRIEDRICH AND KARL JETTMAR IN NORTHERN PAKISTAN[1]

Irmtraud Stellrecht

Searching for Traces in Mainz

If for a current occasion the history of university institutes is to be filled with content, this can be done from many points of view. A pragmatic, albeit one-sided, periodization follows the terms of office of the chair holders—the 'great men' of the past. From this perspective, the first period of the Institute for Ethnology and African Studies at the University of Mainz is called 'Adolf Friedrich'; it marks the 'primeval times', 1947 to 1956. The phase from 1961-64, the third period, is called 'Karl Jettmar'—Friedrich's 'grandson' at the Mainz chair for ethnology. In between lies the 'Wilhelm Mühlmann' period from 1957 to 1960—a deviation from the right cultural-historical path—the dominant research direction of the discipline of ethnology in Germany at that time.

Today, great men in the history of the institute rarely play a role anymore in the institute's present life—they usually only keep their permanent place in its libraries. Here their materialized placeholders can still be found—the special literature acquired by them. In the late 1960s—Adolf Friedrich was already dead ten years at the time, Karl Jettmar in the meantime at Heidelberg University and the institute already in the 'Eike Haberland' period from 1964 to 1968—there still existed in the library of the Mainz Institute an extensive body of literature on ethnography, history and archaeology of Siberia, Central Asia and northern Pakistan much of it in Russian, acquired in the periods of Friedrich and Jettmar. The two anthropologists clearly shared scientific interests, as was obvious to me from the external findings during my time as a student assistant in the library of the Mainz Institute, 1966-68. Through my later regional specialization in northern Pakistan's high mountain area—the joint field research region of Friedrich and

---

1   This paper was first published in German in *60 Jahre Institut für Ethnologie und Afrikastudien Ein Geburtstagsbuch* [Volume 14 of „Mainzer Beiträge zur Afrika-Forschung"], Köppe, 2006 [ISBN 9783896458148].

Jettmar—and through discussions with Karl Jettmar during my time from 1982 to 1986 at the South Asia Institute, University of Heidelberg, it became increasingly clear to me that the scientific and personal consensus of the two ethnologists was limited, even if their life paths ran parallel in phases and were even closely intertwined for a short time.

Friedrich and Jettmar had a number of things in common. They both came from the dominant cultural-historical school of German-Austrian ethnology, from Frankfurt and from Vienna. In their attempts to reconstruct cultural-historical phases they initially both concentrated on 'early hunters' and drew their inspiration from Russian-language literature on Siberia. In 1955 they even set out for their first field research in northern Pakistan together, committed to the same cultural-historical research program as members of the German Hindu Kush Expedition. But their commonality also had its limits. There were differences in scientific point of view as well as personality; right from the start of the field research in Pakistan, these emerged clearly and can be grasped in Friedrich's scientific field diary.

Impressionist vs. Constructionist

The expedition—Adolf Friedrich, Karl Jettmar, Georg Buddruss and Peter Snoy—had been traveling in northern Pakistan for four weeks, in the valleys south of the provincial capital of Gilgit. They just stayed in one place for a short time and then moved on. On June 12, 1955, Friedrich and Jettmar were in the Tangir Valley. Friedrich entered the research results of the last few days in his diary: settlement history, migration, ethnic composition. He also noted his personal physical and mental state. The day before he had to stop interviewing a storyteller; having experienced a sudden loss of memory, he could no longer follow the conversation and therefore was no longer able to correlate. However, Friedrich only puts this irritating blackout as a secondary entry. In the first place he notes a remark by Jettmar that must have been made between June 9th and 12th and is obviously still working on him. Friedrich states without comment: "Karl Jettmar describes my way of doing ethnology as 'impressionist ethnology'. He characterizes himself as a constructionist; he must construct." (Friedrich Diary, June 12, 1955, p. 112).[2]

What provoked Jettmar to express this typification? The preceding June 9th entries may be clues. Friedrich was in a good mood; he had

---

2   Friedrich's original diary, formerly in possession of Peter Snoy, is now kept in the
     Lindenmuseum, Stuttgart.

heard interesting things, met friendly people, including shepherds, and associates:

"A shepherd often carries a lamb in his arm: the image of the good shepherd... The shepherds and goat herders in archaic typology, as they are described in the OT [Old Testament] and the Greek mythical-epic and bucolic literature and how they are depicted in the relief and seal images of the Middle Eastern cities and states, as [Giovanni] Segantini has just captured them again; and how they probably belong to the unresearched steppe and mountain landscape from Tibet to the Middle East, the Mediterranean and North Africa up to the Canary Islands."

A little later is the entry: "Karl Jettmar heard: if there are two brothers in Darel [neighbouring valley of Tangir], one would be a farmer, the other a shepherd." Friedrich's comment on this plain statement by his colleague followed, in brackets: "Cf. Cain and Abel. The reverse in Sumer: the shepherd slays the peasant." (Friedrich Diary, June 9, 1955, p. 109). Did Friedrich irritate his colleague Jettmar in conversation through such associations? Only a little later, the two field researchers also demonstrate their diversity when analyzing ethnographic data. Just arrived in Darel, Friedrich notes on June 16: "Before I left, K. J. [Karl Jettmar] said [after a walk to the village of Sheko] that he now sees the correlation between the order of the *kot* and the *patis*.[3] (I had said the day before, the real sociological structural tendency of the *pati* classification has not yet become apparent to me)." (Friedrich Diary, June 16, 1955, p. 121). Jettmar had already constructed the whole picture with bold lines and sent Friedrich, who was still undecidedly pushing single cultural elements back and forth, into the corner of the scrupulous procrastinator. The choice of words in the diary during these first months of field research corroborates this impression: Friedrich "assumes" or "has an assumption"—Jettmar, on the other hand, already "says" or "finds".

Friedrich the impressionist, Jettmar the constructionist—this dictum contains some truth that goes beyond the personal and leads to the history of ethnology in German-speaking countries. I will therefore take Jettmar's remark as an opportunity to embed the scientific biographies of the two ethnologists in the larger context of discipline-specific development. In addition, I will also follow the two into the field in northern Pakistan with a question that is already echoed in the diary citations above: how did Friedrich and Jettmar combine their

---

3   I.e. between the structure of villages (*kot*) and kinship (*patis*).

scientific convictions with their new experience of field research—the confrontation with the real 'culturally other'? After all, both of them had practiced ethnology for about twenty years 'from the armchair', empathizing with the 'cultural other' without much hesitation, just like that—thus understanding him before they met him in flesh and blood. In order to find the answer to this question, I will trace the scientific biography of Adolf Friedrich and Karl Jettmar, whose first phase will end with the definition of their scientific positions before they left for field research in Pakistan in 1955. Friedrich's and Jettmar's publications up to this year provide evidence of this. For the second phase—field research—the source material is different.

When Friedrich died in Pakistan on April 24, 1956, he left a scientific field diary. For decades it acted as a quarry, from which northern Pakistan specialists broke ethnographic chunks. Self-doubts within our discipline and towards its subject, as well as the historicization and contextualization of field research and field researchers, have meanwhile fundamentally changed the epistemological value of this diary.[4] Today we can read it as precious evidence of a field research experience that was never transformed into ethnographic representation. The predominantly factual style of the diary makes it likely that Friedrich was thinking of a potential readership while writing—close colleagues, perhaps also students—but nevertheless he speaks first of all to himself, not to an imagined audience. For Jettmar, the source material is different; here the results of his field research are only available in their published form intended for the scientific readership. In these publications, Jettmar appears as an enthusiastic field researcher who tells his readers about exciting discoveries in northern Pakistan and shows that, up there in the mountains, what is still tangible on the surface actually originates from deep historical layers.[5]

Adolf Friedrich—The Scientific Biography

Adolf Friedrich's scientific oeuvre begins in 1939 and ends in 1955, a year before his death. In almost all publications Friedrich explores, with variations, the great theme of his scientific and personal life—religion; the focus of his field research in northern Pakistan was also on this topic. The oeuvre is relatively small, but it is sufficient to trace how

---

4   The international literature on this topic is extensive. As an example, I will only
     mention one thematically relevant essay at the peak of the Writing Culture debate:
     Köpping 1987.
5   Cf. Karl Jettmar's list of publications in Snoy (1983: 16ff).

Friedrich's theoretical position in religious ethnology has changed. His religious-ethnological field research in northern Pakistan can therefore also be measured against these writings. Friedrich's scientific and personal biography is complex. Therefore I shall discuss them in more detail than those of Jettmar.

Studies and PhD

Adolf Friedrich was born in 1914. He grew up between Mainz and Frankfurt, in Hofheim am Taunus. After graduating from high school in 1933 and doing an internship at a bank, Friedrich decided to study ethnology in Frankfurt, fascinated by Leo Frobenius (1873-1938) (Jensen 1956: 189). He chose Indology and ancient history as minor subjects and thus opened up for himself the opportunity to work on the religions of 'primitive people' and ancient 'advanced cultures' in a comparative way.

Friedrich learned from Frobenius the cultural-morphological variety of cultural history. In Frankfurt, traces of past major cultural phases were sought, still tangible in fairy tales, myths and rock carvings, but also in living religious ideas and practices. In 1938 Friedrich received his doctorate with a thesis on "African Priesthoods" (published 1939). He was still a fully dedicated pupil of his master Frobenius: on hundreds of pages he compiled proof after proof or, as one critic later bitingly pointed out, poured out his entire card index (Lehmann 1957: 98). In this way, by classifying and assigning cultural elements, Friedrich wanted to contribute to the construction of the 'big house' of African cultural history—with the aim of finally setting up systematic spatio-temporal sequences of cultural areas and cultural layers. In this first work, religious ideas and practices were not yet an object of research *sui generis* for Friedrich, but only a means to a cultural-historical purpose.

War Years and Habilitation

A new phase began for Friedrich in the same year as his doctorate: Frobenius died and he himself was drafted into military service, remaining a soldier from the beginning of the Second World War until 1945. His scientific home—the Frobenius Institute in Frankfurt—changed during this time. Frobenius' successor, Adolf E. Jensen (1899-1965), was relegated as 'politically unreliable' in 1940; many employees were drafted as soldiers. Friedrich nevertheless continued his scientific work under difficult conditions as a soldier and even found 'his' topic: the religion of the 'early hunters' and thus also shamanism.

Friedrich worked on his new scientific focus in two extensive essays until 1943. He obtained the ethnographic evidence from Western literature, but increasingly also from Russian-language Siberian literature; in the Soviet Union (as a soldier?) "he had access to rare literature on Siberian ethnology" (Nachtigall 1956: 303). Friedrich was able to use these ethnographies written before, but also after, the Russian Revolution for his research goals, without encountering ideological limits: written within an evolutionist or Marxist paradigm, they had much in common with the use of ethnographic data by German cultural historians to reconstruct pre- and early history, although the interpretation was based on diametrically different assumptions.

From 1941 until the beginning of field research in 1955, Friedrich developed his own scientific point of view based on examples of Siberian religions. In his first Siberian publication in 1941, "Research on Early Hunting" (1941: 20-43), he wrote about a universal claim to knowledge. 'Early hunters', once spread over four continents, and today's residual hunter groups show astonishing similarities in religious ideas and practices, according to archaeological traces and ethnographic reports. The earliest cultural phase of mankind, so he concluded, can therefore be reconstructed using later ethnographic examples. Frobenius had already called for an investigation of the primordial stratum of hunters. Friedrich, however, took the immediate research stimulus from Hermann Baumann (1902-1972); he researched early hunters in Africa, but was only able to reconstruct the formative experience of the primordial hunting culture— the intimate relationship between man and animal—in the present almost entirely from fairy tales and myths (Friedrich 1941: 26).

Friedrich derived his own research strategy precisely from this African deficit: he deliberately chose a region that promised a surplus of relics— Siberia. Nowhere else than in Siberia is the hunter's way of life and thinking "so diverse and to such a large extent shaping existence preserved up to the present day". Here the primordial hunting experience that has congealed into an 'idea'—a pure concept of things underlying the phenomena—is still alive today: the identification of man with animal through assimilation or transformation. In contrast to Africa, in Siberia this ancient 'idea' is "*still believed... as* in its time of origin" (Friedrich 1941: 20, 29, 34ff, emphasis I.St.); it shapes the present—in truth the historical—worldview. The shaman operated in this scenario at that time, and still does today. His religious knowledge and his actions come partly from the primordial strata of hunters; that's why he integrates past and present in his person (Friedrich 1941: 41). Friedrich's conclusion therefore was that recent belief is identical with primordial belief and that the belief in the central 'idea' that originates from the early hunters is presently combined with cultic acts, forming a unity. Friedrich leaves it open as to whether or not those involved today experience the cult with all their senses, just like their ancestors did in prehistoric times.

Friedrich expanded the hunter topic in 1943 in his work "Bones and Skeletons in the Imaginary World of North Asia". For his argument he uses a motif in which, according to his conviction, the identification of humans and wild animals is condensed into the most crucial belief of prehistoric hunters. As narratives, but also living practice, shows, Siberian hunters collect as many bones as possible from killed animal prey; from these bones the animals are then revived by powerful spiritual beings. The idea of resurrection from the bones, crucial for the primordial hunting culture, was later reassigned to non-hunting cultures and even transferred from animals to humans. The idea of resurrection is now linked to the skeleton of the human corpse and also determines ideas about life after death (Friedrich 1943: 204). Friedrich demonstrates the transfer of this basic idea from an older to a younger cultural layer on the basis of data from the 'high cultures' and 'high religions' of Iran, India, Tibet and Central Asia.

Here, too, in Friedrich's chain of evidence, the shaman plays the role of the hinge between cultural layers. He still experiences his initiation in Siberia as a process of being reduced to a skeleton while alive and afterwards resurrected from the bones (Friedrich 1943: 210). Shamans are therefore living witnesses of the historical transformation of key concepts and religious beliefs of early hunters. However, shamans are not just mere vessels of a sedimented body of knowledge or passive representatives of different temporal strata, but—as can be proven by a still vital Siberian ethnography—rather actively re-enact earlier religious ideas in their current cultic performances. From this argument of Friedrich's, one can deduce that a cultural historian—like him—should work closely with shamans in field research, observe their religious practice and unlock their archived knowledge.

"Bones and Skeletons" was a habilitation thesis submitted to Hermann Baumann in Vienna in 1942; programmatic commitments to tasks and goals of the discipline could be expected. One dictum is particularly relevant to our topic: "ethnology is a historical discipline" (Friedrich 1943: 189). Research can methodically proceed in two ways: on the one hand through "observations of living peoples"—that is, relic research in the present; on the other hand through a "critical inspection" of old, "regional written traditions". Friedrich states decidedly that this second method is far superior to current field research. In old sources the spirit is still alive, so to speak, because they were written in temporal proximity to "still strong dominance of deeply rooted old religiosity"; they are "more informative about prehistory... than European fieldwork can achieve." Friedrich was well prepared for this armchair research through his subjects, Indology and ancient history; in addition, he was an accomplished expert on the Old Testament (Jensen 1956: 191).

This practical research strategy, formulated by Friedrich in 1942, when opportunities for field research were unrealistic, is by no means just a virtue that grew out of necessity. Rather, this is a theoretically supported argument that leads directly to the center of cultural morphology, i.e. to the Frobenius Institute in Frankfurt. In both Siberian essays, in 1941 and 1943, Friedrich unlocks the meaning of his ethnographic data by means of cultural morphological convictions—as laid out by Frobenius and later taken further by his successor, Jensen.[6]

Friedrich adopted three interpretative approaches that were typical for Jensen. They are worth taking a closer look, as, for Friedrich, they later became the decisive scientific stumbling block with Jensen.

First: according to Jensen, the "law of development" of the most important economic resource was "transferred to human life" in an early period; there is identification between man and the specific resource that is mainly used (Friedrich 1943: 204). Jensen demonstrated this concept for the "early planters" and Friedrich took up this concept and transferred it to the previous cultural layer of the hunters: they too try, in the past as well as today, to become one with the animal as the most important resource and, at the same time, "the most impressive environmental power" (Friedrich 1943: 216).[7]

Second: according to Jensen, this early period was creative; the idea of the "law of development", which linked the world and man together,

---

6   Jensen did not present his concept of cultural morphology in its entirety until 1948 in „Das religiöse Weltbild einer frühen Kultur" ("The Religious Worldview of an Early Culture"). But when he set out for field research in Ceram (Seram) in 1937 and also after his return when he developed the concept as an instrument of interpretation for his research results, Friedrich was in his close vicinity—in Frankfurt.

7   For Jensen, first the killing and then the resurrecting of the main economic resource was a concept of belief typical for planters, an idea that was adopted secondarily by hunting groups via diffusion. In contrast to this, Friedrich classifies the correspondence of this concept for planters as well as hunters differently: for him it genuinely belongs to the belief system of hunting cultures.

was then still direct experience or "perception", while today "application" and mere "expression" dominate, when myths of origin are re-enacted in the cult. Friedrich uses Jensen's arguments for three purposes. First of all, religious action today—including the practices of the shaman and those involved in the shamanistic seance—is only a re-enactment, without real creative experience; secondly, it is precisely this cultural degradation in the course of time that makes the evaluation of earlier written evidence so superior, in their temporal proximity, in contrast to the creative "perception" of contemporary relic field research. And thirdly, Jensen had convincingly demonstrated for Friedrich, when using the example of the culture of Ceram (an island in Indonesia, today Seram), that, regardless of historical degradation processes, the unity of myth and cult in its present-day staging enables the ethnologist privileged access to the creative impulses of earlier cultural layers—to their hours of birth. It is precisely this research approach focused on ideational relics that Friedrich adopts and declares to be far superior to previous cultural-historical reconstructions on the basis of material relics (Friedrich 1941: 20). Friedrich obviously wrote the two Siberia papers in consultation with Hermann Baumann, holder of the Chair of Ethnology in Vienna since 1940. Baumann's appointment there had been politically motivated and therefore ensured that the institute could continue to work undisturbed even in war. In Frankfurt, on the other hand, ethnology was weakened after Jensen's *venia legendi* had been revoked in 1940. Friedrich therefore submitted his habilitation thesis to Baumann in Vienna.[8]

---

8   Friedrich and Baumann shared scientific interests. Was there also common political ground between them? In his obituary for Friedrich, Jensen is silent on the motivation and circumstances of Friedrich's change of university—from Frankfurt to Vienna. But apparently he was not formally integrated as a member of the Vienna Institute (Linimayr 1994: 154ff.). There are only two direct manifestations of the political climate at the Vienna Institute which can be grasped in Friedrich's oeuvre. First a programmatic demand in his habilitation thesis for future inclusion of "racial studies" as a historical discipline into cultural-historical research—that was entirely in line with Baumann's colonial political program. Second, two articles in „Afrika. Handbuch der angewandten Völkerkunde" ("Africa. Handbook of Applied Ethnology"), edited by Hugo Bernatzik: „Die Ngumi" ("The Ngumi") and „Mischlinge, Asiaten und Juden" ("Mixed Races, Asians and Jews"). The handbook was part of the colonial policy program of Viennese ethnology between 1940 and 1945. It is unclear when Friedrich wrote these articles, as the handbook was only published after the war, in 1947 (cf. Linimayr 1994: 138ff.). According to a communication from E. W. Müller, Mainz, many employees working on Bernatzik's manual were probably concerned with practical advantages, such as payment or exemption from military duties.

Between Mainz and Frankfurt

The war was over and the ethnological landscape was rearranged. Baumann fled from Vienna in the spring of 1945; Jensen returned to Frankfurt in the same year, became director of the museum of ethnology and, at the same time, the Frobenius Institute, received his *venia* back and in 1946 was appointed to the newly established chair for culture and ethnology at the University of Frankfurt. Friedrich was also back in Frankfurt; he taught there as associate professor from 1946 (Jensen 1956: 189) and was also involved by Jensen in the activities of the Museum of Ethnology.[9] But already one year later, in 1947, Friedrich was finally established professionally: at the age of only 33 he received the call to the newly created professorship for ethnology at the University of Mainz, supported by a benevolent recommendation from Jensen.

Friedrich's contact with the Frobenius Institute remained close, both personally and scientifically, even after his appointment in Mainz. Jensen even got Friedrich a permanent teaching assignment in Frankfurt, from 1947 to 1955. For all these reasons, it is surprising to come across an article by Friedrich from 1951 in *Paideuma*, the scientific journal of the Frobenius Institute, in which he abruptly turns away from Jensen as if in great excitement. The reason for Friedrich's essay "Knowledge and Religion"—a veritable anti-Jensen pamphlet—was the appearance of Jensen's "Myth and Cult among Primitive Peoples" (1951). In this book, Jensen programmatically develops a cultural morphological study of religion based on the "worldview of an early culture", i.e. of Ceram. The real cause for Friedrich's distancing was certainly a different one: Friedrich had turned away from his former religious-ethnological convictions, as he had earlier advocated them in his Siberian essays, and turned towards (religious) phenomenology. From now on he was no longer primarily concerned with history, but first with the question "of the meaning and nature of the phenomena studied" (Jensen 1956: 190). The pamphlet "Knowledge and Religion" therefore marks an important stage in Friedrich's scientific biography.

What is Religion?

What is interesting in our context is not so much Friedrich's changed scientific approach—it was neither particularly new nor surprising

---

9   Friedrich contributed a scientific brochure to the exhibition „Jägerkultur und Tierbild" ("Hunter Culture and Animal Image") (Friedrich, 1946).

in the context of the Frobenius Institute—than his justification of the phenomenon of religion and the definition of its 'essence'. Both can be made the starting point for questions to his field research on religion and ethnology in Pakistan. I will therefore only take up those thoughts of Friedrich that are relevant to this goal.[10]

The argument that Friedrich builds up against Jensen is clear: religion has nothing to do with reason, logic, knowledge, but with emotions and holistic experience. Through subjective meaning people fill old religious forms again and again with qualitatively new 'unfoldings' and experience them in this way as authentic. The *homo religiosus* is therefore not a timeless, but a historical being, "at this point in time and in this place" (Friedrich 1951: 107); the meaning of his religious ideas is always bound to space and time. So what does religion comprise for Friedrich? The answer can be reduced to the simple denominator: exactly whatever Jensen just had decidedly excluded as contamination of the primordial in his book, with the help of logical-reasonable argumentation. For Friedrich, religion is piety without reason and logic, turning towards the extraordinary, to emotional shock. Religion is meaning even without a reasonable explanation, "concealed in mystery, something interwoven into the creation, to be discovered, never to be mastered and incumbent upon man to constantly search for it anew—something that lets him forebear heights and abysses and makes him stammer". (1951: 110).[11] Religion, because it does not conclude logically-causally, is based "in the associative faculties of man, in his sense of analogy".

As if overwhelmed, Friedrich continues: "In the field of religion, the paradox of life comes to light most directly, the Janus-headed, the *'quia absurdum'*, its contradiction between depth of meaning and arbitrariness, between goodness and cruelty, between beauty and decay, between pain and joy." Even the forgetting of the creative and divine primordial process, which Jensen had just defined as a 'sacrilege', is brought in again by Friedrich and reinterpreted: "Such forgetting [belongs] to the daimonion of man... to the deficiency imposed on him" (1951: 110).

---

10 The following will only deal with Friedrich's argument against Jensen, not with the presentation of Jensen's concept *sine ira et studio*. Jensen's approaches are discussed, interpreted and embedded in their scientific context in Kramer 2005: 27ff, as well as in Streck 1997: 149ff.

11 Friedrich adds in brackets: "cf. [Apostle] Paul, prophets [of the Old Testament], Eskimo [Inuit], shamans; but, in my opinion, also the religion of the old planters that Jensen describes".

Friedrich has now determined what belongs to religion, what drives people to it and how religious ideas are cognitively constructed. It is from here that he carries out the final attack on Jensen: cult is not just an act of contemplation on "primeval mythical processes", but also an enthusiastic presentation of content of tradition. Cult invigorates, enhances, stimulates, strengthens, encourages, assures feelings and senses. The divine is felt and experienced by the cult participants—as present and timelessly real. Cult integrates the expectation of reward and salvation, the "dichotomy of the paradox", the riddle, the uncanniness, but also the everyday "exigencies". As if in a frenzy, Friedrich counts up, but then suddenly he pauses and creates distance: he is talking about the "people living in a natural environment", not about the modern city dwellers "released from nature". Man bound to nature is completely different: he "moves more broadly into the life of nature", perceives differently what is happening there; he thinks in analogies instead of making causal-reasonable inferences; he associates "first and foremost from the point of view of what preoccupies him, what pressures him, what he is striving for" (1951: 113), always holistically, with feelings and senses, not particular.

The discussion about Jensen's book was started almost humbly by Friedrich: he only wants to point out certain loopholes, not to put forward a counter-thesis (1951: 104). What emerges, however, is a scathing critique: Jensen's image of man is deficient because he measured the nature-bound man against himself, the modern man, and made him equal to himself through the common denominator of reason. Friedrich therefore also draws a damning conclusion about Jensen's field research on Ceram: "The author has deprived himself of an understanding of the way of life of primitive people" (1951: 113).

The essay "Knowledge and Religion" clearly has the character of a confession. Friedrich acts like an innovator; he does not rely on a broader scientific consensus.[12] How could one describe the *homo religiosus* Friedrich brings to the fore here? With his typification of people bound by nature, he has in an indirect way also defined himself—"the city dweller released from nature"—as a deficient being. Friedrich is precisely that modern, nature-distant person who with his causal-logical thinking can no longer find access to holistic-religious experience. He senses the loss; he suffers from the incompatibility of reason and religion, also in the form of scientific research and

---

12 Apart from the Bible, Friedrich cites only two sources: Friedrich Schleiermacher and the religious philosopher Jean Gebser.

argumentation. Does Friedrich describe his own religious longings via the detour of the "natural man"? The answer to these questions we can safely leave to Jensen. In his obituary for Friedrich, 1956, he deals with him, in a peculiarly detailed way, as a scientific as well as a private person. The obituary reads like a belated comment on Friedrich's essay "Knowledge and Religion" and, at the same time, as a request for understanding for the dead colleague.[13]

Before Field Research

The tenor of Jensen's obituary, also in the choice of words, shows that everything about Friedrich was extreme.[14] Science—for Friedrich that was passionate dedication and ardent zeal in order to reveal the true and essential of phenomena studied, a highly emotional endeavour and a relentless search for knowledge. Ethnology as the study of other cultures and especially other religions—that was science and self-discovery at the same time, the search for a common denominator, for the general human, for a shared basic and worldwide experience of the various concepts of the divine and thus the quest for ultimate epistemological meaning. According to Jensen, his deep (Protestant) religiosity and ecclesial bonds did not hinder Friedrich's vision. The penetration of other beliefs—that conformed with his serious, reverent and untiring effort to understand. It was a never-ending endeavour to empathize with other people's thinking, i.e. to grasp these other worlds with an inwardly turned movement down to the finest nuances, and then turned outwards again, to portray them in forceful language that arose from inner fulfilment, be it Inuit or Siberian hunters. The study of Siberian shamanism—for Friedrich that meant to grasp the fascination of the psychic and moral power of people with supersensory gifts, their willingness to endure agony and loneliness, to sacrifice themselves in order to help others. His preoccupation with the prophets of the Old Testament arose out of the same admiration for these lonely, chosen ones who submitted to the calling and accepted their mission for the good of the people in the course of initiation rituals that were full of privation.

What Jensen outlined with strong words in the obituary,

---

13 The obituaries of Friedrich's pupils Ernst W. Müller (1956) and Horst Nachtigall (1956) also emphasize his religiosity. Jensen was generous enough to publish Friedrich's anti-Jensen pamphlet as editor in *Paideuma*, the journal of the Frobenius Institute.

14 In the following, I will be guided by Jensen's terminology.

Friedrich had in fact implemented in his last two essays on Siberia; they appeared almost at the same time of his leaving for Pakistan (1954; 1955). Friedrich immerses himself in the religious world of the Siberian "primitive peoples" and describes them in vivid, even dramatic language. Shamans again appear among them, but now they are suffering, enduring individuals of flesh and blood, ready to bear responsibility. It is true that they too internalize the timelessness of the primordial era during the trance, but simultaneously they are "intensely interwoven with everyday life"—prisms of the existential experience of the whole group in the here and now.

Friedrich's position on religion and ethnology at the time of his departure to Pakistan—his phenomenological-holistic approach—raises the question of how he intended to proceed methodically in the field and how he planned to later transform his research results into ethnographic writing. Friedrich did not explicitly comment on this; the conclusion that he draws at the end of his essay "Knowledge and Religion" can, however, be interpreted as an indirect but clear indication. There Friedrich—via the detour of criticism of Jensen's all too great research rationality—demands how the ethnologist should approach cultural otherness: it must precisely not be grasped with reason; it must precisely not be clarified in all its aspects in an analytically isolating manner; the unfamiliar may even remain unfamiliar. Ethnographic writing is therefore the description of this unfamiliarity: the phenomena "must be preserved in the scientific representation and must not be explained away." And then apodictically: "The humanities scholar should beware of making a naturally intricate process, endowed with light and shadow, too transparent." (Friedrich 1951: 114) From the considerations and demands of Friedrich in "Knowledge and Religion" one can derive a methodical strategy for his field research—his participation in "Myth and Cult", i.e. in the New Year celebrations of the Kalash in northern Pakistan: no insisting inquiries in order to resolve contradictions between statements, but instead allowing competing descriptions and interpretations as well as accepting contradictions. No scientific attempts to create order and logic through classification, but instead approving the unordered nature of the unfamiliar. Avoiding questions about ultimate reasons and true causes, but instead leaving as they are associations and conclusions by analogy, metaphors and metaphorical comparisons. Deliberately turning away from statements about the generalized, typified cultural other, who speaks in hegemonic attitude as representative for his whole community and authoritatively portrays his own experience as the experience of everyone and, instead, listening to the many voices with an emphatic understanding for individual experience.

Karl Jettmar—The Scientific Biography

Karl Jettmar's professional path is more straightforward and less tormented than that of Friedrich, but just like him, he struggled for knowledge until his death in 2002—not about 'primordial' and at the same time personal experience, but rather about temporally and spatially comprehensive historical contexts in Central Asia.

Studies and Career Path

Karl Jettmar was born in Vienna in 1918 as the son of a well-known painter and professor at the Academy of Fine Arts. In 1936 he began studying at the University of Vienna. There he found an ideal combination of subjects for his specific interests: ethnology, folklore and prehistory. In his dissertation, "The Blacksmith in the Germanic World" (1941), he could therefore treat the topic from the interconnected perspective of his three university subjects. Jettmar wrote his doctoral thesis while on leave from military service; from 1940 he was a soldier, first in Russia, then in France. In 1945 he returned home from American captivity and remained unemployed for eight long years; he made his way as a postman, toy seller, and translator, but never gave up his scientific ambitions.

During the period of unemployment, Jettmar began systematically to learn Russian in order to gain access to Soviet archaeological[15] and ethnological research. Jettmar turned this linguistic qualification, at that time rare in Western ethnology, into a scientific profile and a lifelong publication strategy: he continuously evaluated the Russian-language archaeological specialist literature and published its results for Western scientists. In this way, he built up an immense knowledge of the early history of Siberia and Central Asia and was gradually able to think through these issues independently and in ever larger contexts, beyond the mostly narrowly specific findings of Soviet archaeology, and publish his own interpretation.[16] All of Jettmar's essays before he left for Pakistan belong to this type of publication. With only one

---

15 Archaeology used here in an inclusive sense: prehistory and early history with a focus on excavations, but also including written records.
16 Jettmar later integrated the partial results into major works on the early history of Central Asia and Siberia.

exception, he deals with archaeological topics. The titles speak for themselves: they are about the origins of Turkish tribal formations, the emergence of reindeer and horse breeding, the "original homeland" of the Indo-Europeans and Tungus tribes, the first appearance of the nomadic horsemen, the development of the Scythian animal style—for Jettmar, problems of the beginning and genesis of cultural elements or complexes, their diffusion and the reconstruction of cultural-historical processes were always at the centre of attention. One could say in the words of Jensen and the early Friedrich: he was looking for "primordial times" and "early history", but at that time Jettmar understood it to mean something completely different from the Frankfurt school.

Jettmar had received his cultural-historical training in Vienna in the 1930s. However, his scientific reference point after 1945 was no longer the first (or earlier) Viennese school of his student days, dominated by Father Wilhelm Schmidt (1868-1954), but the second (or later) one, which had developed after the end of the war, *inter alia*, around Robert von Heine-Geldern (1885-1968). The culture area concept, Vienna style, had lost its methodological claim to scientific uniqueness—and with it the validity of its systematized, rigid sequences. Heine-Geldern in particular had always been one of its greatest critics. He also worked in the field of cultural-historical 'relational research', not with a universal historical interest, but with limits in space and time. He first identified cultural complexes on the basis of an organic relationship between their elements; he used abundant archaeological elements as evidence of his constructions and also searched specifically for evidence of dating. The next step was to establish a historically secure relationship between such spatially and temporally limited cultural complexes.[17] Jettmar opted for this methodological approach, even if, later, he often criticized Heine-Geldern's daring conclusions (Johansen 2002: 135f.). But with his own bold leaps over great spaces and long periods of time, Jettmar did not lag behind Heine-Geldern in his early writings.

Jettmar was already 35 years old as a part-time private scholar when he received a guest assistantship for one semester at the Frobenius Institute in Frankfurt, in 1953. Friedrich held his courses there every week. It was then that the two must have met and entered into scientific dialogue.[18] The likelihood of this contact is also implied

---

17 Cf. on the old and new Vienna schools, Contag (1971: *inter alia* 22ff) and Gingrich (1999: 147ff).

18 Perhaps Friedrich and Jettmar met in Vienna as early as 1941—both on leave from military service, one for his habilitation, the other for his doctorate.

by a publication by Jettmar from this period that was, for the first time, less archaeological and more ethnological.[19] In 1954, Jettmar was back in Vienna, and in the same year there he got his first permanent employment at the Museum of Ethnology, albeit on a subordinate level, but nevertheless highly welcome. In the meantime, however, another hope had become reality: on February 20, 1954, the main board of the German Research Foundation (Deutsche Forschungsgemeinschaft, DFG) approved funds for the implementation of the German Hindu Kush Expedition. Friedrich is its scientific director and takes this leadership role very seriously. Jettmar, in contrast, is a simple academic member, as is the Indologist Georg Buddruss (1929-2021) and the ethnology student Peter Snoy (1928-2012).

The Research Program of the German Hindu Kush Expedition

The DFG priority program, which several ethnology professors applied for in 1953, bore the simple name "Ethnology". Its scientific assessment was positive and, in February 1954, the approval for the sub-project "northern Pakistan" had been received.[20] All sub-projects of the program were linked by an overarching research problem that was to be solved through field research on all continents. There was also a second political and methodological goal: German ethnology wanted to build on its "old tradition" of field research "before the First World War" in order to become internationally competitive again. A DFG referee summed up the intention of the ethnological applicants: "Only with field research can the academic training of the ethnologist be considered complete; unfortunately, when selecting the participants, it was occasionally observed that young people no longer had the courage and the spirit of enterprise to travel overseas"—no wonder,

---

19 On the basis of Russian sources, Jettmar published an essay in 1954 about something that was then a classical cultural-historical topic: "Totemism and dual system among the Selkups of Siberia". In the same year, Friedrich published an essay on the "Consciousness of a primitive people...", *inter alia* the Selkups; in it he refers positively to Jettmar's investigation "on the same subject" (Friedrich 1955: 54).

20 The last financial problems were resolved at a meeting in Frankfurt on January 22, 1954, in the presence of the DFG President. The application for the overall program, as well as for the Pakistan sub-project, are no longer available in the DFG archive. Friedrich kept the application secret from expedition colleagues (verbal communication from Georg Buddruss); the application does not exist at the Mainz Institute either. My sources are therefore only protocols of results from DFG referees as part of the approval procedure and documents on accounting problems. I would like to thank Michael Schuster, DFG, for making the files available.

one might add: many ethnologists, professors and students alike, had only recently gained more international experience of a very specific kind than they would have liked. Jensen, represented with his own sub-project, was able to build on his expedition experience of the 1930s; Friedrich and Jettmar, on the other hand, were newcomers to field research.

The overriding problem of the priority program was classically cultural-historical: "lifestyles and cultural styles" defined by their economic specialization—hunter-gatherers, peasants, pastoralists—should be examined, as well as later historically emerged economic "mixed formations". They are not to be understood here as a 'mixture' in the sense of an integration of two 'cultural styles' into a single new form, but rather as 'superimposed layers'. That is, the cultural layers involved in such a process lie in the historical and temporal sense vertically one above the other, but in the present they are positioned horizontally side by side, although still clearly distinguishable through characteristic cultural elements. The historical process can be made recognizable by separating the "mixed formation" into its original individual cultural formations, according to the assumption of the cultural-historical school of ethnology. For this reason, the study of mixed formations was considered heuristically particularly fruitful for cultural historians.

In the Frankfurt school around Jensen, the type of 'mixed formation' was formulated in a specific way. According to Jensen's basic concept—the transformation of the 'law of development' of the most important economic resource of a specific culture into an intellectual and creative idea that produces a holistically integrated worldview—the concept of 'mixed formation' was defined as the historical overlay of two worldviews. They are difficult to distinguish from each other in the present; their original meaning may have changed. Only those researchers who persistently question 'informants' about earlier cultural forms and their meanings can arrive at the formal and meaningful arrangement of the layers. In the Pakistan sub-project[21] and in Jensen's sub-project, Ethiopia, the same mixed formation of 'cultural styles' should be examined—the pastoralists and peasants as well as their 'special relationship' to one another. In Pakistan there were "mountain

---

21 The sub-project was carried out under the title "Ethnological research trip to northern Pakistan and Eastern Iran". I will not go further into the "East Iran" project that the Indologist Georg Buddruss carried out in northeast Afghanistan, in Nuristan (formerly "Kafiristan").

peasants" and "mountain pastoralists" on the one hand, as "relatively pure representatives of their individual style of economy and life" and on the other hand as representatives of "a mixed style of economy and of life". Discerning separation and mixing of these styles was the aim of the research.

What made northern Pakistan so exemplary? The scientific literature on this high mountain region was extremely limited, but it showed one thing nonetheless clearly: hidden in the mountains of the western Himalayas and Hindu Kush there is a paradise for cultural historians; Friedrich had discovered it in regional literature.[22] Here, 'cultural styles' with their typical elements lay side by side in a strictly confined space: alpine pasture and intensive farming with developed terracing and irrigation technology, classic elements of hunting cultures, shamanism, feasts of merit, megalithic stone structures,[23] mythical echoes of headhunting, sacred kingship. The northern Pakistan mountain region clearly had a retreat and residual function for long-lost South- and Central Asian cultural complexes; it was an exemplary link in a chain of similarly layered mountain regions between the Caucasus and Nepal.

Where can we identify Jettmar and Friedrich in this research program? Up to now, Jettmar had dealt almost exclusively with Central and North Asian archaeology; this now became exactly his qualification for the program. He was responsible accordingly for the reconstruction of the long historical waves that had reached the Pakistan highlands from the Central Asian lowlands. So the research program fitted him like a glove, albeit with a certain caveat. Jettmar came from the Heine-Geldern research approach; 'mixture' in Vienna, unlike in Frankfurt, was studied with the help of archaeological data.[24] Field research therefore demanded a new way of working from Jettmar: he now had to find his way into the depths of cultural history from the opposite end in terms of time—from acting and speaking people of the present towards the archaeological evidence of the past.

Friedrich's point of departure was completely different. Perhaps the most important reason for giving up his hitherto negative attitude towards field research lay in his new scientific standpoint: whoever

---

22 See, in the present bibliography, the entries for Buddruss & Snoy (2006) for the original German version, and Buddruss & Snoy (2008) for the English translation.
23 For the connection of these elements to complexes in the cultural-historical school see Braukämper (2001: 214ff).
24 The DFG file mentions another of Jettmar's qualifications, which was unusual for the time: he is "familiar with the problems and methodology of American and English ethnology".

wanted to interpret near-natural people intimately had to come into direct contact with them at least once (even if Jensen, in his obituary, assumes Friedrich had a purely professional-pragmatic reason for his entry into field research). But in truth Friedrich was highly reluctant to actually undertake field research (Jensen 1956: 192). Did the 'new' Friedrich find his place in a research program that so obviously bore Jensen's signature? Apparently without problems.[25] The question of origin and cultural-historical layers remained with Friedrich. Only the present now demonstrated itself to him more as complex: it had acquired its own weight and value, in addition to its status as the last link in a cultural-historical sequence of layers. For Friedrich, this re-evaluation of the present was the challenge of field research. If he wanted to remain true to his point of view, as vehemently advocated in his later religious-ethnological writings, he had to discover the culturally other as a religious individual close to nature in the context of his own field research. In the division of tasks that Friedrich designed for himself and Jettmar at the beginning of June 1955, already four weeks on site in Pakistan, there is no trace of these intentions. Rather, Friedrich completely submits to the given general research program and notes in his diary: "In the following, I will try here and there to particularly point out moments that seem to me to belong to the primordial [layer] of this type of existence and culture. Karl Jettmar will probably prefer to devote himself to the problem of cultural-historical influences and mixtures." (Friedrich Diary, June 6, 1955, p. 54).

The field research cooperation between Friedrich and Jettmar lasted only two months, until August 1955. Friedrich moved from Gilgit to the west, to Chitral, Jettmar to the east, to Baltistan in order to search for hunting rituals and shamans. The two met again in October 1955 in Rawalpindi; in November they finally parted ways. Friedrich travelled back to the mountains, to the Kalash in Chitral. Jettmar set off for Kabul to continue his research in northeast Afghanistan with 'Kafir' groups. However, he could not realise this plan: he fell seriously ill in Kabul and returned to Vienna in March 1956.

Field Research as Experience

Field research as a scientific and personal experience has been the subject of numerous anthropological investigations in the last decades.

---

25 At least this applies as long as we do not know Friedrich's DFG application for the sub-project Pakistan.

The results were an asset for the subject: the fact that field research is a reflexive process was accepted, albeit with many shades in individual cases. This critical historicization also gave a long-known truth a specific human content: field research transforms the field researcher. There are now many examples in the anthropological literature, beyond the famous diary of Bronislaw Malinowski, of crisis experiences and deep turning points, but also of increasing awareness and consolidation of already existing scientific convictions through field research. Adolf Friedrich and Karl Jettmar were also changed by field research, each in a different way.

Karl Jettmar—Ethnology as a Leading Science

Jettmar's fieldwork in northern Pakistan was brief—two months with Friedrich in the valleys south of Gilgit and another two months in Baltistan—but it was enough to provide the cornerstone of a fast-rising career. As early as 1957, one year after his return, the research results were made into his habilitation thesis submitted to the University of Vienna. But still in the same year, even before the habilitation procedure was completed, he was appointed as successor to Heine-Geldern and became assistant professor for 'Ethnology and Palaeoethnology of Asia' at the University of Vienna.

The required interdisciplinary orientation of the professorship seemed to correspond fully to the cultural-historical reconstruction program that Jettmar so ideally combined in his person, according to his university education and previous interests. But what Jettmar had experienced as a field researcher in Pakistan had a decisive influence on the way he continued his research after his return: he had left as a prehistorian and returned as an ethnologist. When he accepted the call to the purely ethnological chair at the University of Mainz in 1961, this change was also formally implemented. However, it was already readable in Jettmar's publications as early as 1957.

What had happened in the course of Jettmar's field research? The personal contact with shepherds and peasants, hunters and shamans in northern Pakistan and the observation of everyday economic activities in the high mountains had opened up Jettmar's hitherto narrow archaeological view and convinced him of the fertility and necessity of field research. The contact with the Frankfurt school—Jensen's worldview approach, respectively the justification of integrated cultural complexes through a dominant idea, strongly linked to the dominant specific economic form—had stimulated him. Jettmar did not adopt the narrow cultural-morphological concept of Frankfurt ethnology; instead, 'ideology', as a system of ideas and above all religion, became decisive for his research strategy, in order to prove processes of cultural and historical change. His theoretical point of view was clear: religious ideas and practices in general and as lived, believed and passed on in the highlands of Pakistan are in principle resistant to cultural change. This precisely is an advantage for the cultural historian; he can use this resistance or resilience as a methodical instrument.

As a result of his field research experience, Jettmar began to redefine the relationship between ethnology and archaeology according to his own ideas. The programmatic text "Ethnology and problems of domestication" (1967), already published after moving from Mainz to Heidelberg University in 1964, can be seen as the conclusion of this innovative stage. Ethnology had, at this point in time for Jettmar, finally ceased to be allowed to serve the dominant archaeology only as a handmaid. From now on he wanted to elevate ethnology to the status of a scientific authority in matters of 'reflection' and model building, for the dry discipline of archaeology (Jettmar 1967: 155). Ethnology was to provide Jettmar in this process with basic data for a genuine "intellectual adventure" (Jettmar 1967: 151). He described his own position in the context of this historical bridge-building as an "optimistic ethnologist" and "critical prehistorian" in one person, explicitly under the umbrella of a "cultural anthropology", in reference to his Heidelberg colleague Wilhelm E. Mühlmann (Jettmar 1967: 159).

Ethnographic field research was the dominant medium of knowledge gathering for Jettmar from 1955 onward, but always in the service of his primary research interest—cultural-historical reconstruction. Patient participation and observation, meticulous data recording over weeks or even months was never his concern; Rather, Jettmar was always on the move, ceaselessly searching for evidence and proof. If one looks at the movement patterns of his numerous field research trips up into the 1990s, they illustrate his focused search in selected valleys of the mountain region for still existing traces of a past that spanned far beyond northern Pakistan. Jettmar then used his findings like bait on a fishing rod, which he cast from the elevated position of the highlands far into the lowlands, preferably of the north, towards Central Asia. His profound archaeological and historical knowledge determined the direction and scope. In these cultural-historical reconstructions, physical-geographical and other environmental conditions of the high mountain region clearly receded for him as factors influencing cultural processes.

The experience of field research had actually changed Jettmar's scientific research approach, albeit within an already given and still maintained cultural-historical constructivist framework. Viewed in this way, Jettmar recognized himself clearly in the Tangir Valley as early as 1955 when he apodictically told Adolf Friedrich: "I am a constructionist—I have to construct."

Adolf Friedrich—*Via dolorosa* to "Myth and Cult"

The journey to the scientific high point of the field research program—the Winter Festival or New Year's Festival of the Kalash in Chitral—began, for Adolf Friedrich, in early November 1955. Four months of 'field research expedition' had already passed as movement from place to place; during this time the first signs of the disease, from which he died some months later, became apparent.

Friedrich is in a positive mood in this preliminary phase of Kalash research. He observes attentively and notes down his observations in his diary unemotionally. Enthusiastic or all-too-free associations are the exception. Even when he found his favourite Siberian motif—the resurrection of the hunted animal from its bones—as a living narrative tradition, or met his first shaman in person, he remained surprisingly distanced. Friedrich shows emotion, however, when simplistic explanations are served up to him in response to questions as to the meaning of cultural practices, such as "only for beautiful" as a verbatim answer of a local interpreter, to his inquiry about a specific ornament in a mosque (Friedrich Diary, July 14, 1955, p. 179). Such answers are fundamentally wrong for him. Then he digs deeper and deeper until he can prove to his partner in conversation from the information finally given, willy-nilly, that there is always meaningful depth behind a banal surface. Maybe these disappointments made it clear to Friedrich how difficult it is to gain access to experience and, at the same time, meaning. But at least Friedrich is the old cultural historian again: he meticulously examines huge stones as he passes by; they could be relics of a "megalithic culture".

In mid-November 1955, Friedrich arrives in the settlement area of the Kalash in the Pakistan-Afghan borderland, together with Peter Snoy. So far the Kalash had successfully resisted the pressure of Islamisation and are therefore still to be considered *kafirs*. In mid-December they celebrate their 'pagan' New Year festival. A myth gives meaning to the ritual acts. Friedrich would like to be familiarized with as many details as possible before the festival begins. Immediately after arriving on November 14th, he began his interviews (Friedrich Diary, November 15th, 1955, p. 451ff) and thus, in the first few days of his stay, learned about Balumain, the main deity of the festival. Balumain came to the Kalash in primordial times; since then he appears once a year, at the New Year festival (Friedrich Diary, November 19, 1955, p. 468).

Friedrich grasps Balumain with both hands, so to speak, and does not let go of him until he leaves the Kalash in early April. His preoccupation with festival and deity goes through three research phases between mid-November, 1955, and end of March, 1956: before the festival, questioning—first a theoretical approach; then, during the festival—participation and observation; finally, after the festival, further interviews—the scientific penetration. This sequence of knowledge building should lead to ever-greater clarity, but the research reality looked different: the complexity of the event grew under Friedrich's questions, as more and more versions and contradictions in ritual and myth emerged.

As the diary shows, this experience was stressful for Friedrich. What did he expect, what did he want to achieve? Let's go back to his theoretical convictions shortly before his departure for Pakistan: for Friedrich, field research was documentation and cultural-historical interpretation of ancient myths and cults, but also an apprehensive understanding of the depth of religious experience of nature-bound individuals during and through practice. Knowing shamans could provide guidance in such a process, but also additional informants have to be included. Starting from this approach one can follow Friedrich's personal process of gaining knowledge in three research phases.

Friedrich already encountered contradicting versions of the festivities in the first research phase. He does not want to come to terms with that: "I am now trying to put each of today's two reports in an order, because, within the narration of every informant, it went pretty much criss-cross" (Friedrich Diary, November 24, 1955, p. 484). Then Friedrich, supported by an interpreter, asks for further descriptions of the festivities, one festive day after the other. Nevertheless, the difference between the narrated versions cannot be resolved; it is even getting bigger and bigger.

Already in the first research phase, however, Friedrich found 'his' Ogotemmêli[26]—the shaman Bodok. More and more he becomes

---

26   The famous, philosophically gifted main informant of Marcel Griaule (1965).

Friedrich's indispensable "main informant". As an initiated shaman—
Friedrich was already aware, at least in theory—Bodok is a source
of knowledge that originates in different cultural strata; but as a
religious practitioner of the present, he is, at the same time, able
to experience the New Year festival in its full and deep meaning
and can tell Friedrich about it. Bodok is a flexible and constructive
interlocutor. In a never-ending and highly creative dialogue, he and
Friedrich elaborate together "Myth and Cult" of the Kalash New
Year festival—even if Friedrich would certainly not agree with my
characterization of this cooperation.

Friedrich can observe the program of the second research phase,
the practice of myth and cult, at least in part himself—although his
illness worries him more and more, he is still mobile. He describes
very precisely, with clear sympathy and high sensitivity for colors,
smells and noises, as well as in meaningful, sophisticated and vivid
language, sacrificial rituals and the actions of the festival participants.
Their appearance, their body language, their facial expressions emerge
impressively before the reader's eye. Friedrich is particularly attentive to
children and empathizes with them. He embeds people and their actions
in the snow-covered winter landscape of the high mountain environment,
which he portrays in an atmospheric way. Everything academic-
theoretical and all that tormented him seems to have fallen away.

The third research phase, which begins after the festival—
Friedrich is now more tied to the house due to illness—is entirely
dominated by the shaman Bodok. The dialogue between them is
now well established. Friedrich asks questions (sometimes he writes
them down verbatim), Bodok answers some immediately, some days
later. Bodok: "I had to think. Today I'm ready to narrate" (Friedrich
Diary, January 19, 1956: 582ff). Through Friedrich's stimulating
questions and Bodok's reflection, the simple Balumain of the month
of November unfolds into an increasingly differentiated god by
March; his horse, on which he rides in at the New Year festival, also
participates in this leap of complexity. Friedrich not only draws on
Bodok's specific stock of knowledge as an expert in traditions. He
should also remember his many former shamanistic trances at the
sanctuary of Balumain on the occasion of the New Year festival and
unveil what he 'saw'—according to Friedrich's expectations this
information at last might turn out to be true, condensed meaning,
emerging from cultural depths. The diary allows us to participate in
these dialogues: "I ask if there is a story that Balumain's horse has 7, 8

or 9 legs. Bodok replies: I heard Balumain's horse has 6 legs backwards, one leg forward." (Friedrich Diary, January 29, 1956, p. 582)

"I ask Bodok if he, in a trance near the Tok tree,[27] has seen earlier whether the horse of Balumain's is a stallion or a mare? I explain to him: in the first information he provided about Balumain, he definitely and clearly told me when I asked: Balumain is female. Later he explained to me: Balumain is male and female, from one side he shows the figure of a bearded man, from the other that of a woman. I now ask: because among the Katir [a neighboring group of the Kalash] 'Balo' are only female fairy spirits who are eager for horses [and] since Balumain is so closely connected to his horse—is it possible that Balumain's bisexual character is structured in this way: Balumain in human appearance (as a human being) equals feminine; Balumain in horse appearance equals stallion male? Bodok replies: Balumain always comes by horse. He gives his instructions from the horse. In the pastures he always sits on his horse. Balumain loves his horse very much." (Friedrich Diary, January 29, 1956, p. 582h)

Friedrich never lets go of Balumain's androgyny; could his feminine aspect be identical with the goddess Kushumai? "I ask Bodok whether I could write down as follows: 'If the Betan [i.e. the shaman] sees Balumain as a man, it is Balumain; if the Betan sees Balumain as a woman, then it is Kushumai.' Yes, Bodok answers, this is correct" (Friedrich Diary, p. 598).[28] And so the dialogue about Balumain's diversity in unity and his horse goes on, page by page.

In the deepening process of the third research phase, Balumain's first appearance in prehistoric times becomes more and more Friedrich's topic. The details are worked out with Bodok, then Friedrich uses them to draft an ordered system in the style of Jensen: all Kalash gods are assigned chronologically and hierarchically to worldviews typical of certain economic forms, an earlier "pastoralist-nomadic" and a later sedentary-agricultural life (Friedrich Diary, p. 602ff). But Friedrich's consistent ordered systems break down again and again under the power of further information. Even before Bodok has answered former questions satisfactorily, new and complicating facets emerge. For example, Balumain suddenly has a brother—and again a long-winded clarification process begins (Friedrich Diary, p. 600ff), which

---

27 A sacred tree that plays an important role in the ritual.
28 From January 1956, the exact chronological assignment of the entries is no longer clear.

becomes more and more difficult as new information has to be reconciled with earlier, within Friedrich's ordering process.

For Friedrich, Bodok has meanwhile not only become a particularly knowledgeable expert, but also the highest authority for right or wrong. He submits information to Bodok from other informants, for hegemonic decision-making: "Bodok made corrections to this report. We got into a thorough discussion." (Friedrich Diary, p. 665). Or: "Yesterday I was in Krakal [a neighboring village]... The people of Krakal know disturbingly little about the past and folk customs. Unad Beg, who is still the best and has already told me some important things, apparently has little to eat at the moment; the old man's brain no longer functions accurately. Bodok was here today, correcting the Krakal information and adding to it." (Friedrich Diary, March 1, 1956, pp. 762f.) But then also doubts: "I ask Bodok whether he gave me this information in order to answer my question positively, or whether this was a tradition that he had heard from older members of his people? Bodok replies: 'I heard this from an old man: our ancestors received such instruction from Balumain. This is what I heard within the traditions. I only have to think and remember'." (Friedrich Diary, p. 689)

What appears so strange about Friedrich's consistently pursued clarification procedure? Less the question-and-answer game between ethnologist and informant or a certain scurrility of the dialogues; not even the attempts to get to the meaningful root of a problem. Arrogance would also be out of place—what ethnologist does not remember the deficits of his own field research when reading someone else's field diaries! Rather, what makes it so strange is the rift. On the one hand Friedrich as the inquisitive ethnographer in the field 1955/56, who wants to know everything; who does not accept the inexpressible and does not take for granted anything that is not logically accessible to him; who cannot bear to leave something in the dark and therefore wants to illuminate everything as brightly and sharply as possible. On the other hand, Friedrich silently working in his study in Mainz in 1951, who, as a result of his attack on the field researcher Jensen and his overly rational effort to understand the cultural other, demanded that otherness must not be rationally grasped and represented as analytically isolated aspects—it can keep its otherness and thus remain untidy; not everything can or should be explained.

What led Friedrich to this break with his past? We can only guess. Did the polyphony—the multitude of voices and versions—virtually enforce his attempts to create order? Was there a conflict, behind his endeavours to understand, with an ethnological core belief widespread at the time: every ethnic group around the world has a consistent and monophonic canon of traditional knowledge with a unique attribution of meaning, just as Russian Siberian ethnographers presented it? There, it was conveyed, the entire group knew only one single version of a myth or a ritual—the very version the ethnographer noted down, often that of a shaman as the mouthpiece of the group. Was the reason for Friedrich's ever more one-sided bond to Bodok based on the example of the Siberian ethnographies? Or do we find an answer for the rift also in Friedrich's character, as Jensen describes him: unrelentingly in search of the true, the essential and knowledge—i.e. there must be a valid answer to every question? And finally: could not Friedrich's advancing illness also have led to his increasing thematic narrowing and, as it seems to me, to his hectic pace in data collection, paired with a disillusionment about the quite normal cultural other.

In any case, with the help of the diary, it can be stated with certainty that in the overwhelming experience of field research, Friedrich was only able, in exceptional cases, to tie in with his earlier life as a pure scientist. Nothing shows this more clearly than his relationship with the shaman Bodok. From a theoretical point of view, for Friedrich he had to be the embodiment of altruistic suffering for the benefit of the Kalash community, in other words, one of those impressive personalities that he admired so much in Siberian ethnography and in the Old Testament. But Bodok remains a mere expert who is questioned; even the description of his past initiation experiences just fills a single page in the diary. What is striking, however, is that when Friedrich himself takes part in social events or when informants report on such events in colourful detail and in a flow of words, that is, when Friedrich foregoes constant questioning, then he can tie in with thoughts about community and *collective* experience, just as he developed them in his last two essays before leaving for Pakistan (cf. e.g. Friedrich Diary, pp. 478, 549ff, as well as his lengthy reports on his participation in the New Year's rituals).

How would Friedrich have 'represented' the results of his field research in an ethnographic monograph? Actually an idle question, but it has its appeal in the light of the Writing Culture debate. As we have learned from many examples, the path from field research to ethnographic representation, often written only after a long time has passed, does not follow the claimed research logic; rather, the connection between the field and the study at home is broken in multiple ways. It can therefore by no means be ruled out that Friedrich would have healed the break between his scientific-theoretical convictions and field research in the process of writing as a learning experience and reconciled the illusive clarity of the results within a new interpretation with his previous commitment to ambiguity and ambivalence of the cultural other, according to his earlier published commitment: "The humanities scholar should beware of making a naturally intricate process, endowed with light and shadow, too transparent".

Adolf Friedrich and Karl Jettmar in Ethnological Memory

The memory of ethnology under its aspect as a university subject is filled with much content—with publications of all kinds, but also with biographies of its representatives, which *ex post facto* and taken together can be used as food for thought about ethnographic practice. Adolf Friedrich and Karl Jettmar left both behind.

Jettmar's extensive published oeuvre impressed and influenced research on northern Pakistan and thus also on Central Asia. In particular, the study of the rock carvings and inscriptions of northern Pakistan, to which Jettmar has devoted himself intensively since 1980, further consolidated his international reputation. After Jettmar retired for reasons of age, their study was continued by the Academy of Sciences in Heidelberg until the mid-2010s. Results of this continued research, published after Jettmar's death in 2002, contributed in an indirect way to his lasting appreciation within South Asia and Central Asia research, quite rightly: Jettmar had been a highly creative and erudite 'cultural anthropologist'—for that is what he increasingly saw himself as.

Friedrich had once given Jettmar the opportunity to do field research. He made full use of it and later passed it on to his own students—including me. Not all field research carried out in northern Pakistan by cultural anthropologists, geographers and linguists since the 1980s, however, met with Jettmar's approval; he regretted that cultural-historical issues were no longer the focus. Only when written sources from early historical times and the Middle Ages were opened up (he used them increasingly himself for the interpretation of rock carvings), or when the interaction between the physical-geographical high mountain environment and cultural processes was the focus of research (he meanwhile viewed the neglect of environmental factors as a deficit in his own research), Jettmar could reconcile himself with the new type of research in 'his' northern Pakistan.[29]

---

29 This applies above all to projects within the interdisciplinary priority program of the DFG "Karakorum Cultural Area", 1989-99 (coordination: Irmtraud Stellrecht).

What remains of Friedrich? On the one hand, for the regional specialist, there is important new ethnographic material on the New Year festival of the Kalash. Since their winter festival remained the focus of international, albeit no longer German, research, Friedrich's ethnographical data opened up an additional perspective on this festival event and also stimulated comparison and reflection on the connection between the context of field research and its results.[30] On the other hand the diary can be considered as an opus *sui generis*—a valuable document for 'field research as experience', the significance of which goes far beyond the ethnographic context of northern Pakistan and Friedrich's personal experiences there.[31]

The German Research Foundation (DFG), too, was left with something of Friedrich: an open file; the final accounts for funds spent by him in Pakistan were missing, for understandable reasons. It was not until 1970, i.e. 14 years after his death, that this financial aftermath of Friedrich was settled with an annotation in the file: "recipient has died, statute of limitations". A second and similar problem had also been resolved in the meantime: the whereabouts of a "personal loan" from the DFG to Friedrich of "10 tropical suitcases, standard design, and 2 Petromer lamps". With a handwritten note, probably from 1967,[32] this file was also brought to a final point with reference to Friedrich's closest scientific associate at the Mainz Institute: "Devices according to the information provided by Dr. Sulzmann no longer usable".

---

30 See in particular Loude & Lièvre (1984); Parkes (1983; 1984).
31 In the history of German anthropology Friedrich is rarely remembered. An exception is Streck (1997: 153f); he compares Friedrich's scientific positions with those of Jensen.
32 The copy of the document is not clearly legible.

Literature

Bernatzik, Hugo A. 1947. *Afrika. Handbuch der angewandten Völkerkunde*. 2 vols. Innsbruck: Schlüsselverlag.

Braukämper, Ulrich. 2001. „Der ‚Verdienst-Komplex'. Rückblick auf einen Forschungsschwerpunkt der deutschen Ethnologie". *Zeitschrift für Ethnologie* 126, 209-36.

Contag, Jürgen. 1971. *Zur Methodik der deutschsprachigen Völkerkunde*. Marburg University, unpublished dissertation.

Friedrich, Adolf. 1939. *Afrikanische Priestertümer. Vorstudien zu einer Untersuchung*. Stuttgart: Strecker und Schroeder.

———. 1941. „Die Forschung über das frühzeitliche Jägertum". *Paideuma* 2 (1-2), 20-43.

———. 1943. „Knochen und Skelett in der Vorstellungswelt Nordasiens". *Wiener Beiträge zur Kulturgeschichte und Linguistik* 5, 189-247.

[———]. [1946]. *Jägerkultur und Tierbild. Ausstellung des Frobenius-Instituts an der Johann Wolfgang Goethe-Universität und des Städtischen Museums für Völkerkunde in Frankfurt am Main*. Frankfurt/M.

———. 1951. „Erkenntnis und Religion". *Paideuma* 5, 103-14.

———. 1955. „Das Bewusstsein eines Naturvolkes von Haushalt und Ursprung des Lebens". *Paideuma* 6 (2), 47-54.

———. 1955/56. *Diary (Tagebuch)* [Written during his field research in Pakistan, unpublished].

Friedrich, Adolf & Georg Buddruss. 1955. *Schamanengeschichten aus Sibirien*. Translated from Russian and introduced by Adolf Friedrich and Georg Buddruss. München-Planegg: Barth.

Gingrich, Andre. 1999. *Erkundungen. Themen der ethnologischen Forschung*. Wien: Böhlau.

Griaule, Marcel. 1965. *Conversations with Ogotemmêli. An Introduction to Dogon Religious Ideas*. London: Oxford University Press.

Jensen, Adolf E. 1948. *Das religiöse Weltbild einer frühen Kultur*. Stuttgart: August Schröder.

———. 1951. *Mythos und Kult bei Naturvölkern. Religionswissenschaftliche Betrachtungen*. Wiesbaden: Franz Steiner.

———. 1956. „Adolf Friedrich †, *22. April 1914—† 25. April 1956". *Paideuma* 6 (4), 189-93.

Jettmar, Karl. 1941. *Der Schmied im germanischen Raum*. Wien University, unpublished dissertation.

————. 1957. *Zur Kulturgeschichte eines Dardvolkes. Siedlungsgeschichte, Schamanismus und Jagdbrauchtum der Shin*. 2 vols. Wien University, Habilitation dissertation, unpublished

————. 1967. „Ethnologie und Domestikationsproblem". *Studium Generale* 20 (3), 149-60.

Johansen, Ulla. 2002. „Karl Jettmar, 1918-2002". *Zeitschrift für Ethnologie* 127, 133-38.

Köpping, Klaus-Peter. 1987. „Authentizität als Selbstfindung durch den anderen. Ethnologie zwischen Engagement und Reflexion, zwischen Leben und Wissenschaft". In Hans Peter Duerr (ed.): *Authentizität und Betrug in der Ethnologie*. Frankfurt/M.: Suhrkamp, 7-37.

Kramer, Fritz. 2005. *Schriften der Ethnologie*. Frankfurt/M: Suhrkamp.

Lehmann, Friedrich R. 1957. „Der omulodi-Glaube. ‚Schuldig' oder ‚unschuldig' im Bereiche des ‚Todeszauber-' oder ‚Hexenglaubens' in Afrika". *Jahrbuch des Museums für Völkerkunde zu Leipzig* 16, 62-109.

Linimayr, Peter. 1994. *Wiener Völkerkunde im Nationalsozialismus. Ansätze zu einer NS-Wissenschaft*. Frankfurt/M., Berlin, Bern: Peter Lang.

Loude, Jean-Yves & Viviane Lièvre. 1984. *Solstice paien. Fêtes d'hiver chez les Kalash du Nord-Pakistan*. Paris: Presses de la Renaissance.

Müller, Ernst Wilhelm. 1956. „Adolf Friedrich, Nachruf". *Tribus* 6, 145.

Nachtigall, Horst. 1956. „Adolf Friedrich †". *Zeitschrift für Ethnologie* 81, 303-6.

Parkes, Peter. 1983. *Alliance and Elopement: Economy, Social Order and Sexual Antagonism among the Kalasha (Kalash Kafirs) of Chitral*. Oxford University, unpublished dissertation.

————. n.d. *Chaomas: The Winter Festival of the Pagan Kalasha*. Unpublished ms.

Snoy, Peter (ed.). 1983. *Ethnologie und Geschichte. Festschrift für Karl Jettmar*. Wiesbaden: Franz Steiner.

Streck, Bernhard. 1997. *Fröhliche Wissenschaft Ethnologie. Eine Einführung*. Wuppertal: Edition Trickster im Peter Hammer Verlag.

INDEX

ARCHAEOLOGY

Peristan in General

Aerde, Marike van, 2019
Allchin, F. Raymond, 1981
Court, C. Auguste, 1839
Dambricourt Malassé, Anne & C.
 Gaillard, 2011
Dani, Ahmad H., 1989a, 1998, 2001
Denwood, Philip, 2007
Eggermont, Pierre H.L., 1984
Francfort, Henri-Paul, 1991
Fussman, Gérard, 1986
Jettmar, Karl, 1989b, 1993a, 1994, 1995,
 2002, 2003b, forthcoming in 2022
Johansen, Ulla, 2002
Khan, Rafiullah & I. Shaheen, 2015
Kuwayama, Shōshin, 2002
Neelis, Jason, 2002, 2011, 2012a, 2012b,
 2013, 2014
Olivieri, Luca Maria, (ed.) 2010b
Olivieri, L.M. & Ghani-ur-Rahman,
 (eds.) 2011
Parpola, Asco, 2015
Scerrato, Umberto, 1997
Sims-Williams, Nicholas, 1989, 1992
Staley, Elizabeth, 1966
Witzel, Michael E.J., 2004b, 2019
Zahir, Muhammad, 2016b, 2017

Baltistan

Benassi, Andrea & I. Scerrato, 2008
Bruneau, Laurianne, 2007
Jettmar, Karl, 1990a

Chilas, Shinaki and Indus Kohistan

Bandini-König, Ditte, (ed.) 1999, (ed.)
 2003, (ed.) 2005, (ed.) 2007, (ed.)
 2009, 2011
Bandini-König, D., M. Bemmann & H.
 Hauptmann, 1997
Bandini-König, D. & O. von Hinüber,
 (eds.) 2001

Bemmann, Martin, (ed.) 2005
Bemmann, M. & D. Bandini-König,
 (eds.) 1994
Cacopardo, Alberto M., 2008
Carther, Martha, L., 1993
Dani, Ahmad H., 1983a, 1983b, 1995
Ebert, Jorinde, 1994
Faccenna, Domenico, 1980
Fussman, Gérard, 1989c, 1993, 1994b
Fussman, G. & D. König, (eds.) 1997
Fussman, G., K. Jettmar & D. König,
 (eds.) 1994
Gnoli, Gherardo, 1980
Hauptmann, Harald, 2007, 2008, 2013
Hauptmann, H. & M. Bemmann, 1993
Hinüber, Oskar von, 1983, 1989, 2004,
 2009
Humbach, Helmut, 1985, 1994
Jettmar, Karl, 1985a, 1985b, 1991, 1992,
 1993b, 1993c, 2008
Jettmar, K. & V. Thewalt, 1985
Jettmar, K., D. König & M. Bemmann,
 1993
Jettmar, K., D. König & V. Thewalt,
 (eds.) 1989
Khan, M. Nasim, 2000
König, Ditte (= Bandini-König), 1994
Neelis, Jason, 2017
Rehman, Saeed ur, 1990
Scerrato, Umberto, 1980
Thewalt, Volker, 1983, 1985, 1998-2000
Tusa, Sebastiano, 1985
Twist, Rebecca L., 2011
Zahir, Muhammad, 2019

Chitral

Ali, Ihsan, C.M. Batt, R.A.E. Coningham
 & R.L. Young, 2002
Ali, I., D. Hamilton, P. Newson, M.
 Qasim, R. Young & M. Zahir, 2008
Ali, I., I. Shah, A. Hameed & A. Ahmad,
 2010
Ali, I., I. Shah, A. Samad, M. Zahir & R.
 Young, 2013, 2016

Ali, I., I. Shah, R. Young & A. Samad,
    2010
Ali, I. & M. Zahir, 2005a
Ali, I., M. Zahir & M. Qasim, 2005b
Allchin, F. Raymond, 1970
Cacopardo, Alberto M., 2007
Gaillard, Claire, et al., 2002
Khan, Fawad, 2013
Khan, M. Nasim, 2002, 2020
Samad, Abdul, et al., 2012
Young, R., M. Zahir, A. Samad, I. Ali &
    I. Shah, 2012
Zahir, Muhammad, 2016a, 2016b

Dir and Panjkora Basin

Court, C. Auguste, 1839

Gilgit/Yasin and Astor

Bräker, Annette & H.H. Geerken,
    2017
Burton-Page, John, 1986
Fussman, Gérard, 2004
Hakal, Muezuddin, 2014, 2015, 2016, 2019
Hallier, Ulrich W., 1991
Hauptmann, Harald, 2007, 2008
Hauptmann, H. & M. Bemmann, 1993
Hinüber, Oskar von, 1983, 1989, 2004,
    2007, 2009, 2014
Humbach, Helmut, 1980a, 1980b
Jettmar, Karl, 1993b, 1993c, 2008
Litvinsky, B.A., 2002
Mock, John, 2013a

**Hunza/Nagar Valley and other
Burushaski-speaking areas**

Bräker, Annette & H.H. Geerken, 2017
Dani, Ahmad H., 1985, 1995
Hauptmann, Harald, 2007, 2008
Hauptmann, H. & M. Bemmann,
    1993
Neelis, Jason, 2000, 2006

Kalasha

Zahir, Muhammad, 2020

Ladakh and Da/Hanu

Benassi, Andrea & I. Scerrato, 2008
Bruneau, Laurianne, 2007, 2010, 2013,
    2015
Vernier, Martin, 2007
Vohra, Rohit, 1993

Nuristan

Filigenzi, Anna, 2020
Klimburg, Maximilian, 2016
Potts, Daniel T., 2016

**Pamir, with Wakhan, Badakhshan,
Kashgar/Yarkhand**

Dambricourt Malassé, Anne & C.
    Gaillard, 2011
Mock, John, 2013b, 2016a, 2018a, 2018b

Swat and Swat Kohistan

Burton-Page, John, 1986
Court, C. Auguste, 1839
Di Castro, Angelo A., 2015
Falk, Harry, 2009
Filigenzi, Anna, 2010, 2011, 2015, 2016,
    2019
Klimburg, Maximilian, 2016
Olivieri, Luca Maria, 1998, 2008, 2009,
    2010a, (ed.) 2010b, 2011,
    2013, 2015a, 2015b, 2015c, 2016a,
        2016b, 2016c, 2017, 2018
Olivieri, L.M. & A. Filigenzi, 2018
Olivieri, L.M. & Ghani-ur-Rahman,
    (eds.) 2011
Olivieri, L.M. & M. Vidale, 2004, 2006
Scerrato, Umberto, 1997
Stacul, Giorgio, 1987, 2001
Stein, M. Aurel, 1930
Tribulato, Olga & L.M. Olivieri, 2017
Tucci, Giuseppe, 1997
Young, Ruth, 2003

BIBLIOGRAPHY

Peristan in General

Allan, Nigel, 1998
Baart, J. & E.L. Baart-Bremer, 2001
Kristiansen, K. & I. Ross, 1973
McCoy Owens, Bruce, Th. Riccardi Jr. &
    T.T. Lewis, n.d. [1987]
Schmidt, R.L., O.N. Koul & V.K. Kaul,
    1984
Söhnen-Thieme, R. & O. von Hinüber,
    1994b
Stellrecht, Imtraud, (ed.) 1998a

**Hunza/Nagar Valley and other
Burushaski-speaking areas**

Berger, Hermann, 1985

Kalasha

Cacopardo, Augusto S., 2012
Canonne, Marie & J. Herment, 2020

Nuristan

Børdahl, Per E., 2021a, 2021b

**Pashai and other "Dardic"-speakers of
Afghanistan**

Ovesen, Jan, 1979

Swat and Swat Kohistan

Olivieri, Luca Maria, 2015a

ETHNOLOGY

Peristan in General

Abaeva, Tamara G., 1971, 1980
Alekseev, Sergej V., 2012
Allan, Nigel, 1986, 1999
Anonym, 1934
Backstrom, Peter C. & Carla F. Radloff,
    1992
Barrow, Edmund G., 1888

Bashir, E. & Israr-ud-Din, (eds.) 1996
Baskhanov, Mihail K., A.A. Kolesnikov,
    M.F. Matveeva, (eds.) 2015
Baskhanov, M.K., A.A. Kolesnikov, M.F.
    Matveeva, A.I. Gluhov, (eds.) 2017
Bhatt, Ram P., H.W. Wessler & C.P.
    Zoller, 2014
Bonvalot, Gabriel, 1889
Buddruss, G. & P. Snoy, 2006 2008
Cacopardo, Alberto M., 2005, 2019
Cacopardo, A.M. & A.S. Cacopardo,
    2001, 2011
Cacopardo, Augusto S., 2016a
Cockerill, George K., 1895
Dani, Ahmad H., 1989b
Dittmann, Andreas, 1997, (ed.) 2001
Drew, Frederick, 1876
Ehlers, Eckart & H. Kreutzmann, (eds.)
    2000
Forsyth, Thomas D., 1875
Frembgen, J. Wasim, 1989, 1999b, 2003
Girdlestone, Charles, 1874
Gornenskij, Ioann, 2000
Grjunberg, A.L. & I.-M. Steblin-
    Kamenskij, 1974
Haserodt, Klaus, 1989
Holdschlag, Arnd, 2005
Illi, Dieter W., 1988, 1991
Israr-ud-Din, (ed.) 2008
Izzatullah, Mir, 1872
Izzet Ullah, Mir, 1842
Jensen, Adolf E., 1956
Jettmar, Karl, 1986a, forthcoming in
    2022
Johansen, Ulla, 2002
Kaverin, Sviatoslav I., 2019, 2020
Klimburg, Maximilian, 1997, 2005,
    2007c, 2008d
Kreutzmann, Hermann, 1994, 1995,
    1998a, 1998b, (ed.) 2000, 2003,
    2004a, 2017a
Kristiansen, K. & W. Witek, (eds.) 2001
Kussmaul, Friedrich & P. Snoy, 1972
Leitner, Gottlieb W., 1872a, 1872b
Lentz, Sabine, 2000
Lines, Maureen, 1988
Mock, John, 1998a
Moorcroft, William & George Trebeck, 1841

Morgenstierne, Georg, 2001
Neve, Arthur, 1913
Noci, Francesco, 2006
Olivieri, L.M. & Ghani-ur-Rahman,
    (eds.) 2011
Parkes, Peter, 1996a, 2003, 2004, 2005
Parkin, Robert, 1987b
Rennell, James, 1792
Rieck, Andreas, 1997a
Scerrato, Ilaria E., 2005
Scerrato, Umberto, 1983b, 1984, 1985,
    1997
Schmid, Anna, 2002
Schmidt, Ruth Laila, 2002
Shaw, Robert B., 1871
Skyhawk, Hugh van, (ed.) 2008a
Snoy, Peter, 1983, 1993
Söhnen-Thieme, Renate & O. von
    Hinüber, (eds.) 1994a
Sökefeld, Martin, 1997a
Staley, John, 1966, 1982
Stein, M. Aurel, 1934
Stellrecht, Imtraud, (ed.) 1997a, 1998b,
    (ed.) 1998c, 1998d, 206a
Stellrecht, I. & H.G. Bohle, (eds.) 1998
Stellrecht, I. & M. Winiger, (eds.) 1997
Strand, Richard F., 1997-2021
Streefland, Pieter H., S.H. Khan & O.
    van Lieshout, 1995
Tanner, Henry C.B., 1891
Thornton, Edward, 1844
Torwali, Zubair, 2021
Tsuchiya, Haruko, 1998, 1999
Ujfalvy, Charles E. de, 1883, 1884, 1887,
    1896
Vigne, Godfrey T., 1842
Weinreich, Matthias, 2015
Witek, Wlodek, 2005a, 2005b
Zoller, Claus Peter, 2007, 2018

Baltistan

Benassi, Andrea & I. Scerrato, 2008
Dainelli, Giotto, 1924
De Filippi, Filippo, 1924, 1932
Drew, Frederick, 1879
Faggi, Pier Paolo & M. Ginestri, 1977
Francke, August H., 1899, 1909
Izzatullah, Mir, 1872

Izzet Ullah, Mir, 1842
Jettmar, Karl, 1977
Klimburg, Maximilian, 2007b
Kreutzmann, Hermann, (ed.) 2013,
    2015b
Moorcroft, William & George Trebeck,
    1841
Preller, Charles du Riche, 1924
Rieck, Andreas, 1997b
Sagaster, Klaus, 1984, (ed.) 1989, 1993,
    1995
Samreen, Akita, 2013
Scerrato, Ilaria E., 2010, 2017
Söhnen, Renate = Söhnen-Thieme, 1983
Vigne, Godfrey T., 1842
Wade, Claude M., 1835

Chilas, Shinaki and Indus Kohistan

Akhtar, Aasim, 1997
Andrews, Peter A. & K. Jettmar, (eds.)
    2000
Chaudhary, M. Azam, 1997, 1998
Clemens, Jürgen & M. Nüsser, 2008
Douglas, J.A., 1895
Douglas, J.A. & C.H. Powell, 1894
Faggi, Pier Paolo & M. Ginestri, 1977
Frembgen, J. Wasim, 1999a, 2008, 2014
Godfrey, Stuart H., 1898
GSI General Staff, India, 1928a
Janjua, Zahid J., 1998
Scerrato, Umberto, 1980
Schmidt, Ruth Laila, 2003, 2003-2004,
    2006, 2013
Schmidt, R.L. & M.M. Zarin, 2008
Schweinfurth, Ulrich, 1983
Topper, Uwe, 2000
Wiegand, Jahn, 2009
Zarin, Mohammad Manzar & R.L.
    Schmidt, 1984
Zoller, Claus Peter, 2010

Chitral

Ahmad, Zahir, J.C. Postigo, F. Rahman
    & A. Dittman, 2021
Akhunzada, Fakhruddin, 2018
Akhunzada, F. & M. Liljegren, 2009
Anonym, 1879

Dir and Panjkora Basin

Gilgit/Yasin and Astor

Hunza/Nagar Valley and other Burushaski-speaking areas

Ali, Abida, 2018
Ali, Tahir, 1981, 1983
Baskhanov, M.K., A.A. Kolesnikov, M.F.
   Matveeva, A.I. Gluhov, (eds.) 2017
Bräker, Annette & H.H. Geerken, 2017
Butz, David & N. Cook, 2018
Charles, Christian, 1981
Csáji, László K., 2011, 2018
Davies, Wendy, (ed.) 2004
Felmy, Sabine, 1986, 1989, 1993
Frembgen, Jürgen W., 1983, 1984, 1985,
   1986a, 1986b, 2022
Frembgen, J. Wasim, 1988a, 1988b,
   1992, 1996, 2005, 2007, 2017
Fremont, Annette, 1984
Fussman, Gérard, 1991
Godfrey, Stuart H., 1898
Holden, Livia, (ed.) 2018
Hussain, Shafqat, 2015
Kreutzmann, Hermann, 1986, 1988,
   1993, 1996b, 1999, 2002, (ed.)
   2006a, 2006b
Lorimer, David L.R., 1927, 1981
Lorimer, Emily O., 1936a, 1936b, 1938
Munshi, Sadaf, 2016
Nicolaus, Peter, 2015a
Parkin, Robert, 1987a
Pfeffer, Georg, 1984
Schmid, Anna, 1997 2007
Sidky, M. Homayun, 1994, 1996, 1997,
   2003, 2004, 2015
Sidky, M.H. & J. Subedi, 2000
Skyhawk, Hugh van, 2003, 2006, 2008b,
   2021
Skyhawk, H. van, H. Berger & K.
   Jettmar, 1996
Stellrecht, Irmtraud, 1991, 1992, 2006b,
   2007a, 2007b
Tiffou, Étienne, 1993
Tikkanen, Bertil, 1991
Willson, Stephen R., 1999a

Kalasha

Ahmed, Ajaz, 2007
Ahmed, Akbar S., 1986

Alauddin, Mohammad, 2006
Ali, M. Kashif, 2020
Ali, M. Kashif & M. I. Chawla, 2019
Ali, M. Kashif, G. Shabbir & M.I.
   Chawla, 2021
Amella, Marie-Véronique, 2020
Andersen, Peter, S. Castenfeldt & S.
   Soren, 2010/11
Balneaves, Elizabeth, 1952, 1964
Balslev Jørgensen, Jørgen, L. Edelberg,
   C. Krebs & H. Siiger, 1964
Bashir, Elena, 2011
Bianchi, Nicola, 2011
Bibi, Lakshan, 2019
Borriello, Manuela, 1974
Cacopardo, Alberto M., 1974, 1977,
   1985, 1991, 1996, 2009, 2019
Cacopardo, A.M. & A.S. Cacopardo,
   1989, 1992, 1996
Cacopardo, A.M. & S. Pellò, 2021
Cacopardo, Augusto S., 1974, 1985,
   1991, 1996, 1999, 2006, 2008,
   2010a, 2010b, 2011, 2012, 2013,
   2016b
Canonne, Marie & J. Herment, 2020
Carbajo Usano, Matilde, 2020
Cardini, Anna Maria, 2016
Castenfeldt, Svend, 1999, 2016
Castenfeldt, S. & H. Siiger, 2003
Chelazzi, Guido, et al., 2016
Chiellini, Maddalena, 2013
Choudhry, Fahad R., M.S. Park, K.
   Golden & I.Z. Bokharei, 2017
Choudhry F.R., T.M. Khan, M.S. Park &
   K.J. Golden, 2018
Ciruzzi, Sara, 1981
Ciruzzi, Sara, S. Mainardi & M.G.
   Roselli, (eds.) 2004, (eds.) 2007
Cristoforetti, Simone, 2014
Darling, E. Gillian, 1979
Di Carlo, Pierpaolo, 2007, 2009, 2010a,
   2010b, 2010c, 2011b
Everhard, Carol & E. Mela-
   Athanasopoulou, 2011
Fentz, Mytte, 1994, 1996, 1999, 2010
Ferdinand, Klaus, 1974/75, 1999
Frembgen, J.W., 1998
Fussman, Gérard, 1975, 1991
Graziosi, Paolo, 2004, 2007

Allison, John, 1976
Anderson, Dorothy, 2003, 2008
Arbabzada, Nushin & N. Green, 2022
Balslev Jørgensen, Jørgen, L. Edelberg,
　C. Krebs & H. Siiger, 1964
Barrington, Nicholas, J.T. Kendrick & R.
　Schlagintweit, 2005
Barrow, Edmund G., 1888
Bartasheva, Nina L., 1975
Becka, Jiři, 1981a, 1981b
Benveniste, Émile, 1952
Brandl, Rudolf M., 1997
Bucherer-Dietschi, Paul, (ed.) 1988
Buddruss, Georg, 1979b, 1987, 1992,
　2002, 2005, 2008
Cacopardo, Alberto M., 1999, 2009,
　2013, 2019
Cacopardo, A.M. & A.S. Cacopardo, 2001
Cacopardo, A.M. & R. L. Schmidt, (eds.)
　2006
Cacopardo, A.M. & S. Pellò, 2021, (eds.)
　forthcoming
Capus, Guillaume, 1889a, 1890
Castenfeldt, Svend, 1996, 1999, 2021
Castenfeldt, S. & H. Søholt, 1985
Chelazzi, Guido, et al., 2016
Chiellini, Maddalena, 2013
Ciruzzi, Sara, 1981
Ciruzzi, Sara, S. Mainardi & M.G.
　Roselli, (eds.) 2004, (eds.) 2007
Court, C.Auguste, n.d., ca. 1837
Degener, Almuth, 1994, 1995, 1998a,
　2001, forthcoming in 2022
Downes, Edmund, 1873
Dumezil, Georges, 1995
Eardley Harwood, W.S., 1902
Edelberg, Lennart, 1952
Emel'janov, Aleksandr J. & S.I. Kaverin,
　2019
Fentz, Mytte, 1999
Ferdinand, Klaus, 1974/75, 1999
Filigenzi, Anna, 2017, 2020
Fussman, Gérard 1975, 1988, 2012
Giglioli, Enrico H., 1889
Ginestri, Mario, 1977
Griffith, William, 1847
Grjunberg, Aleksandr L., 1969, 1980
Grünberg, A.L.=Grjunberg, 1994a,
　1995a, 1995b

Hackin, Joseph, 1926
Hallet, Stanley I. & R. Samizay, 1975
Herrlich, Albert, 1939-40
Holdich, T.H., 1896
Holzwarth, Wolfgang, 1993, 1994b
Inostrancev, K. A., 1909
Irgens-Møller, Christer, 2005, 2009,
　2021
Jettmar, Karl, 1986b
Johnsen, Ulrich H., 2016
Johnsen, U. H., T. Funder, S. Jones & Taj
　K. Kalash, 2021
Jones, Schuyler, 1978, 1979, 1981, 1983,
　1984, 2003, 2021
Kalter, Johannes, 1982
Katz, David, 1980
Katz, David J., 1982, 1984
Khan, M. Hayat, 1874
Kisljakov, Nikolaj A., 1957, 1963
Klimburg, Maximilian, 1983, 1987,
　1990, 1993, 1999, 2001, 2002a,
　2002b, 2004, 2007a, 2008b, 2014,
　2016, 2019
Kohzad, Ahmad Ali, 1948, 1954
Kristiansen, Knut, 1986, 2008
Kristiansen, K. & W. Witek, (eds.) 2001
Kvaerne, Per, 1986
Lal, Mohan, 1834, 1846
Lavan, Spencer, 1988
Leitner, Gottlieb W., 1874
Lessar, Pavel M., 1888
Levy, Peter, 1973
Lumsden, Harry B., 1860
Lushina, Aleksandra V., 2009
Maev, Nikolay A., 1874
Matveev, Pavel P., 1883
Mayrhofer, Manfred, 1967
Meyendorff, Egor K. de, 1826
Miloserdov, Dmitry Y., 2019
Mit'ko, Oleg A., 2011
Morgenstierne, Georg, 1932, 1973, 1992,
　2001
Motamedi, Ahmad A., 1957, 1983
Neubauer, Hans Franz, 1974a, 1974b
Newby, Eric, 1958
Nuristani, Ahmad Yusuf, 1973, 1994a,
　1994b
Ovesen, Jan, 1986
Parkes, Peter, 1987, 1991

Pamir, with Wakhan, Badakhshan, Kashgar/Yarkhand

Pashai and other "Dardic"-speakers of Afghanistan

Pathan

Swat and Swat Kohistan

GENETICS

Peristan in General

Di Cristofaro, Julie, et al., 2013
Guha, Biraja S., 1938
Hemphill, Brian E., 2009
Mohyuddin, Aisha, et al., 2002
Narasimhan, Vagheesh, N. Patterson, P.
    Moorjani, et al., 2019
Semino, Ornella, et al., 2004
Witzel, Michael E.J., 2019

Baltistan

De Filippi, Filippo, 1924, 1932

Chitral

Aziz, Shahid, M. Nawaz, S.G. Afridi &
    A. Khan, 2019
Blaylock, Sarah R. & B. Hemphill,
    2007
Hemphill, Brian E., 2020
Hemphill, B.E., I. Ali, S. Blaylock & N.
    Willits, 2013
Hemphill, B.E., M. Zahir & I. Ali, 2017
Mazumdar, S.K., 1976

Gilgit/Yasin and Astor

Mumtaz, Mah Noor, H. Ihsan, S. Aziz,
    Hizbullah, S.G. Afridi, S. Shams &
    A. Khan, 2019

Kalasha

Bakker, Peter & A. Daval-Markussen,
    2016
Balslev Jørgensen, Jørgen, L. Edelberg,
    C. Krebs & H. Siiger, 1964
Bigoni, Francesca, 2016
Hellenthal, Garrett, et al., 2016
Mansoor, Atika, et al., 2004
Massari-Mariottini, Claudia, 1974
Mazumdar, S.K., 1976
Mohyuddin, Aisha, et al., 2002
Qamar, Raheel, et al., 2002
Qasim, Ayub, et al., 2015

Ladakh and Da/Hanu

De Filippi, Filippo, 1924, 1932
Syama, Adikarla, V.S. Arun, G.
    ArunKumar, et al., 2019

Nuristan

Balslev Jørgensen, Jørgen, L. Edelberg,
    C. Krebs & H. Siiger, 1964
Massari-Mariottini, Claudia, 1974
Mazumdar, S.K., 1976

Pathan

Firasat, Sadaf, et al. 2007

GEOGRAPHY

Peristan in General

Anonym [Davies, Robert H.], 1862
Barrow, Edmund G., 1888
Bashir, E. & Israr-ud-Din, (eds.) 1996
Baskhanov, Mihail K., A.A. Kolesnikov,
    M.F. Matveeva, (eds.) 2015
Baskhanov, M.K., A.A. Kolesnikov, M.F.
    Matveeva, A.I. Gluhov, (eds.) 2017
Bonvalot, Gabriel, 1889
Buksh, Munshi Faiz, 1872
Cacopardo, Alberto M., 2005
Cockerill, George K., 1895
Court, C. Auguste, 1836
Curzon, George N., 1898
Davies, Robert H., 1862
Dittmann, Andreas, (ed.) 2001
Forsyth, Thomas D., 1870, 1875
Girdlestone, Charles, 1874
Haserodt, Klaus, 1989
Israr-ud-Din, (ed.) 2008
Izzatullah, Mir, 1872
Izzet Ullah, Mir, 1842
Kreutzmann, Hermann, 1994, 1995,
    2004b, 2007
Leitner, Gottlieb W., 1950
Moorcroft, William & George Trebeck,
    1841
Rennell, James, 1792
Shaw, Robert B., 1871

Skrine, Clarmont P., 1925
Staley, Elizabeth, 1966
Stein, M. Aurel, 1934
Thornton, Edward, 1844
Vigne, Godfrey T., 1842
Younghusband, Frances E., 1895
Yule, Henry, 1872a, 1872b
Yule, H. & H. Cordier, 1913-16

Baltistan

Dainelli, Giotto, 1924
De Filippi, Filippo, 1924, 1932
Izzatullah, Mir, 1872
Izzet Ullah, Mir, 1842
Kreutzmann, Hermann, 2015b
Moorcroft, William & George Trebeck, 1841
Vigne, Godfrey T., 1842
Wade, Claude M., 1835

Chilas, Shinaki and Indus Kohistan

Clemens, Jürgen & M. Nüsser, 2008
Douglas, J.A. & C.H. Powell, 1894
Godfrey, Stuart H., 1898

Chitral

Anonym, 1879
Barrow, Edmund G., 1888
Bonvalot, Gabriel, 1889
[Buksh, M. Faiz =] F.B., 1883
Gurdon, Bertrand E.M., 1903
Hayward, G.S.W. & Mahomed Amin, 1869
Khan, Raja, 1845
Leitner, Gottlieb W., 1950
Rose, Horace A. & E.B. Howell, 1908
Schomberg, Reginald C.F., 1934, 1936
Younghusband, Frances E., 1895

Dir and Panjkora Basin

Khan, Raja, 1845
Rose, Horace A. & E.B. Howell, 1908

Gilgit/Yasin and Astor

Anonym 1879, 1882
Barrow, Edmund G., 1888

Clemens, Jürgen & M. Nüsser, 2008
Fischer, Reinhard, 1998
Godfrey, Stuart H., 1898
Hayward, George W., 1871
Kreutzmann, Hermann, 2015b
Schomberg, Reginald C.F. 1947

Hunza/Nagar Valley and other Burushaski-speaking areas

Baskhanov, M.K., A.A. Kolesnikov, M.F. Matveeva, A.I. Gluhov, (eds.) 2017
Charles, Christian, 1981
Godfrey, Stuart H., 1898
Kreutzmann, Hermann, 1993, (ed.) 2006a, 2006b
Younghusband, Frances E., 1895

Kashmir

Vigne, Godfrey T. 1842

Ladakh and Da/Hanu

Dainelli, Giotto, 1924
De Filippi, Filippo, 1924, 1932
Moorcroft, William & George Trebeck, 1841
Vigne, Godfrey T., 1842

Nuristan

Barrow, Edmund G., 1888
Bartasheva, Nina L., 1975
Court, C. Auguste, 1836
Lumsden, Harry B., 1860
Maev, Nikolay A., 1874
Newby, Eric, 1958
Rennell, James, 1792
Ritter Carl & V.V. Grigorjev, 1867
Thesiger, Wilfred, 1957

Pamir, with Wakhan, Badakhshan, Kashgar/Yarkhand

Barrow, Edmund G., 1888
Baskhanov, Mihail K., A.A. Kolesnikov, M.F. Matveeva, (eds.) 2015
Baskhanov, M.K., A.A. Kolesnikov, M.F. Matveeva, A.I. Gluhov, (eds.) 2017

Curzon, George N., 1898
Forsyth, Thomas D., 1875
Hayward, G.S.W. & Mahomed Amin,
    1869
Izzatullah, Mir, 1872
Izzet Ullah, Mir, 1842
Kreutzmann, Hermann, 2017b
Shaw, Robert B., 1871
Yule, Henry, 1872a, 1872b
Yule, H. & H. Cordier, 1913-16

**Pashai and other "Dardic"-speakers of
Afghanistan**

Simpson, William, 1879

Swat and Swat Kohistan

Rose, Horace A. & E.B. Howell, 1908

HISTORY

Peristan in General

Abaeva, Tamara G., 1973, 1987
Alekseev, Sergej V., 2012
Allen, Nick, 1999
Anonym [Davies, Robert H.], 1862
Anonym, 1934
Barrow, Edmund G., 1888
Bartol'd, Vasily V., 1896
Bashir, E. & Israr-ud-Din, (eds.) 1996
Baskhanov, Mihail K., A.A. Kolesnikov,
    M.F. Matveeva, (eds.) 2015
Baskhanov, M.K., A.A. Kolesnikov, M.F.
    Matveeva, A.I. Gluhov, (eds.) 2017
Bonvalot, Gabriel, 1889
Bredi, Daniela, 1994, 1996
Buksh, Munshi Faiz, 1872
Cacopardo, Alberto M., 2005, 2016,
    2019, forthcoming in 2022
Cacopardo, A.M. & A.S. Cacopardo,
    2001
Cacopardo, Augusto S., 2016a
Court, C. Auguste, 1836, 1839
Curzon, George N., 1898
Dani, Ahmad H., 1989a, 2001
Daushvili, Georgij Dž., 2014

Davies, Robert H., 1862
Denwood, Philip, 2007
Dittmann, Andreas, 1997, (ed.) 2001
Eggermont, Pierre H.L., 1984
Forsyth, Thomas D., 1870, 1875
Frembgen, J.Wasim, 2003
Fussman, Gérard, 1986, 1989b
Girdlestone, Charles, 1874
Grombtchevsky, Bronislaw L., n.d.,
    1889-91
Grombčevskij, B.L. = Grombtchevsky,
    1891a, 1891b, 1891c
Haidar, Mirza M. Dughlat, 1895
Hill, John E., 2003
Holzwarth, Wolfgang, 1994a, 1998b,
    1999
Israr-ud-Din, (ed.) 2008
Jettmar, Karl, 1989a, 1995, 1996, 2003a,
    forthcoming in 2022
Jettmar, K. & E. Kattner, (eds.) 2003
Johansen, Ulla, 2002
Kaverin, Sviatoslav I., 2020
Keay, John, 1977, 1979
Khan, Husain, 1984
Khan, Rafiullah & I. Shaheen, 2015
Klimburg, Maximilian, 1982, 2005
Kogan, Anton I., 2012, 2014
Kreutzmann, Hermann, 1998a, 1998b,
    2004b, 2007, 2008a
Kushev, Vladimir V., N.L. Luzhetskaia,
    L. Rzehak & I.M. Steblin-
    Kamensky, (eds.) 1998
Kuwayama, Shōshin, 2002
Leitner, Gottlieb W., 1950
Litvinskij, B. A., 1968
Mock, John, 2013c
Moorcroft, William & George Trebeck,
    1841
Müller-Stellrecht, I., 1981
Munphool Meer, 1872
Nasr-ul-Mulk, 1935
Neelis, Jason, 2002, 2011, 2012a, 2012b,
    2014
Neve, Arthur, 1913
Parker, Edward H., 1897b
Parkes, Peter, 1996a, 2003, 2004, 2005
Parpola, Asko, 1988, 2002a, 2002b,
    2012, 2015
Prontera, Francesco, 2017

Rapin, Claude, 2005
Rawlinson, Henry C., 1869
Rennell, James, 1792
Rizvi, Janet, 1994
Schmid, Anna, 2002
Schmidt, Ruth Laila, 2002
Skrine, Clarmont P., 1925
Snoy, Peter, 1983
Söhnen-Thieme, Renate & O. von
    Hinüber, (eds.) 1994a
Stellrecht, Imtraud, (ed.) 1997a, 1997b,
    1997c, 1998b, 1998d
Stellrecht, I. & M. Winiger, (eds.) 1997
Thornton, Edward, 1844
Thuillier, Henry R., 1898
Tsuchiya, Haruko, 1998, 1999
Vigne, Godfrey T., 1842
Witzel, Michael E.J, 2019
Younghusband, Francis E., 1890, 1895
Yule, Henry, 1872a, 1872b
Yule, H. & H. Cordier, 1913-16
Zeisler, Bettina, 2010
Zoller, Claus Peter, 2018

Baltistan

Bredi, Daniela, 1994, 1996
Emerson, Richard M., 1984
Francke, August H., 1909
Hashmatullah Khan, A.-H.M., 1987
Holzwarth, Wolfgang, 1997
Khan, Husain, 1984
Khan, Yar M., 1985
Moorcroft, William & George Trebeck, 1841
Sagaster, Klaus, 1984
Sheikh, Abdul G., 1998
Söhnen, Renate = Söhnen-Thieme, 1983
Vigne, Godfrey T., 1842
Wade, Claude M., 1835

Chilas, Shinaki and Indus Kohistan

Chaudhary, M.Azam, 1998
Dani, Ahmad H., 1983a, 1983b
Douglas, J.A., 1895
Frembgen, J.Wasim, 1999a, 2008
Godfrey, Stuart H., 1898
GSI General Staff, India, 1928a
Hashmatullah Khan, A.-H.M., 1987

Hinüber, Oskar von, 2004
Jettmar, Karl, 1993b, 1993c
Schmidt, Ruth Laila, 1985, 2003-2004
Twist, Rebecca L., 2011

Chitral

Anonym, 1879
Baig, R. Karim, 1994, 1997
Barrow, Edmund G., 1888
Bashir, Elena, 1995
Bonvalot, Gabriel, 1889
[Buksh, M. Faiz =] F.B., 1883
Cacopardo, Alberto M., 2007, 2009, 2019
Cacopardo, A.M. & A.S. Cacopardo,
    1995, 2001
Cobb, Evelyn H., 1951
Dittmann, A. & M. Nüsser, 2002
Eggert, Peter, 1990
GSI General Staff, India, 1928b
Gurdon, Bertrand E.M., 1903, 1933
Hayward, G.S.W. & Mahomed Amin,
    1869
Holzwarth, Wolfgang, 1996, 1998a
Howard, J.E., 1889
Israr-ud-Din, 1979
Khan, Husain, 1991
Khan, Raja, 1845
Kreutzmann, Hermann, 2008b
Leitner, Gottlieb W., 1950
Mock, John, 2017
Munphool Meer, 1869
Munphool Pundit, 1870
Murtaza, M. Ghulam, 1982
Nasr-ul-Mulk, 1935
Parker, Edward H., 1897a
Parkes, Peter, 2001a, 2003, 2008
Plattner, Stewart, 2002
Rahman, Hidayat ur, 2010
Raverty, Henry G., 1864a
Rustamov, Uzbek A., 1956
Scott, Ian Dixon, 1937
Younghusband, Frances E., 1895

Dir and Panjkora Basin

Cobb, Evelyn H., 1951
Court, C. Auguste, 1839
Khan, Raja, 1845

Gilgit/Yasin and Astor

Anonym, 1879, 1882
Barrow, Edmund G., 1888
Bräker, Annette & H.H. Geerken, 2017
Bredi, Daniela, 1994, 1996
Cacopardo, Alberto M., 2009, 2019
Chohan, Amar Singh, 1997, 1998
Dani, Ahmad H., 1987a, (ed.) 1987b
Fischer, Reinhard, 1998
Godfrey, Stuart H., 1898
Göhlen, Ruth, 1997
GSI General Staff, India, 1928a
Hashmatullah Khan, A.-H.M., 1987
Hayward, George W., 1871
Hinüber, Oskar von, 2004, 2014
Holzwarth, Wolfgang, 2006, 2008
Jacobsen, Jens-Peter, 1995
Jettmar, Karl, 1990b, 1993b, 1993c
Khan, Yar M., 1985
Litvinskij, B.A., 1993
Löhr, Johannes, 1997a, 1997b
Lužeckaja, Nina L., 1998
Marhoffer-Wolff, Maria, 1997
Mock, John, 1998b
Munphool Meer, 1869
Munphool Pundit, 1870
Parker, Edward H., 1897a
Schmidt, Ruth Laila, 1985
Schneid, Monika, 1997

Hunza/Nagar Valley and other Burushaski-speaking areas

Chohan, Amar Singh, 1997
Flowerday, Julie, 2018
Frembgen, Jürgen, 1985, 1986a
Frembgen, J. Wasim 1988a, 1988b, 1992, 1996, 2005
Godfrey, Stuart H., 1898
Grombtchevsky, B.L., 1889-91
Holzwarth, Wolfgang, 2006
Khan, Nazim, 1936
Kreutzmann, Hermann, 1999, 2006b
Lužeckaja, Nina L., 1998
Müller-Stellrecht, Irmtraud, 1978, 1983, 1984
Neelis, Jason, 2006
Parker, Edward H., 1897a

Sidky, M. Homayun, 1996, 1997, 1999
Stellrecht, Imtraud, 2006b, 2007a
Tuite, Kevin, 1998
Younghusband, Frances E., 1895

Kalasha

Cacopardo, Alberto M., 2009, 2019
Cacopardo, A.M. & A.S. Cacopardo, 1992, 1996
Cacopardo, A.M. & S. Pellò, 2021
Cacopardo, Augusto S., 1991, 1996, 2006, 2011
Jansari, Sushma, 2014, 2017
Lurje, Pavel B., 2021
Mayrhofer, Manfred, 1967
Parkes, Peter, 2008
Plattner, Stewart, 2002
Pstrusińska, Jadwiga, 1999, 2003
Rahman, Hidayat ur, 2010
Witzel, Michael, E.J., 2004a
Zoller, Claus Peter, 2018

Kashmir

Kogan, A.I. 2009, 2012, 2014
Munphool Pundit, 1870
Neve, Arthur, 1913
Vigne, Godfrey T., 1842

Ladakh and Da/Hanu

Chohan, Amar Singh, 1997
Francke, August H., 1909
Moorcroft, William & George Trebeck, 1841
Sheikh, Abdul G., 1998
Vigne, Godfrey T., 1842
Vohra, Rohit, 1983, 1985, 1988, 1993, 1995

Nuristan

Abaeva, Tamara G., 1978, 1984, 1987
Allen, Nick, 1999, 2000
Anderson, Dorothy, 2003, 2008
Anonymous Missionary, 1896
Arbabzada, Nushin & N. Green, 2022
Barrow, Edmund G., 1888

Pamir, with Wakhan, Badakhshan, Kashgar/Yarkhand

Pashai and other "Dardic"-speakers of Afghanistan

Kohzad, Ahmad A., 1955
Ovesen, Jan, 1983

Swat and Swat Kohistan

Cobb, Evelyn H., 1951
Court, C.Auguste, 1839
Di Castro, Angelo A., 2015
Mankiralay, Abd al-Haq Jashni, 1987, 1992
Olivieri, Luca Maria, 2009, 2010a
Raverty, Henry G., 1862
Tucci, Giuseppe, 1997

LINGUISTICS

Peristan in General

Allchin, F. Raymond, 1981
Baart, J.L.G., H. Liljegren & T. E. Payne, (eds.) 2022
Backstrom, Peter C. & Carla F. Radloff, 1992
Bashir, Elena, 1996a, 2003
Bashir, E. & Israr-ud-Din, (eds.) 1996
Buddruss, Georg, 1975, 1976, 1993
Daushvili, Georgij Dž., 2014, 2015
Degener, A. & E. Hill, (eds.) 2022
Di Carlo, Pierpaolo, 2011a, 2016
Driem, George van, 2001
Èdel'man Džoj I., 1980, 1982, (ed.) 1999, 2011
Fussman, Gérard, 1989b
Grierson, George A., 1900b
Grjunberg, A.L. & I.-M. Steblin-Kamenskij, 1974
Hegedűs, Irén, 2005
Hock, H. Heinrich, 2015
Hock, H.H. & E. Bashir, (eds.) 2016
Israr-ud-Din, (ed.) 2008
Kogan, Anton I., 2003, 2005, 2008, 2015, 2016, 2019, 2021
Kreutzmann, Hermann, 1995, 2017a
Kristiansen, K. & I. Ross, 1973
Kristiansen, K. & W. Witek, (eds.) 2001
Kuiper, Franciscus B.J., 1978
Kushev, Vladimir V., N.L. Luzhetskaia, L. Rzehak & I.M. Steblin-Kamensky, (eds.) 1998

Liljegren, Henrik, 2014, 2017, 2019
Liljegren, H. & F. Akhunzada, 2017
Liljegren, H., R. Forkel, N. Knobloch & N. Lange, 2021
Liljegren, H. & N. Haider, 2015a
Liljegren, H. & E. Svärd, 2017
Litvinskij, B. A., 1968
Morgenstierne, Georg, 1927, 1935a, 1935b, 2001
Parkin, Robert, 1987b
Parpola, Asko, 1988, 2002a, 2002b, 2012, 2015
Ringdal, Nils J., 2008
Rysiewicz, Zygmunt, 1956
Schmidt, R.L., O.N. Koul & V.K. Kaul, 1984
Skyhawk, Hugh van, (ed.) 2008a
Söhnen-Thieme, Renate & O. von Hinüber, (eds.) 1994a
Strand, Richard F., 1997-2021, 2001, 2022
Tikkanen, Bertil, 1999, 2008
Torwali, Zubair, 2021
Turner, Ralph L., 1926-28, 1966
Vasil'ev, Mihail E. & A.I. Kogan ,2013
Weidert, Alfons 1973
Weinreich, Matthias, 2015
Witek, Wlodek, 2005a, 2005b
Witzel, Michael E.J., 2004b, 2019
Zoller, Claus Peter, 2016a, 2016b, 2017, 2018, 2022

Baltistan

Bashir, Elena, 1996a
Kogan, Anton I., 2019, 2021

Chilas, Shinaki and Indus Kohistan

Barth, F. & Morgenstierne, G., 1958
Bashir, Elena, 2007b, 2009
Fitch, Martin & G. Cooper, 1985
Rensch, Calvin R., S.J. Decker & D.G. Hallberg, 1992
Schmidt, Ruth Laila, 1985, 2003, 2004, 2006, 2013
Schmidt, R.L. & R. Kohistani, 2008
Schmidt, R.L. & O.N. Koul, 1983
Zoller, Claus Peter, 2005

Mela-Athanasopoulou, Elizabeth, 2014
Mørch, Ida, E. & J., Hegåard, 2008
Nelson, David N., 2020
Trail, Ronald L., 1996
Trail R.L. & G.R. Cooper, 1999
Trail, R.L. & A. Hale, 1995
Witek, Wlodek, 2005a
Zoller, Claus Peter, 2018

Kashmir

Ahmed, Musavir, 2016, 2019
Schmidt, Ruth Laila, 1981, 2004
Schmidt, R.L. & O.N. Koul, 1983

Ladakh and Da/Hanu

Bielmeier, Roland, 1994
Kogan, Anton I. 2019, 2021

Nuristan

Bailey, T. Grahame, 1927
Bakker, Peter, K.F. Bøeg & Y.U.
    Goldshtein, 2021
Benveniste, Émile, 1952
Blažek, Václav & I. Hegedűs, 2012
Buddruss, Georg, 1977, 1979a, 1987,
    1992, 2005, 2006a
Buddruss, G. & A. Degener, 2015, 2017
Cathcart, Chundra, 2011
Degener, Almuth, 1994, 1995, 1998a,
    1998b, 2001, 2002, 2016,
    forthcoming in 2022
Degener, A. & E. Hill, (eds.) 2022
D'jačok, Mihail T., 2004
Èdel'man Džoj I., 1980
Elfenbein, Josef, 1999
Fussman, Gérard, 2012
Grierson, George A., 1911
Grjunberg, Aleksandr L., 1980, 1981
Grünberg, A.L.=Grjunberg, 1994a,
    1994b, 1995a, 1995b
Halfmann, Jakob, 2021, 2022
Hamp, Eric, 1966, 1968, 1969, 1977,
    1993, 2002
Hegedűs, Irén, 2002, 2011, 2012, 2017,
    2018, 2020a, 2020b, forthcoming
    in 2022

Ivanow, Wladimir, 1932
Konow, Sten, 1911, 1913
Kristiansen, K. & W. Witek, (eds.) 2001
Kushev, Vladimir V., N.L. Luzhetskaia,
    L. Rzehak & I.M. Steblin-
    Kamensky, (eds.) 1998
Liljegren, Henrik, forthcoming in 2022
Lurje, Pavel B., 2021
Morgenstierne, Georg, 1932, 1935a,
    1935b, 1945a, 1952, 1992, 2001
Nelson, David N., 1986, 1993, 2018
Parpola, Asko, 2002a
Pisowicz, Andrzej, 2008
Raverty, Henry G., 1864b
Reichert, Pierre, 1983, 1986, 1990/91,
    1998
Rybatzki, Volker, 2013a, 2013b
Sihler, Andrew L. & J. Greppin, 1997
Sköld, Hannes, 1927
Strand, Richard F., 1997-2021, 1999,
    2016, forthcoming in 2022
Trumpp, Ernst 1866
Turner, Ralph L., 1931-32, 1932
Werba, Chlodwig, 2016
Witek, Wlodek, 2005a

**Pamir, with Wakhan, Badakhshan,
Kashgar/Yarkhand**

Bashir, Elena, 2001b
Buddruss, Georg, 1979a, 1986, 1998
Capus, Guillaume, 1889b

**Pashai and other "Dardic"-speakers of
Afghanistan**

Dvorjankov, Nikolaj A., 1964
Grierson, George A., 1900a
Grjunberg, Aleksandr L., 1996
Lehr, Rachel, 2014
Morgenstierne, Georg, 1945b
Rybatzki, Volker, 2013a, 2013b

Swat and Swat Kohistan

Baart, Joan L.G., 1997, 1999
Baart, J.L.G. & M. Zaman Sagar, 2004
Barth, F. & Morgenstierne, G., 1958
Bashir, Elena, 2010a